# Super Mad at Everything All the Time

"*Super Mad at Everything All the Time* takes on the important subject of political culture, in particular, the political talk which results from the transformation of American political culture in the past several decades. While this change was the product of several factors, this book makes a compelling case that changes in media systems, broadly defined, is one of the primary factors that drove this change. While the subject is quite complex, Dagnes' argument and writing makes the book an accessible, and importantly, highly interesting read."
—Jody Baumgartner, *Distinguished Professor of Political Science, East Carolina University, USA*

"Professor Dagnes has written an essential guide for anyone interested in understanding the polarized media landscape in the age of Trump."
—Howard Polskin, *President, Founder and Chief Curator, TheRighting*

"*Super Mad at Everything All the Time* expertly delineates the deep political divisions in the country. But, we did not get here by accident. Dr. Dagnes provides a clear and compelling examination of the history of the how and the why that have brought us to this point in our political and media discourse. An outstanding contribution to the field."
—Danilo Yanich, *Professor, School of Public Policy & Administration, University of Delaware, USA*

Alison Dagnes

# Super Mad at Everything All the Time

Political Media and Our National Anger

Alison Dagnes
Department of Political Science
Shippensburg University
Shippensburg, PA, USA

ISBN 978-3-030-06130-2      ISBN 978-3-030-06131-9   (eBook)
https://doi.org/10.1007/978-3-030-06131-9

Library of Congress Control Number: 2018966127

Cover design by Fatima Jamadar

This Palgrave Macmillan imprint is published by the registered company Springer Nature Switzerland AG
The registered company address is: Gewerbestrasse 11, 6330 Cham, Switzerland

*For Jerry Mileur*

# ACKNOWLEDGEMENTS

I feel tremendously lucky to be able to thank so many great people who have helped me with this book. Being a professor at Shippensburg University gives me a big advantage because extraordinary faculty, students, and staff surround me.

Big thanks go to my colleagues, especially Niel Brasher who assisted in myriad ways at every step, Mark Sachleben, Lonce Bailey, Curtis Berry, Cynthia Botteron, Kara Laskowski, James Greenburg, and Lawrence Eppard, who offered critiques and advice with frequency and kindness, and Sara Grove who consistently set the bar high in friendship, mentorship, and collegiality.

My students went above and beyond the call of their duties, and several undergraduates willingly read chapter drafts to point out words that were grating: Thanks to Thomas Fisher, Ryan Oister, Madeleine Lampert, Alex Ruquet, Sara Smith, Dylan Nichols, Emily Keating, and especially Adam Friscia.

Our graduate students Julia Frey, Madeline Mulhall, Heather Day, Amber Quivers, and Matt Osenbach were superstars. Special thanks go to Audrey Mcgarrell who created the single best book cover that could not be used because of copyright laws, but trust me: It was perfect.

Several Ship alumni including Tom Dunn and Megan Silverstrim assisted me throughout the process. Tyler Williams probably helped this writing project more than anyone did, and his interest, guidance, and wise counsel are greatly appreciated.

Special recognition goes to Stephanie Jirard and Marin Hagen who offered abundant and substantial support in gracious ways. Heather Lennon, Michelle Ephraim, Rachel Hamilton, and Eleanne Hattis supplied kindness and advice. Much gratitude goes to Eunice Johnson who was an inspiration and a source of encouragement when I needed it most. Thanks to the comedian John Mulaney who does not know me, but who nonetheless gave me the book title and additional inspiration throughout the text.

Many thanks to the anonymous reviewers who read and critiqued, and a special thanks to whomever suggested I explain my methodology more carefully because that inspired the Preface. In this next section of the book, I detail each of my interviews with journalists, scholars, and political professionals to explain the substantive assistance of each expert. I thank the interviewees here *en masse* for their time and insight, and go into specifics in the next chapter.

Finally, the ultimate thanks go to my family: My father, Dennis Spokany, is my hero who supplies endless wit, wisdom, and unconditional love. My sister Monica Gocial makes my sun rise and set every single day. My daughters Maddy and Caroline are my whole heart, and my husband Pete is my collaborator in all and the walking embodiment of kindness, which makes everything worthwhile.

Although everyone named here would probably take the blame for any mistakes in this book, all of that falls to me.

# CONTENTS

# PROLOGUE

In the fall of 2015, I was waiting for my daughter at her volleyball practice, which was held in a community gym in my small, central Pennsylvania town. This was Rec League volleyball so a small group of 13-year-olds was practicing their serves and spikes, and an even smaller number of parents were sitting in bleachers waiting for their children. There were so few parents in attendance, none of whom I knew, that I was able to sit alone at the top of one set of bleachers and grade papers. Out of the periphery of my vision, I saw a man whom I did not know turn to look up at me. He had been sitting much lower down on the next set of seats, and when he moved his whole body to face me I raised my head and made eye contact. He opened his mouth and spoke:

> "I'll tell you what. This country is gonna be MUCH better when Donald Trump is president."

I was caught totally off guard, completely surprised, without an idea of what to say. I must have stared at him blankly because he went on:

> "And I'll tell you what. When Obama was elected, I KNEW this country was gonna fail and it did. You know why? Because he's not an American. And he don't even salute the troops!"

At this point, I was able to get out a "What?" and the man continued:

> "I gotta friend at Letterkenny [Army Depot] and he says Obama don't even salute the troops and my friend served in Iraq and he knows that Obama don't even salute the troops and he's not a real American."

I realized at this point that my mouth was actually hanging open because I was flabbergasted; I could not figure out where this came from, who this guy was, or how to respond. Luckily, I did not need to reply because the man was wound up and spinning like a top:

> "And I'll tell you what. I got nothing against women. I like women. My boss is a woman and she don't take no bullshit from no one and I like women. You know what I'm saying? So I don't got no problem with a woman president. Not Hillary -- she's shady as fuck. But a woman president? I got no problem with that. You know who would make a good woman president?"

Blank stare.

"Sarah Palin."

In what felt like ten minutes but was probably closer to two or three, my new friend railed against the Democrats, Obama, "illegals," and Hillary in a stream of expletive-laden vitriol and anger. I was dumbfounded and literally rendered speechless, so totally thrown by his fury and by the topic that I couldn't find the words to respond to a single thing he said. As abruptly as he began, the man stopped talking, motioned to the stack of graded papers on my lap, and asked: "You a teacher?" I nodded. "That's cool." And with that, he turned back around and focused once more on his iPhone.

I could not believe what had just happened, so I did the only thing a smarty-pants professor would do: I went home and I blogged about it. The next day, I told the story to my students and they laughed (especially at the "Hillary is shady" part) while they nodded and said "Yeah. That's nuts. But he's right, Donald Trump is great," which pulled me up short again. Wait. What? I was well-versed and well-read in American politics, the system, and the politicians; I knew the lay of the political land. Furthermore, I read *The Washington Post* and *The New York Times* every day. I had push alerts on my phone from *CNN* and *Politico*. Donald Trump was great? The guy who said Mexicans were rapists? The guy who said John McCain was not a hero because he was a prisoner of war? The guy who made fun of the disabled, used explicitly racist and misogynistic language? *That* Donald Trump? What was I missing?

Turns out, I was missing a segment of the country who got their news from different places than I did. At the time this happened, I acknowledged (in my blog post) that I lived in a filter bubble where very few people thought about Sarah Palin anymore. I admitted that we were deeply divided as a country and I wrote: "We have stopped talking to each other and have started talking past one another." At least I got that right. Almost everything else, I got wrong. I woefully underestimated the power of the media, especially the outlets that I did not consume. I did not watch *Fox News*, but then again I did not watch any cable news because it was all too howling and loud. I did not read *Breitbart* and *Drudge*, but I did not read *Huffington Post* or *Daily Kos* either. I figured that my media choice did not matter, because we were debating the same issues from varying perspectives using the same information and the same set of facts. I was very wrong.

In order to find out why I was so far afield, I decided to re-examine the modern political media system. I have spent the better part of my life consuming, working within, and researching the American political media, but the past decade brought mammoth changes to a system I thought I understood. There were explanations that, taken individually, were correct but incomplete. I tried to plot a course where I could examine the whole media and put the pieces together in a way that made sense, but it was a mess. I was lost, dissatisfied with my results, unhappy with the confusion I was creating in my own mind. This is where the wisdom and kindness of a sexagenarian named Eunice saved the day.

In 2012, Eunice and I sat together at a community dinner where I was brought in as the guest speaker, there to talk about that year's elections. We so thoroughly enjoyed our time together that we made plans to meet for coffee, and our conversations have continued for years. As I was struggling through this mess of information, I confided to Eunice that I felt disoriented. She offered me the piece of advice that changed the trajectory of the research project: interview an expert. Eunice argued that if I could find that one key authority to question, they could help guide me through the topic. This may sound like an easy recommendation, but it was more prescient than Eunice could have imagined. She was right: I needed expert advice to help me make sense of this, and because the American political media are so expansive in size and power, I realized that I needed more than one expert. I needed several dozens.

I sorted the general areas to investigate and I let my interview request letters fly. I began to talk with Communications Directors from think tanks because I (correctly) assumed they would understand the scholarly nature of my query. I was lucky enough to speak with three people from important DC institutes: Khristine Brookes, Communications Director at Cato; Bridget Lowell, Communications Director at Urban; and Darrell West, Vice President at Brookings. I went into these interviews without a set of specific questions, because I had no idea where the research was going. Instead, I asked them what they thought of the modern media system in Washington and how they did their job. Ms. Brookes led me through the new ways that think tanks engage the public and opened my eyes to the amplification of discourse because of all the competition for airtime. Ms. Lowell and I talked about the importance of authenticity and the new nature of data-driven journalism. And Dr. West had a lovely and brilliant observation about how to plant the seeds to change our angry discourse which informed my conclusions while it also gave me hope.

The answers I received from the think tank leaders led me to interview three more communications experts, these from interest groups. I spoke with Joe Bonfiglio, President of the Environmental Defense Action Fund; Kaylie Hanson-Long, Communications Director NARAL Pro-Choice America; and Jason Pye, who had been the Comms Director at FreedomWorks but shot up the ladder to become Vice President of Legislative Affairs. Mr. Bonfiglio and I had one of the best conversations in memory about the state of the political parties and the new strength of activists. I have incorporated his insight into more academic talks than I can count, and although I could not use it all in this work, I could write another book just to reference his insight. Ms. Hanson-Long discussed the different communication techniques of liberals and conservatives, and the way interest groups are increasingly personalizing their messaging. I was connected to Mr. Pye by my former student Tyler Williams, and my visit to FreedomWorks was one of my favorites, even though everyone there cheerfully acknowledged that I was not exactly their target audience. Pye led me through the wilds of an activist group with candor and insight so incredibly useful, I decided to open the book with him.

Thanks to these first interviews, I had a sharper focus and moved toward the issue of polarization. I met with political ad guys from both sides of the aisle: Julian Mulvey (Democrat), a partner at Mulvey Devine Longabaugh, and from Guy Harrison and Brad Todd, both partners at OnMessage (Republican). Our discussions were valuable as they helped me to understand our divisions and the resulting changes to the profession of politics. Mr. Mulvey and I discussed authenticity in a highly mediated world, and he had incredible insight into the generational differences of various audiences; his take on polarization was one of the best I have heard and I return to his perception regularly. Guy Harrison from OnMessage was introduced to me by another Ship alumnus, Tom Dunn. Tom and Guy talked to me about how they make ads in an age of cord cutting, how Democrats speak collectively and Republicans speak individually, and how every election cycle brings innovation and new challenges. Brad Todd, fresh off his own book tour, described to me the new Republican landscape in terms that I had not considered, and now I cite him with frequency. He expanded on Mr. Harrison's discussion of advertising innovation and told me about the new models for mobile. It was a delight to talk with my former student, Tom Dunn, about his work and he gave me a skillful analogy that I use throughout the book and in all of my teaching about American politics: You gotta put your jersey on and know what team you're rooting for. I learned several things from all of these gentlemen: that keeping up with the technology is a necessity, that the new media system is a blessing and a curse, and that our smartphones give up more information about us than we could have predicted.

I knew that I needed to ground this work in what academics call "the literature," and so I decided to read a hearty number of books and journal articles and then interview scholars in this field. I was fortunate to speak with some of the biggest names in American political behavior, all of whom patiently answered my questions about their work. This gave me even more to think about. I spoke with the Doctors Kevin Arceneaux from Temple University, Lara Brown of George Washington University, Lisa George from Hunter College, Roderick Hart from the University of Texas at Austin, Matthew Levendusky of the University of Pennsylvania, and Michael Wagner from the University of Wisconsin. Vin Arceneaux and I talked about social media and how our filter bubbles can lead to political overconfidence, and he made the prescient observation that our social identities have been so politicized it is now difficult to see another side of an argument. Lara Brown provided fascinating historical context for our current political era and layered in the technology and financial imperatives of the media in a brilliant overview. Dr. George offered a priceless summary of the economics of the news media, tracing the development of advertising through the centuries to explain how to follow the money in an increasingly complicated commercial industry. Dr. Hart was the first person to make the observation that President Trump's tweets were modern day press releases, something repeated to me several times throughout my interviews, but since Rod was the first to note this I give him full credit. Rod's consideration was rooted in an optimism that was rare throughout my research, and he argued that the strength of our democracy could be found in our grassroots discussions.[1] Dr. Levendusky and I spoke about the effects of the partisan media, what the next big thing would be, and how the political system has changed. Michael Wagner noted that journalists found "costly" talk to be newsworthy, and that one solution is to make an effort to listen more. I also spoke with David Levinthal who is a reporter and editor at the Center for Public Integrity, and who writes about the confluence of money in politics. He was especially instructive on the topic of academic funding by conservative billionaires and led me to even more research in this area. All of these scholars helped put the research into context and connect the theories with practice.

After that, I interviewed journalists from print, television, and digital outlets. In the process, I scored newsroom tours from Paul Farhi from the *Washington Post* and Sara Fischer, Media Reporter at *Axios,* and I took up too much time in the *Baltimore Sun*'s newsroom with David Zurawik. Mr. Farhi and I spoke about money in media, and he gave me the quote I used as the title of a conference paper: "Everyone hates the media but they still use it." He also gave me a positive spin on the benefits of a flattened media system, which was supremely helpful. Sara Fischer shared her encyclopedia-level media knowledge, which provided the structure for much of this book, and her observations about the right-wing media circle were invaluable. I could have easily spoken to Dr. Zurawik for weeks to gain even more from his instrumental insights into biases and balances. His faith in journalism as a profession was encouraging and delightful.

I spoke with Eliana Johnson, the National Politics Reporter from *Politico,* who graciously gave me her time and attention as she was in between running down a story and appearing on *Meet the Press*. Ms. Johnson provided me with a great lesson in modern Washington media, and Lloyd Grove, Editor at Large of *The Daily Beast*, told me about gatekeeping and the value of traditional journalism norms. Matthew Sheffield, Staff Writer at *Salon*, offered a mastery of conservative ideological philosophy that matched his knowledge of the modern media and was vital in my framing of conservative and right-wing media. I went "home" to my alma mater *C-SPAN* and spoke with the award-winning Brian Lamb, and we discussed money and the new rules of journalism, which veer far away from what they used to be. He gave me a copy of Walter Williams' "Journalist's Creed," which hangs in the National Press Club and which I quote at the end of this book. I talked at great length with my fellow SPANial, Steve Chaggaris, who was the Political Director of *CBS News* at the time, and I interrupted the birthday celebration of *CBS* White House Correspondent Major Garrett[2] who provided experienced opinions about the distrust in the media today, as well as a thorough explanation of the current broadcast news environment. I even interviewed someone from the *CNN* investigative unit who asked to remain anonymous because the climate in Washington had so politicized working for *CNN*.

Armed with information about the ways of Washington and the meaning of the messages, I continued my queries to drill down on the right-wing media. I had learned an incredible amount from everyone up to this point, and I realized that there was a separation between the right-wing media and the rest of the media. To figure out what was happening and why, I spoke with three tremendous experts in this area: Jared Holt, Research Associate at People for the American Way; Howard Polskin, writer of *TheRighting*, a daily tip sheet that aggregates the top stories on the right-wing media Web site; and Will Sommer, Reporter at *The Daily Beast* and the author of *The Right Richter*, a tip sheet on the right-wing media. Jared Holt was especially helpful in our discussion about deliberate efforts to delegitimize the mainstream media, and shortly after our interview, he single-handedly brought down Alex Jones from social media (Marcotte 2018). Will Sommer and I discussed epistemic closure, high-context culture, and the rise of conspiracy theories. He also checked and added to my diagram of the right-wing media circle, which proved to be instrumental in my research. And Howard Polskin provided me with enough material to write a second book, especially in the area of topics covered within the right-wing media circle, the politics of fear, and the effect of a polarized media on our broader political culture. These interviews were more explanatory and instructive than Eunice could have predicted. What had been a tangle of ideas had come into clear focus. It took two years for me to make sense of it all but Eunice was correct: I had needed experts to show me the way. It is my greatest hope that I made sense of their wisdom and can add productively to the larger discussion about political media in a polarized age.

After all of these interviews and after more research, I found that there was not a two-sided political media system which divided news and commentary into left and right. Instead, a small, tightly closed circle contains right-wing media outlets. With the exception of *Fox News*, which is the focal point of the circle, these outlets are not journalistic: Their mission is not to uncover difficult truths or break news and speak truth to power. They have a negative objective, which is to cast aspersions on those they oppose. They provide commentary and analysis, some of which is brilliantly written and argued, practically none of which is self-effacing. Those within the right-wing media circle compete against one another only for an audience, and even in this regard, they are generous with their support of one another, featuring players from other organizations on varying platforms. They do not challenge others within their sphere; they do not race to break news that contradicts the narrative or politicians that they support. They have their own set of facts, truths, and explanations, and these do not match up *at all* with those outside the circle.

I was able to more fully understand the anger of the man from the volleyball practice in 2015. He is one of many Americans who feel ignored by politics, by the "establishment" leaders in Washington and the media that cover them. The news and information my volleyball buddy receives is very different from the media I consume, which is highly problematic because we cannot communicate effectively without a common set of ideas, facts, and truths. We do not have to agree with one another politically, but we should be able to have a conversation that is informed by the same reality. He and I live in the same town, but we might as well live in different countries because we are so deeply divided in our understandings of the world around us. Our sharpest resemblance is how angry we both are, although we are angry about different things. We are not alone in our frustration and it feels like the whole country is annoyed, indignant, and unwilling to compromise. The rest of this book explains how we became so furious. My hope is that by understanding the reasons we have grown so divided, we can try to unite, if only to lower the political temperature and repair our discord.

Shippensburg, USA                                                    Alison Dagnes

## NOTES

1. I strongly recommend Roderick Hart's book, *Civic Hope*, which expands on this point.
2. True story.

## REFERENCE

Marcotte, Amanda, "Meet Jared Holt, the guy who's getting Alex Jones kicked off the internet". *Salon*, August 8, 2018. https://www.salon.com/2018/08/08/meet-jared-holt-the-guy-whos-getting-alex-jones-kicked-off-the-internet/.

# CHAPTER 1

# Two Truths

Jason Pye is in his thirties with a hipster beard, cool-nerd glasses, and a big smile. He wears baggy pants and a hoodie around the offices of FreedomWorks where he is the Vice President for Legislative Affairs. Pye says that he is one of the oldest guys in the office and that Millennials dominate his libertarian advocacy group specifically, and DC politics in general. Cans of Mt. Dew litter the FreedomWorks desks, which may be one reason Pye talks so fast, and the overall vibe of the office is something that Aaron Sorkin would have created if he were writing a TV show about an ideological activist group in the twenty-first century. Pye came to FreedomWorks without a college education or any formal political experience: He was a blogger.

Jason Pye is successful at FreedomWorks, the firebrand organization that takes great pleasure in shuttering the government, because of his ability to craft messages quickly and stay on-brand. His brand is libertarianism. Pye speaks about the future of political communication in terms of "rapid reaction" and "hits" and "followers" which fits in neatly within the political messaging environment of today: Quick and immediate missives are blasted from far and wide on capricious platforms. Jason Pye is at FreedomWorks at a time when the American public wants their political alerts in strident bursts of ideological fervor; fast, direct, and emotional, delivered so the public can respond and react with equal zeal and feeling. The modern American political media climate is crowded with voices from countless places, where politicos jockey for attention, and the public is fired up and fuming. Jason Pye is good at his

© The Author(s) 2019
A. Dagnes, *Super Mad at Everything All the Time*,
https://doi.org/10.1007/978-3-030-06131-9_1

job; accordingly, the right-leaning portion of the American public hears from (and about) FreedomWorks often. The job of the FreedomWorks communications staff is to keep their members angry and active, because the best way to motivate a political base is through wrath and alarm. Most political messaging, from FreedomWorks, or any other political activist, ends with what is termed a "call to action," a direction for the public to do something. Most calls to action are answered because of anxiety and anger.

FreedomWorks is located on Capitol Hill, close to the action of government, blocks from both Congress and the Supreme Court, and is an easy cab ride to the White House. In that way, FreedomWorks represents the norm of traditional American politics; they are located in the right spot and the office is chock-full of eager recent graduates of Political Science programs. But beyond the standard-issue cubicle furniture and whiteboards where they plot government shutdowns, FreedomWorks represents the new Washington. It is not just the beer kegs that are tapped in their kitchen (signaling a bro-culture of ideological warriors), but the cell phones, monitors, and data that dominate their workspaces and dictate every action and response. The new political communication landscape is hard-wired and built for speed. This is for a good reason: The country is similarly connected, and the public is just waiting to hear from FreedomWorks—or the Environmental Defense Fund or the National Abortion Rights Action League or any of the other political groups that play such a big role in American politics today. Other interest groups may not have the kegs tapped in their kitchens, but their Communications Directors and Legislative Affairs reps share Jason Pye's intensity and drive. They will tell you that politics today is a war and the first side to reach the most people will win. It is more than the reach in the "emails sent" way; it is the persuasion and the connection to a specific, segmented, and ideological audience. It is about reaching an American public who are super mad at everything all the time, and keeping them that way.

A growing number of people who work in politics embrace the new Washington media culture. While many have noted the expansion of government, what has grown even more profoundly are the numbers of political consultants, interest group activists, and unelected advisors who play critical roles in the policymaking process. There are more political players in DC today who have to communicate to both politicians and to the voting public, and luckily they do not have to fight for limited coverage in a few select newspapers, or for precious airtime on three television channels. Everyone involved in politics has had to raise their communications game in the last decade because media technology has changed so dramatically, which has consequently magnified the landscape. The media have exploded in size, form, and reach, and as a result there are seemingly endless outlets to utilize in political communication efforts. Politicians and other political actors need this media system in order to reach the public, and they clamor for the attention of a disparate and finicky audience. Forget Warhol's twentieth-century idea that everyone gets their 15 minutes of fame; in today's political media environment, everyone has to put in their 15 minutes of face time just to keep the whole thing running. Because the media are ubiquitous, and because the public chooses not to escape from the relentless push-notifications and alerts, Americans are awash in news and information. There are so many places to find news content, politicians and politicos have to work hard to attract serious attention while news outlets have to elbow away a mounting volume of competition. The current political messaging landscape has a sizeable (and growing) number of people all vying for attention from an audience that has too many options.

This is at once democratizing because the abundance of voices leads to a diversity of perspectives, but also tricky because the media terrain is so vast and crowded that it is hard to be heard over the din. The word "media" is the plural of "medium," and today there are many different platforms on which to communicate, and all are interlinked. There are no stand-alone political programs or forums; something broadcast on TV or radio will also have a Web site, something online will also stream video content, all print media have journalists who blog, tweet, and podcast, and everyone wants you to like them on Facebook. Jason Pye knows that in the old days, a well-placed newspaper story or cable news story about FreedomWorks would suffice, but today these outlets are only one piece of a very large puzzle.

Pye keeps his eye on news organizations and trade publications, on bloggers and pundits and fellow activists, and now more than ever FreedomWorks interacts with their members on social media. What used to be a fairly linear public relations push to sell policy (or an ideology or a candidate) is now far more serpentine. It is also focused on two separate and disparate audiences: As a figurehead of FreedomWorks, Jason Pye needs to communicate with other political players in Washington, and so he is frequently quoted in mainstream political outlets like *The*

*Hill* and *USA Today*. This is his inside game: Capitol Hill reporters likely know that they should find Jason Pye for a good quote about economic liberty. As a figurehead of a group that remains ideologically connected to the Tea Party, Pye also needs to communicate with a more specific audience of ideologues, and so he is quoted on *Breitbart*, *Newsmax*, and *Hot Air*. These outlets are within a right-wing media circle that is tightly closed and specific: This circle includes talk radio shows, Web sites, media conglomerates, and *Fox News*, and its mission differs from the mission of rest of the political media. This right-wing circle exists because of a long-standing opposition to the so-called liberal media, and because of its origin story this circle has a negative objective: Their purpose is to support conservative ideals but even more to oppose those outside of their bubble. If the rest of the mainstream media (to include liberal, centrist, and conservative outlets) work to break stories with scoops and investigative reporting, the right-wing media circle works to oppose an enemy. Jason Pye pitches his press releases to the broader press, but much of the time the outlets within the right-wing media circle are the ones that run them because they share a philosophy. Vehemently anti-Washington, raging against liberals and the institutions of government that have left them behind, the right-wing media circle encapsulates resentment. Much of the content produced within this circle is not journalism in classic sense of breaking stories, but it is considered "news" to a segment of the population who has no use for any other media source because they simply do not trust them.

It would be false equivalence to say there are two equal ideological media bubbles since the right-wing circle is small, focused, and closed off, while the rest of the mainstream media exists around it. Yet those inside this right ring see themselves fighting against everyone who opposes them, and this battle is one constant source of their fury. Concurrently, while the mainstream media is not a tightly controlled circle, today the public can sense a similarly intense anger in the press, felt across a wide expanse of programs and platforms, focused on much of what the right-wing media circle espouses, targeting the politicians supported by the right. In this manner, there are two opposing media sides today even though they may be differently constructed and varying in size, scope, and mission. Journalism today is a combative industry, reflective of the genuine fury all over politics. The American political system has always been ideologically divided, but now the political media are divided as well with audiences on both sides pointing at the other saying

"Can you believe what those people are saying?" There are now two very different news narratives informing the public. Both narratives expose and feed our anger.

The right-wing media and the mainstream news media might be separated by ideology but they operate in similar ways: They both race the clock to be first with a story because being first means more attention (and more profit) from a content-hungry public. They both feature journalists and media stars who bounce from program to program, across platforms in order to gain recognition, capture an audience, and sell their media brand, and they also include politicos like Jason Pye who lend expertise and authority to their content. They are dedicated to delivering stories to their audiences that they will find interesting, stories that make the public feel strongly. Yet despite these structural similarities, the missions of these two media sets are different and so their product is too, which means that their audiences have dissimilar information experiences. The mainstream media break news and varying outlets will build on a big story, adding facts and analysis to make it their own. Within the right-wing media circle, the commentators and reporters will provide their own take on a situation that stays in line with what others in the circle articulate. One important quality of outlets within the right ring is how unified they are in their messaging, how uncritical they are toward one another.

The broader mainstream media is so vast that it cannot maintain such a united purpose. Everything outside of the right ring includes liberal Web sites such as the *Huffington Post* and *Salon*, centrist news organizations such as *The New York Times*, *Washington Post*, *Axios*, and the *PBS Newshour*, and conservative sources such as *The Wall Street Journal*, *The Weekly Standard*, and *The National Review*. Certainly, there are ideological clusters within the mainstream media but they are not as cohesive, reinforcing, or unified as those in the right-wing circle.[1] Size matters here, too: Within the right-wing circle, there are only a few dozen outlets while the mainstream media includes many, many more. This means that it is easier for the right ring to stay on-message, while the rest of the mainstream media have a harder time doing this.

Additionally, the ambitions of the mainstream news media differ from their right-wing counterparts as well. The professed journalistic dedication to the First Amendment may come off as sanctimonious, but the craving for professional success and the profit imperatives of news organizations support the self-aggrandizing. In modern news journalism, newspapers, television networks, and Web sites are rewarded for breaking news, either through major scoops or minor scooplets. The intense competition between the *Washington Post* and *The New York Times* (and the resulting financial gains for both) is one example of how those engaging in actual journalism are compensated for their efforts. To stay profitable, a news organization has to supply something, and the mainstream news media supplies breaking news, while the right-wing media circle furnishes the counter narrative.

Political media organizations from both sides face the challenges of financial solvency, but again this reveals itself in different ways. Within the right-wing media circle, speed is important and the competition among these outlets is to be first. There is very little real competition between these organizations given the bunker mentality of this partisan press corps, but the right-wing media outlets do race against each other to attract as many clicks and hits as possible. This is how they make money. The financial imperatives of the mainstream media are more complicated since (a) legacy outlets in the mainstream press have had to transform themselves in the face of a rapidly evolving technological landscape and (b) the competition among news organizations is ferocious. Time, technology, and circumstance collided to force the mainstream media to renovate and that transition has been rocky. Mainstream news organizations, be they legacy or digitally native, now have a very different set of tools to use in an evolving media environment, but they have had to learn how to use these tools while on the job. They are reliant upon the journalistic norms of traditional politics but are now tied to the new American media mandates of speed and splashy content while news competitions pop up like mushrooms. The political media business is both booming and struggling at exactly the same time.

Understandably, with all of the content available today the public can be overwhelmed by political storytelling that comes in the form of news, analysis, opinion, headlines, rumors, conspiracies, and satire. There is an abundance of material now, all coming from outlets who are trying hard to capture our attention, yet in the boom times there are also drawbacks. While the public can access information with unprecedented speed, and while this *should* be a good thing for American democracy, we are veering sharply into concentrated discord. Never before has the public had as much access to data, analysis, and opinion from such a wide array of sources, but far from inspiring, we have cocooned ourselves in bubbles that comfort and reaffirm but do not challenge or encourage. Polls consistently show that the American public is distrusting of the news, of our elected officials, of our neighbors. We are polarized in ways that are deeply painful and seem lasting, and in the course of this polarization we are fast losing the ability to compromise for the better of the whole.

This book is about political media and their role in our devolving national political discussion. Marshall McLuhan wrote in 1967 that the "medium is the message," where a media form has a profound impact on how a message is understood, but today there are too many questions that McLuhan could not have foreseen. What transpires when everyone has access to a medium and anyone can become a messenger? What happens to the news media in this content-heavy climate? What occurs when there is so much information that Americans are drowning in it? When politicking turns into a machine-gun spray of reactions and positions? When the once vaunted information institutions are shunned in favor of targeted hits and social media, and the news organizations struggle to survive?

Politics becomes angry, loud, and urgent, and the media help to spread the discontent. There are now two sets of truths in American politics making it impossible to find common ground. The public is super mad at everything all the time.

## OUTLINE OF THE BOOK

Nothing happens all at once, nor does one single thing trigger an enormous cultural shift. The American public did not wake up one day and wonder "why is everyone yelling at each other?" because we have gradually grown accustomed to the noise and have progressively contributed to it. We did not go from three broadcast channels to Twitter overnight. Spiro Agnew might have called the media "nattering nabobs of negativism" in 1970, but at that time the public writ large did not hold the Fourth Estate in such snarling disdain. There are four primary reasons that we have the political media we have today, and all of them are interconnected.

1. For there to be a divided media system, the ground had to be fertile for a separation. For fifty years, conservatives have disparaged academics, the government, and the media as being liberally biased, to the point that alternatives to all three were pursued.

2. Technological advancements made the media faster and more personal, shifting print to broadcast, broadcast to cable, and then moving everything online. This lead to the creation of niche narrowcasting which generated partisan news.
3. The new, conservative alternative to the perceived liberally biased media was profitable and produced imitators, the technology available furthered the growth of a separate right-wing media bubble.
4. Our deepening political divide that has been growing through the decades has intensified into a sharp polarization, and this has now spread to apolitical areas of our lives. The public cocoons itself in ideological filter bubbles, especially in regard to media choice.

We have the political media system that we do because of all of these components, all put together. In this book, however, they are addressed independently first and then brought together.

## SHIFTS IN THE POLITICAL CLIMATE

A hyperpolarized media must be built upon a foundation of anger, and Chapter 2 delves into the history and development of this foundation. There are several important factors that lay the groundwork for the political communicating we do today, all of which have to do with trust. While many Americans may adhere to the belief that the country has always been great and has grown progressively greater with time, those who long for the old days often speak of the lost faith in our leaders. The public used to trust experts, elected officials, and newsmen far more than today, in part because of events that sparked social and political changes which then produced a backlash against liberalism and ideas about higher learning, governing, and journalism. Derision of these institutions became constants in conservative dogma, which grew and flourished in the mid-twentieth century. Without the constant rejection of politics and the news media, the hunger for something new would not be there to drive innovation and adaptation, nor would the vehemence against the news industry land so solidly. A polarized media is only possible if doubt is cast on these existing institutions.

In the 1960s and 1970s, the government grew in size and leaned forward to assist groups who had heretofore been victims of discrimination. Also during this time, the news media's coverage of the Vietnam War and Watergate further contributed to a perception that the press was at war against the government. The conservative backlash against political liberalism and the media's role in challenging the institutions of power prominently featured the discouraging characterization that the government is defective and the media are biased. This provided the basis of a lasting debate between intellectuals and policymakers about the size, role, and competence of the Washington establishment. It also had an alarming influence on what is called "external efficacy," the belief that the political system is not only valuable but also responsive to the needs of the people. The nation was founded with a healthy dose of skepticism, but in the past half century, this cynicism has grown into something more intense.

This distrust is directed against three separate entities: experts and academics, the government, and the media. Since the 1950s when conservatives began to rail against the elite and effete professors on college campuses, public sentiment about colleges has cooled. Vilifying academics and their scholarship is one problematic element of the shifting cultural landscape because arguably research and education are important for progress. Also, investigation is one of the primary tools in policymaking and the data produced by researchers can be valuable. Education is foundation for future generations, and is thus important for the health of the nation. So the conservative arguments that scholarship and higher learning are liberally biased have had two important effects. The first is the growing unpopularity of university professors among Republicans, which has secondary effects on Republican college students.[2] The second is a concerted effort to create and fund specifically conservative academic programs, think tanks, and entire colleges as alternatives to the perceived liberal institutions of knowledge. Chapter 2 explores this in more depth, but (spoiler alert) the upshot is a contribution to growing informational divide.

Another facet of this distrust concerns hostility toward the government. According to a Pew Research Center study, only 19% of Americans actually trust the federal government to work. The problems are obvious: The government is too big and unwieldy, and according to Pew, "frustrating and badly managed" (Center, Beyond Distrust: How Americans View Their Government 2015). Many involved in governing, especially those inside the Washington bubble, are surprised by the aspersions cast against a system that is, though imperfect, fairly strong. Many of the arguments opposing the federal government stem from DC's geographic distance from the rest of the country and the public's lack of policymaking knowledge. Most Americans do not follow politics closely; in the height of the 2016 presidential election, an especially attention-grabbing period, a poll showed that only 39% reported paying "close attention" to politics, up from 2015 where only 31% reported the same thing (Auter 2016). Hence, most Americans do not care too much about Washington, the complex policymaking process that unfolds there, or the denizens of the capitol city. Additionally, the allegations of governmental ineptitude, while erroneous as a sweeping indictment of a generally admirable system, are rooted in some truths. In the last century, the federal government has exploded in size which has led to some inefficiency and incompetence. New federal agencies, departments, and programs all need bureaucrats and staffers to run them, so the sheer magnitude of the federal government is formidable. With an institution this big and with so many rules and personnel, there is also room for improvement (or reduction). Finally, with this size comes an immense scope of regulation that aims to assist all Americans, but we have varying ideas about how much government we want and need. Those on the left like the idea of an activist government to help those who need it, but those on the right take the view that such a massive government can adversely harness business in the name of protection. This big American government now includes programs that favor groups who had been left out of the process before, and with this favoritism comes the inevitable backlash against the programs and the people they serve. Where you stand on these issues depends on where you sit, but if your stand is that the government infringes upon personal rights and leaves you out of the bargain in the process, then the government is not the solution—it's the problem.[3] Much of the public is untrusting and angry, disconnected and disaffected, hating a Washington that seems both far away and damaged.

The third focus of distrust is against the media. As the majority of this book examines the political media, and Chapter 2 goes into depth concerning the evolution and development of bias claims against it, suffice it to say here the argument that the news media are destructively and antagonistically liberal is fundamental for the development of the partisan system we have today. What began in the early 1950s as a conservative cry against a so-called liberal media has now developed into entirely distinct information systems, designed to cater to ideologically specific audiences. The rejection of a left-leaning media began well before *Fox News* was built, but *Fox's* launch in 1996 amplified the call to arms against the mainstream media. An article by Bruce Bartlett[4] argues that the liberal slant of journalists was perceptible enough in the 1970s and 1980s to help create an audience hungry for the creation of a counterbalance (Bartlett 2015). *Fox News* became, and remains, so wildly successful that it consistently smashes the competition to pieces. The network has spawned imitators and alternatives, but *Fox News* remains the center of the right-wing media circle. When the Internet expanded options exponentially so too did the ideological selections available, and thus Americans are choosing political sides when they choose a news source. A survey by the Pew Center clearly showed that the public today are not only polarized in their politics, their media diet is similarly split (Center 2014). Since the options are plentiful the competition is fierce, and in order to claim and keep an audience, news outlets will profess their trustworthiness over all others, and as they do so, cast suspicion on their competition; hence, a viewer's *distrust* is born. The *Fox News Channel* slogan "fair and balanced," according to Bartlett, "implied its competition was neither" (Bartlett 2015). Today, this kind of boastful chest-thumping about conviction and excellence is commonplace among political media organizations, which means that when Americans select the ideological flavor of the news that best suits their existing belief system, they also hear that their choice is valid above all others.

Adding fuel to the fire, politicians and candidates (most notably President Trump) now take great joy in insulting the news media. It might feel as if all politicians whine about the press, but the 2016 election brought something new which continues today. President Trump began his near-constant assault against the journalists covering him during the 2016 campaign, and still refers to much of the press as "fake news," going so far as to call the press corps the "enemy of the people," historically a way authoritarian governments attack a free press. Thus, not only does a news audience hear opposition against other outlets from the journalism industry itself, the attentive public hears their elected officials throwing shade at the media too. With very few people actually defending the press, it is easy to see why the distrust festers. It also helps to explain why the news media are in a defensive crouch: When the President of the USA uses the bully pulpit to call your industry dishonest, one can get a complex.

The overall mood about American politics is grim, which is unsurprising given the fifty years of ridicule against the institutions that are most important to our democracy. Chapter 2 explores these criticisms, going back to trace the origination and development of the arguments to show why this contributes to our political outrage.

## TRANSFORMATION OF THE MEDIA IN STRUCTURE AND ECONOMICS

At the same time the distrust in our political institutions was growing, the media were growing as well and so part of Chapter 3 examines the technological advances that have been transformational. The political media system is an unwieldy behemoth today because innovation allowed messaging platforms and information outlets to explode in size and number: Technological advancements took the media of fifty years ago and blew it to pieces. First, cable altered television and provided (seemingly) endless minutes dedicated to particularized interests and issues. Then Internet technology gave us (literally) endless sites devoted to precise issues and interests. Fifty years is not a terribly long stretch of time; the expansion of the media in just five decades is dramatic. This new technology forced everything else to change along with it, most notably journalism.

Because of the vast expanse of news media outlets and the dazzling array of platforms upon which we consume information, there is now more time to fill. But in what was a horrific piece of timing, just as news organizations began to develop their ability to disseminate information constantly, they had less money with which to operate. Financial troubles have hindered news organizations for several important reasons. First, because there is so much competition, it is hard to get and keep an audience; second, because it is incredibly difficult to monetize online content, a media form that began without cost to consumers now demands remuneration in order to continue; and finally, with changing information forms come expensive upgrades. Consequently, the existing financial models of newsgathering became practically obsolete and news organizations have been scrambling to keep their heads above water. Accordingly, Chapter 3 also examines the new financial models of the media and the ways news organizations try to monetize their content.

There are so many different ways to get news and information, which means that newsmakers and policy shapers have to spread themselves across these different platforms, in different ways, and they have to do this *constantly*. Politics has become a relentless business. Election campaigns, which now begin years in advance of the first primary election, have given way to battles for policy. The idea of the "permanent campaign" began in the 1970s when Patrick Caddell, an advisor to President Jimmy Carter, sent a memo to the president saying "governing with public approval requires a continuing political campaign" (Goddard 2016). After that, Sydney Blumenthal expanded on this idea, arguing that because elections were costing so much money, politicians were constantly campaigning for re-election, often at the expense of policy (Blumenthal 1980). The argument went that as technology influenced both the media and polling techniques, elections became more expensive as they became more sophisticated. As a result, politicians spent more time fund-raising than policymaking, hence the "permanent campaign."

Now, this permanent campaign is found in policymaking as well. Because candidates have become so dependent on the media (both news media to cover them, ads to market them, and social to connect with voters), they simply continue this habit after they win an election. In 2005, *Time* magazine columnist Joe Klein wrote about the presidency: "The pressure to "win" the daily news cycle—to control the news—has overwhelmed the more reflective, statesmanlike aspects of the office." In the modern era of the "Twitter Presidency," this is a regrettable understatement, but the pressure to "win" the news cycle now extends well beyond the White House. Once in office, lawmakers at all levels have to stay attentive to the media because of two different needs: They must remain responsive to a connected and focused public who use social media to watch and scold or support their elected officials, and they are also dependent upon the news media to advertise their efforts. Moreover, extending this beyond just politicians, this is the precise formula now for *everyone* involved in politics—they need to connect to the public to win the day and they need that news attention to stay in the public eye. Lawmakers, party advocates, and lobbyists all have to utilize some form of the permanent campaign in order to operate in Washington. This means that while there is now constant messaging, there are enough people to fill the airwaves, pack the Web sites, and supply posts for social media.

And yet there is so much media and only so many minutes in a day, and so those involved in politics know that they must be selective in their communication planning. Chapter 3 also examines how different political professionals utilize this polarized media in order to "win" their battles. It also examines how the political communication helps maintain this split system, how the additional of ideological voices contributes to the increase in volume, and how this has become harmful as the public's cultural divisions worsen.

Journalists are hamstrung by the demands of a 24-hours news cycle that has been shortened to an immediate response system: The need for speed and the imperative to reach a wide audience across many platforms is exacerbated by the fact that information flow is seemingly infinite. Reporters have to file stories, blog, tweet, podcast, and respond immediately to breaking news, all of which takes time and attention. News organizations have adopted the rapid-reaction style of policy advocates and send "urgent" updates and information blasts as events unfurl. There is now the ability to deliver any kind of news and information at any time, and the public has become accustomed to receiving the news on a near-constant basis. There are many more platforms upon which the public can consume information which is a boon for viewers, listeners, and readers but incredibly problematic for news organizations who desperately need an audience in order to drive ratings revenue. At the exact same time that financial woes were hitting newsrooms, news producers needed more hands on deck to tweet, post, blog, and podcast. The demand for more audience amounts to weighty financial pressures on news organizations who must adapt in order to stay attention grabbing.

Additionally, in order to stay current and competitive, and to cross-promote their production, established news outlets are adding even more media platforms to the existing ones in an effort to reach the most people and keep a news organization relevant. This has resulted in new ways for the public to get news beyond print and cable, and new methods by which news organizations attract an audience. Not only are news organizations cutting their cords too, they also now have Web sites, podcasts, YouTube channel videos, Snapchats, Twitter feeds, Hashtags, and Facebook pages. News organizations are constantly expanding their reach to increase advertising with suggestions of whom to follow on platforms such as Twitter and Facebook, expanding their presence across larger media system. In short, we hear plenty from news outlets. They must do this in order to stay solvent and relevant, but it also adds to the clutter in the media climate.

The abundance of media has led to an environment where there are so many voices to listen to, it is often impossible to pick just a few upon which one can focus which also makes it challenging to concentrate or energize around one issue of import. Additionally, in their race for attention many outlets blur fact and opinion and it is increasingly challenging for audiences to understand the difference. As media outlets vie for an audience and financial support, they raise the volume of their communication. This not only contributes to the fury in the zeitgeist, it spreads the fury to the point that the anger can feel inescapable. This, then, leads to the issue of polarization.

## POLITICAL POLARIZATION AND HOW ALL PERSONAL IS NOW POLITICAL

The comedian Dennis Miller is currently writing for *Breitbart*. *Breitbart* is the right-wing blog launched in 2007 as an outspoken antagonist of the left, and it became massively influential during the 2016 presidential campaign as the go-to site for Donald Trump supporters. *Breitbart's* support of Trump grew even stronger when its editor, Steve Bannon, became Trump's most senior advisor in the White House. But Bannon's importance plummeted when he lost both his White House position and then his command at Breitbart. Without Bannon at the helm the site lost both readers and a sharp focus, becoming shrill and anemic instead. For his part, Dennis Miller had risen to great heights as a comedian in the 1990s but his own star began to fall after September 11 when he too became an outspoken antagonist of the left. His once solid fan base found *his* humor to be shrill and anemic; perhaps Miller and *Breitbart's* similar trajectories are synchronistic. Regardless, Miller hit *Breitbart* in 2018 with his typical highbrow analogies and he wrote: "Let's face it, this country couldn't be more Polarized if Jaruzelski was at the North Pole and Walesa had just set up camp at the hemline of Antarctica." Talk about a deep cut! That said, it feels incongruous that a *Breitbart* posting laments the polarized state of the nation: Something is off if the site that grew and succeeded solely because of political polarization is bemoaning our divisions.

Nevertheless, Miller is correct: The nation is politically polarized. Our ideological divisions have been consistent over time, rising at points in our history, falling at times of national crisis when we come together as one. At present, the political system is suffering under crushing affective polarization, when our dislike of a political opponent outweighs even our feeling toward our own side. There is a natural propensity for people to group themselves, and that is explored in Chapter 4, so too are our inclinations to sort ourselves by our political beliefs. In order to win, because winning is the goal, politicians running for office and politicos pushing policy feed on these divisions and exacerbate them further.

The American political climate is toxic in the second decade of the century, and our divisions can be found not only in discussions about politics, but in our conversations about practically anything. The media (especially that of the social variety) help to spread this polarization and deepen the divisions. The public feels the separation from the partisan news system where organizations pick sides, which leads to the issues that arise from the blend of fact and opinion. But now our media spread our divisions beyond news and information to our broader national culture. The public increasingly hears about political protests, boycotts, and rage in distinctly non-political areas such as sports and entertainment. This helps to broaden the antagonism even more, forcing the public to take sides even when they do not want to. It is small wonder that our political media, the system specifically and purposely dedicated to informing the public, both mirrors and amplifies these divisions. Chapter 4 examines the political polarization that helped to establish the divided political media establishment.

## THE RIGHT RING, MAINSTREAM, AND ENTIRELY DIVIDED MEDIA SYSTEM

With so many news choices available, it is natural that people pick an outlet with which they are comfortable. As news channels became overtly partisan, it logically led to a phenomenon known as "selective partisan exposure." This is when people choose a news outlet with a particular ideological bias, thus reinforcing a viewer's existing partisan beliefs. One of the leading researchers in this field is Natalie Stroud, who wrote a book called *Niche News* about how we select the news we consume. Stroud found that, while partisan news may increase political interest and participation, it also led to polarization. In other words, conservatives will select *Fox News* because it delivers information tailored to a right-wing viewpoint and, the theory goes, because they know their beliefs will not be challenged. Audience loyalty to ideological news organizations only encourages these outlets to remain partisan since the success of *Fox News* proves that revenue comes from audience attention and fealty. Political media outlets maintain brand loyalty, and this is where the two separate spheres have taken root.

The fifty-year arguments of liberal bias helped provide the rationale that an alternative was necessary, and with technological assistance and money to be made, a conservative alternative was developed. Tightly closed to those outside of it and self-reinforcing, the right-wing media circle has created their own rules, norms, and messaging styles. This has only been possible because of the polarization that has now led to a complete dismissal of mainstream journalism: When the President of the USA calls American journalism fake, the door opens for whatever alternative messaging that he wants. Yet while President Trump is the current beneficiary of the right-wing media circle's adoration, the bubble is not contingent upon his tenure as president. Since the broader narrative of the right-wing media bubble is oppositional to anyone outside of it, their negative objective outweighs their support of anyone. This is, by the way, totally in line with "negative partisanship," where voter's antipathy toward the opposing party is the driving force behind their decision-making. Those inside the bubble maintain that since the rest of the mainstream media is liberally biased, in the tank for the Washington establishment, and generally corrupt; their intention is to provide a counterargument for all that the mainstream media produces. This counterargument is made with vague consternations, without specific policy proposals, and with tremendous venom. Their antipathy is their brand and the outlets within this bubble wear the brand label proudly.

This is not to say that there is only siloing on the right. An interesting study discussed in *Politico* made the very compelling argument that journalists were in their own bubble by virtue of their geographic locations, which leads to a liberal cocooning. Jack Shafer and Tucker Doherty studied the locations of major news organizations and found: "Concentrated heavily along the coasts, the bubble is both geographic and political. If you're a working journalist, odds aren't just that you work in a pro-Clinton county—odds are that you reside in one of the nation's most pro-Clinton counties" (Shafer 2017). Shafer and Doherty went on to argue that the mainstream media bubble has been exacerbated of late by the very shifts in media technology that have already been addressed here: The shift from print to Internet meant that newspaper jobs around the country have been lost, while jobs on the coasts have been found. Because of this, and because journalists trend more left leaning than right by large, the mainstream media is predominantly liberal.

Yet even though there are biases on both sides, those biases are asymmetric. Because the right-wing media circle argues that they fight against a powerfully dominant liberal adversary, one can be forgiven for believing that there are two separate and equal ideological media circles, but it is more complicated than that. First, the fight is uneven: The bubbles are dissimilarly shaped and unevenly focused. This has much to do with the size of the rest of the media, as the number of mainstream media outlets far outweighs the number of those within the right-wing circle. The mainstream media breaks into varying journalistic categories, which include both liberal silos of commentary and information as well as centrist journalistic outlets. But even with the aforementioned liberal journalism bubble, Shafer and Doherty also maintain that the higher purpose of the news media can overcome the cocooning. Since the point of journalism is to speak truth to power the efforts to maintain an objective eye are also important to the business of the industry: "Many newsrooms really do feel a commitment to reflecting America fairly. Sometimes, correcting for liberal bias can be smart business as well" (Shafer 2017). In this regard, the overall mission of those in the mainstream media makes it an asymmetrical counter to the right-wing media circle: Mainstream journalistic outlets do not purposely strive to combat an ideological opponent, and their journalistic goals offset many of their biases.

There is, of course, a liberal media clique. The liberal blogs that were first launched in opposition to the George W. Bush administration are still popular and lucrative.[5] The op-ed pages of the major national newspapers are predominantly left leaning. Late-night comedians stand firmly and sharply in opposition to those on the right, and Democrats send each other video links and clips confirming their own biases. But, as explained more fully in Chapter 5, the nature of the right-wing media circle is enormously different from the rest of the political media. This gives the public a way to choose their news, and it gives political actors a specific strategy for their communicating efforts. Knowing that an audience is ideologically identifiable allows politicians, campaign strategists, and political professionals new ways to target their message.

It also leads to a complete disconnect in what we think to be true. Operating with totally different facts makes it nearly impossible to have a normal conversation with someone who disagrees with you. At the same time, we are seemingly addicted to the news we receive on a near-constant basis because it feeds our sense of outrage. Our outrage is incessant.

## LIKE A HORSE LOOSE IN A HOSPITAL

The comedian John Mulaney wrote the line that is the title of this book, and one sketch in his expansive stand-up repertoire is the inspiration for more conceptual content because it illustrates how the American public has grown so angry and attentive. Mulaney admits to not being very interested in politics, and his comedy is as apolitical as one can imagine, but times have changed and so too has his material. In a 2018 special taped at Radio City in New York, Mulaney dipped his big toe into the political comedy waters without once mentioning a person, event, or political party. Without naming names, Mulaney compared the Trump Presidency to "a horse loose in a hospital." This feels like exactly the right way to envision our currently unpredictable and completely unfamiliar political climate because as Mulaney says: "I think eventually everything is going to be okay but I have no idea what's going to happen next" (Mulaney 2018). The volatility of modern politics has much of the public on edge, which naturally leads to an increased attention to current events. Because there is a heightened interest in the political and more attention to it, the media feed the increased attention with more political material and this is one reason the public feels overwhelmed by all of the news and information available today. Another reason that Americans feel overwhelmed is that we now have the ability to stay connected perpetually and so we do, because as Mulaney says: "When there's a horse loose in a hospital, you gotta stay updated, so you walk around all day going 'Oh. What did the horse do?'" (Mulaney 2018). The push alerts are endless and the public consumes them even as they complain about feeling exhausted and overcome. News organizations try to stay connected to the public because covering the horse in a hospital is good for business.

For both politicos and the public, when it comes to messaging the most important factor is speed: Those who make and break the news want to do it first and those who receive the news want it immediately. Both need a connection to one another in order to feel not only supported but also successful.

Back at FreedomWorks, Jason Pye has to pay attention to the DC establishment with whom he works and to his members who are as far away from the DC establishment as possible.[6] This means using two different sets of communication skills. To reach the political media, Pye relies on a database of journalists called Meltwater, which allows him to reach out to contacts he has cultivated during his tenure at

FreedomWorks. He also uses Meltwater to reach media orgs who have already given them positive coverage and to that end he has spreadsheets sorted into "good" and "bad" lists and can access those two groups separately. But beyond his own old-school flack approach to PR, Pye also enlists the use of the Pinkston Group, a media firm that specializes in helping politicians and political groups place news and PR stories, euphemistically called "earned media" in various news outlets. The tactic here is to reach as many political outlets as quickly as possible who will give FreedomWorks the kind of notice that they want. So the speed imperative to reach the political media has to come from all of the actors involved because, as Pye said: "the first one to the show wins." Normally, he says, being the first one means a reaction within half an hour and it involves people well beyond the FreedomWorks offices. If Pinkston can get a pro-FreedomWorks story in the right place, it can spread into the media cycle where other outlets will pick it up, potentially becoming larger than a mere press release. This is the payoff for FreedomWorks: Becoming part of the national political conversation helps their brand and gives the group a seat at the table.

In today's increasingly polarized media environment, beyond the wonky policy stories about confirmation hearings and policymaking decisions which are covered in the "industry" media of DC, most of the FreedomWorks coverage is found within the right-wing media circle. Reaching the ideologically attentive American public is important to attract and maintain a membership, and features on right-wing Web sites or mentions on talk radio help keep the FreedomWorks brand popular among its base. To further reach this segment of the public, social media is the instrument of choice. Pointing to their 260,000 Twitter followers and calling Facebook Live the "new Fireside Chat," Pye is very bullish on social media. Going straight to his supporters, he argues, is the best way to prove a movement is (or might be) afoot. The FreedomWorks Facebook page is updated about five times daily, and staffers tweet between two and three dozen times a day. Getting followers to pay attention to FreedomWorks is imperative, but with the deluge of social media output it is important to attract attention beyond the base as well, which means sometimes resorting to explosive messaging that is long on detonation. Those "calls to action" are chock-full of explosive language and beseeching requests. As the rhetoric ramps up, sometimes facts fall to the wayside and there is evidence that the social media output for

partisan activist groups (although not FreedomWorks specifically) is riddled with falsities. A 2016 Buzzfeed report showed that in a review of six
Facebook pages from "hyper partisan" activist groups (three right-leaning, three left-leaning), 38% of the postings on conservative pages were
a mixture of true and false information, and 19% of the liberal postings
were similarly skewed (Silverman 2016). Since the Pew Research Center
found that 44% of the American public follows news on Facebook, this is
a bit alarming (Hermann 2016). However, the popularity of social media
proves its attraction for organizations like FreedomWorks and shows the
downfall of this use:

> The best way to attract and grow an audience for political content on the
> world's biggest social network is to eschew factual reporting and instead
> play to partisan biases using false or misleading information that simply
> tells people what they want to hear. (Silverman 2016)

It is, undoubtedly, easier to fudge the truth when your audience is (a)
predisposed to believe it and (b) are unlikely to challenge your findings.
Additionally, when there are "alternative facts," there is less likely to be
the kind of scrutiny on the truth that there once was. The same kind of
mendacity was studied over at *Fox News*, where several significant studies have proven, as Bartlett writes, "that right-wing bias, including inaccurate reporting, have become commonplace" (Bartlett 2015). Having
an echo chamber, be it on cable or on the web, is as effective as it is
problematic for political communication. Another reason, beyond the
insular audience, that social media is so successful for activists, politicians
and policymakers writ large is because they encourage participation and
engagement. But while this kind of engagement can garner attention,
it also leads to the crowded, angry, and noisy political setting of today.
Political groups attract a slice of the very attentive public who are dyed-
in-the-wool partisans. This is why Pye and his staff supply their members
with the kind of meaty ideological bone that is specifically libertarian,
hostile to the opposition, and deliciously, politically chewy. Most of the
material that ideological activists spout is angry and oppositional; nothing motivates an audience quite like infuriation. In today's media, revenues matter more than ideology and in our polarized political climate,
winning matters more than policy. These two factors combine to produce the divided new system that we have.

One interesting fact is that Jason Pye reads all kinds of political media, from liberal, conservative, and mainstream news sources. He says that he has to read everything to fully understand the issues and the political context in which he operates, and it is clear that a well-balanced diet of news offerings is the best way to fully comprehend the complexity of modern American politics. What he dishes out to the FreedomWorks supporters, however, is far from balanced because nuance does not bring home the attention nor rally the base of support needed to be an advocate in Washington today. And so the messaging from FreedomWorks is strident and filled with rage, and this is how the FreedomWorks members like it. To the followers and supporters of FreedomWorks, the group's tweets, postings, chats, and missives are nectar. They strike at exactly what comedian Stephen Colbert described as "the pure polarization that is a hit of heroin to those who take pleasure from political strife" (Colbert 2016). While this hit may be pleasurable to the devoted public, and while it may mean success for FreedomWorks, much like actual heroin it can be lethal. Political strife may be good for business and media attention, but it is a lousy way to govern.

After fifty years of being told the government is bad and the media are biased, the American public finally believes it. America today is a nation of distrust: People do not trust their elected officials because they think politicians are slick and too "camera ready" and disingenuous. The search for authenticity led the Republican electorate to select as their nominee for president a man whose sole qualification for office was that he was not a politician. When asked what they liked about Donald Trump, many of his supporters said that they liked how he spoke plainly and (in their minds) honestly, and how he had never been elected to office. How much more cynical can we get than to elect someone to lead a nation based on his absolute inexperience in politics? We have worked our way up to this cynicism thanks not only to the politicians who run against Washington as they fight for election, but also to the political media we have consumed for the last half century. News stories about political scandal lend credence to the claim that politicians are liars, political comedy is a constant stream of jokes about the failures of government, and every two years political ads claim that the stakes in an election are high and the consequences are dire. No wonder the American public is politically distrustful.

Americans distrust the news media, not only because politicians tell them to be distrustful of it but also because many news organizations maintain they are the only ones to be trusted. Partisans fill 24 hours of airtime and limitless web pages that help prime an audience to believe only one perspective and to wholly reject opposing thought. The political isolation in which the American public gets their news and information allows people to be genuinely shocked when their prognostications and opinions turn out to be wrong. Instead of learning and correcting, the public then gets angry at a system they think has misled them. Therefore, the cycle of mistrust continues.

In a nation that prides itself on our First Amendment rights and dedication to the ideals of a free marketplace, it is doubtful that there is an easy solution to this problem. As long as there are messaging platforms on which to communicate, people will do so for all kinds of reasons: to connect and to assault. And as long as there is money to be made from political discourse, groups will double down on the hostile rhetoric in order to succeed. Nevertheless, it does present an interesting challenge for the public that could be productive. If we can turn down the volume of political discourse and listen to others, we have a fighting chance. If not, the political system will continue to be fast and loud and, unfortunately, unproductive and slightly mean.

The rest of this book explores how political media is being used and how citizens can adapt to the environment in which we find ourselves without hitting the "mute" button too frequently. Interviews, research, data, and journalism are all used to analyze the landscape and explain how, in the twenty-first century, politics became so loud, and why the American public is super mad at everything all the time.

## NOTES

1. More on this with specific citations will be discussed at length in Chapter 5.
2. This is from a September 2017 study from the Pew Research Center titled "Republicans much 'colder' than Democrats in view of professors."
3. President Ronald Reagan's First Inaugural Address, January 20, 1981.
4. Bartlett, "How *Fox News* Changed America" (New York, 2016).
5. Although not as popular and lucrative as those on the right.
6. FreedomWorks is a libertarian group so the members *hate* the establishment.

24    A. DAGNES

# WORKS CITED

est

Auter, Z. 2016. Number of Americans Closely Following Politics Spikes. *Gallup. com*, September 22. Retrieved from http://news.gallup.com/poll/195749/number-americans-closely-following-politics-spikes.aspx.

Baker, G. 2016. Vice News and the New World of the News. *The Wall Street Journal*, October 30. Retrieved from http://www.wsj.com/articles/vice-media-and-the-new-world-of-the-news-1477879441.

Bartlett, B. 2015. *How Fox News Changed American Media and Political Dynamics*, June 3 Available at SSRN: https://ssrn.com/abstract=2604679.

Bazilian, E. 2014. How Shane Smith Built Vice into a $2.5 Billion Empire. *Adweek*, September 29.

Blumenthal, S. 1980. *The Permanent Campaign*, 1st ed. New York, NY: Simon and Shuster.

Broder, D. 1994. War on Cynicism. *The Washington Post*, July 6: Op-Ed.

Colbert, S., interview by T. Gross. 2016. *Fresh Air*, November 2.

Cottle, M. 2016. Newt Broke Politics—Now He Wants Back In. *The Atlantic*, July 14. Retrieved from https://www.theatlantic.com/politics/archive/2016/07/newt-broke-politicsnow-he-wants-back-in/491390/.

Dickerson, J., interview by S.P. Gabfest. 2016. Host, *CBS's Face the Nation*, December 15.

Epstein, B. 2018. *The Only Constant Is Change: Technology, Political Communication, and Innovation Over Time*. Oxford: Oxford University Press.

Fischer, S., interview by A. Dagnes. 2017. Media Trends Reporter. *Axios*, June 15.

Fried, A. 2012. *Distrust in Government as a Political Weapon*. New York, NY: Scholar Study Network.

Gallup. (2011). *Gallup.org*. Retrieved from http://www.gallup.com/poll/5392/trust-government.aspx.

Garrett, M., interview by A. Dagnes. 2017. *CBS News White House Correspondent*, August 17.

Goddard, T. 2016. *Political Wire*. Retrieved February 14, 2017, from http://politicaldictionary.com/words/permanent-campaign/.

Grynbaum, M. 2017. Trump Strategist Stephen Bannon Says Media Should 'Keep Its Mouth Shut'. *New York Times*, January 26. Retrieved from https://www.nytimes.com/2017/01/26/business/media/stephen-bannon-trump-news-media.html?_r=0.

Hannity, S. 2017. Cable Exclusive: President Trump Sits Down with Sean Hannity at White House. *Fox News*, January 26. Retrieved from http://www.foxnews.com/transcript/2017/01/26/cable-exclusive-president-trump-sits-down-with-sean-hannity-at-white-house/.

Hermann, J. 2016. Inside Facebook's (Totally Insane, Unintentionally Gigantic, Hyperpartisan) Political-Media Machine. *New York Times Magazine*, August 14. Retrieved from http://www.nytimes.com/2016/08/28/magazine/inside-facebooks-totally-insane-unintentionally-gigantic-hyperpartisan-political-media-machine.html?_r=0.

Kenkins, H.S. 2013. *Spreadable Media: Creating Value and Meaning in a Networked Culture*. New York, NY: New York University Press.

Komarow, S. 1989. *House Republicans Elect Gingrich to No. 2 Spot, Chart Battle with Democrats*. Washington, DC: Associated Press.

Lemann, N. 2005. Fear and Favor: Why Is Everyone Mad at the Mainstream Media? *The New Yorker*, February 14.

Miller, A. 1974. Political Issues and Trust in Government: 1964–1970. *American Political Science Review* 68 (3): 951–972.

Mulaney, J. 2018. *Kid Gorgeous at Radio City*, May 1 (J. Mulaney, Performer). Radio City Music Hall, New York, NY, USA.

Nye, J.S. 1997. *Why People Don't Trust Government*. Cambridge, MA: Harvard University Press.

Patterson, T. 2016. *News Coverage of the 2016 General Election: How the Press Failed the Voters*. Cambridge, MA: Harvard Kennedy School.

Pew Research Center. 2014. *Political Polarization in the American Public*. Washington, DC: Pew Research Center.

———. 2015. Beyond Distrust: How Americans View Their Government. *People-press.org*, November 23. Retrieved from http://www.people-press.org/2015/11/23/beyond-distrust-how-americans-view-their-government/.

Reagan, R. 1964. A Time for Choosing. *The Heritage Foundation*, October 27. Retrieved from http://www.heritage.org/initiatives/first-principles/primary-sources/a-time-for-choosing-ronald-reagan-enters-the-political-stage.

Riffkin, R. 2015. Americans' Trust in Media Remains at Historical Low. *Gallup. org*, September 28. Retrieved from http://www.gallup.com/poll/185927/americans-trust-media-remains-historical-low.aspx?g_source=Trust in Media&g_medium=search&g_campaign=tiles.

Rutenberg, J. 2016. Sean Hannity Turns Adviser in the Service of Donald Trump. *The New York Times*, August 21. Retrieved from https://www.nytimes.com/2016/08/22/business/media/sean-hannity-turns-adviser-in-the-service-of-donald-trump.html.

Shaer, M. 2017. How Far Will Sean Hannity Go? *The New York Times*, November 28. Retrieved from https://www.nytimes.com/2017/11/28/magazine/how-far-will-sean-hannity-go.html?partner=socialflow&smid=tw-nytmag&smtyp=cur.

Shafer, J. 2017. The Media Bubble Is Worse Than You Think. *Politico*, April 25. Retrieved from https://www.politico.com/magazine/story/2017/04/25/media-bubble-real-journalism-jobs-east-coast-215048.

Shapiro, A. 2010. Distrusting Government: As American as Apple Pie. *NPR. org*, April 19. Retrieved from http://www.npr.org/templates/story/story.php?storyId=126028106.

Silverman, C. 2016. Hyperpartisan Facebook Pages Are Publishing False and Misleading Information at an Alarming Rate. *Buzzfeed*, October 20. Retrieved from https://www.buzzfeed.com/craigsilverman/partisan-fb-pages-analysis?utm_term=.qlL70PXJy#.yjzRNPdOl.

Spayd, L. 2016. The Truth About 'False Balance'. *The New York Times*, September 10. Retrieved from https://www.nytimes.com/2016/09/11/public-editor/the-truth-about-false-balance.html?_r=0.

Stolberg, S.G. 2012. Gingrich Stuck to Caustic Path in Ethics Battles. *The New York Times*, January 26. Retrieved from http://www.nytimes.com/2012/01/27/us/politics/the-long-run-gingrich-stuck-to-caustic-path-in-ethics-battles.html.

CHAPTER 2

# Upping the Anti's: 50 Years of Vilifying Intellectuals, the Government, and the Media

In 1971, a Richmond, Virginia, lawyer named Lewis Powell Jr. was talking to his neighbor about ways to present a business-positive perspective to the public. Powell's neighbor was Eugene Sydnor Jr., who happened to be the education director of the U.S. Chamber of Commerce. Sydnor asked his friend to write up some of those thoughts and so Powell did, and while today we call it "The Powell Memorandum," the real title of the document was "Attack on American Free Enterprise System." This was not a subtle paper. It aimed to confront the multi-pronged assaults against the American economic system by powerful perpetrators who had it in for businessmen. Powell identified the "varied and diffused" culprits as "the Communists, New Lefties and other revolutionaries who would destroy the entire system" (Powell 1971). This, according to Powell, made sense since those Lefties would be against free enterprise by dint and virtue of ideology. But the real problem emanated from places more pernicious and more institutional:

> The most disquieting voices joining in the chorus of criticism come from perfectly respectable elements of society: from the college campuses, the pulpit, the media, the intellectual and literary journals, the arts and sciences, and from politicians. In most of these groups, the movement against the system is participated in only by minorities. Yet these often are the most articulate, the most vocal, the most prolific in their writing and speaking... One of the bewildering paradoxes of our time is the extent to which the enterprise system tolerates, if not participates, in its own destruction. (Powell 1971)

The real problem, according to Powell, could be directly traced to three distinct entities: the universities and their intellectuals who developed the harmful anti-capitalist theories that flowed from college campuses like daisy chains, the media (both news and entertainment) which had for so long refused to give business its due, and the government which denied pro-commerce policymaking in its collectivism. It was a short, succinct encapsulation of the three largest obstacles to the promotion of liberty.

The Memorandum further describes the sources and tenor of the attack against business, explains the role of the business community in protecting their own interests, and then goes into specific detail about how to combat the assault. The document is a fascinating read, written by a very sharp cookie; two months after Powell sent his Memorandum to the US Chamber of Commerce, President Nixon tapped him to be a Supreme Court Justice. The public was only able to read the paper more than a year after it was initially written, when newspaper columnist Jack Anderson published sections of the writing during Powell's Senate confirmation hearing, and shortly, thereafter, the whole thing was made public by the Chamber itself. Modern authors go back and forth about crediting the Powell Memorandum with shaping the modern conservative movement, but more important (for these purposes, at least) are the Memorandum's prescience when it comes to the strategy against that specific, professed set of liberal enemies: intellectuals, the government, and the media. Powell was building on a foundation of wariness that had been forming during the decades before; a growing conservative antipathy toward the three largest impediments to free enterprise. What Powell did, which was unique at the time, was to construct a strategy for corporate America to combat these three obstacles together.

Powell wrote that college campuses, as hotbeds of both intellectual growth and unfettered liberalism, are the first target against which to strike. Powell conceded that while the "need for liberal thought is essential for a balanced viewpoint," there is not much balance when seemingly everything slants to the left. His remedy: New scholars were necessary for the social sciences, pro-business speakers should visit campuses more frequently, textbooks should be reevaluated and rewritten, and "equal time" should be mandated in the classroom, all in the favor of free enterprise. He also spent a short amount of time advocating for closer ties to new business schools and wrote that attention should be paid to high schools. But really the primary focus was on college campuses.

Powell argued that the next focus should be presenting a business-positive message in the media, especially on television, which was the emerging medium of the time:

> The national networks should be monitored in the same way that textbooks should be kept under constant surveillance. This applies not only to so-called "educational" programs... but to the daily "news analysis" which so often includes the most insidious type of criticism of the enterprise system. (Powell 1971)

Radio was good too, as were scholarly journals, books, and paid ads, but for Powell, TV was where it was at since 1971, television was massively influential. Finally, Powell argued for greater attention to politicians, specifically geared toward direct action. The Powell Memorandum argues that chief executive officers of major corporations should increase lobbying and public relations efforts, especially those aimed at shaping the policies important to business: "This is the lesson that political power is necessary; that such power must be assiduously cultivated; and that when necessary, it must be used aggressively and with determination – without embarrassment and without the reluctance which has been so characteristic of American business" (Powell 1971).

Thus, in one relatively short document was a coordinated strike against the three institutions that most affected political ideology and policymaking. This hostility toward intellectuals, the media and the government did not happen overnight. Powell's ideas were reflective of the political culture of the time, and so his Memorandum landed really well. President Nixon summarized the dominant conservative argument in 1972 when he said: "The press is the enemy. The establishment is the enemy. The professors are the enemy" (Glaister 2008). Powell's plan to focus on academia, the press, and the government was met by a very receptive conservative audience, which embraced the ideas and expanded upon it.

The Powell Memorandum clearly had a lasting effect on how we view these institutions, because we have come to an era in American politics when a segment of the population entirely dismisses them. While it would be easier to blame specific politicians and modern movements for this encouraging distrust, in truth there has been a fifty-year march toward institutional contempt, a slow-boil of accusations and doubt that built to the fever pitch we have today. Our modern, polarized media system could not exist were it not for this foundation of distrust. The disparagement toward the press would not be possible if it did not also extend to the politicians who lead us and to the scholarship used to form policy and make decisions.

The USA was founded on a healthy skepticism toward intellectualism (hence, the broadsides against Jefferson—of all people—as beautifully described by Richard Hofstadter in *Anti-intellectualism in American Life*), the press (the 1798 Alien and Sedition Act), and the government (the Bill of Rights). For the sake of brevity, this examination of our anti's begins in the modern era; the time after World War II when modern political ideologies began to gel and coalesce around central ideas. What we now call the "conservative movement" was born in this postwar period as a reaction against the expansion of federal power. As most political movements originate in reaction against something else, the anti-intellectual, anti-government, and anti-media crusades came about as reactions specifically produced to counter the liberalism of the early and mid-twentieth century. Identifying bias and attempting to remedy an imbalance is not problematic on its own, but the result of this particular rejoinder against liberal intellectuals, the government, and the press has helped to form our current political polarity. Rather than trying to reconcile differences or forge compromise and discussion, hammering away at these institutions has directly resulted in completely detached ideological information systems. Conservative elites spent fifty years arguing that college professors, the government, and the media cannot be trusted. At some point, a segment of the conservative public bought into the argument. One important consequence of this derision is the polarization we have today and the separate spheres of news and information that have resulted.

## ANTI-INTELLECTUALISM

It is on college campuses, the conservative argument goes, that the problematic seedlings of liberalism are planted. Institutions of higher learning serve two purposes: Scholars research and write, publishing the kind of work that is used when formulating policy; and academics also teach our children. Professorial instruction of students is fundamental for the development of a new generation of Americans in all fields, and accordingly, universities are viewed as tremendously influential in shaping discourse and thought. Early in American history, a select few Americans went to college, which meant that university attendance was something of an elitist endeavor. As literacy rates rose in the late 1800s and more colleges were founded, the number of college graduates began to grow, but not expansively. So although there were more colleges in America only a select segment of the population had degrees, and as a result, a university education was regarded as special and important. The learned men were the successful ones, which led to the idea of college attendance as an aspirational undertaking. Two important pieces of legislation increased college attendance in the second half of the twentieth century: the GI Bill encouraged World War II veterans to go back to college (calling it the "pathway to the middle class") and then affirmative action programs encouraged minority students to apply to colleges and universities. Mid-twentieth century, America saw more people going to college than ever before and that number kept growing. Add the baby boom to these two legislative actions and the percentage of American college graduates doubles from 7.7% in 1960 to 16.2% in 1980 and then doubles *again* to 33.4% in 2016 (Statista 2017).

All of the fresh new collegiate faces meant two important things: Despite the appeal of higher learning and the obvious benefits of a college degree, Americans remained mistrustful of "eggheads"[1] and had a general suspicion of smarty-pants professors. There was a historical foundation for this. As the historian Richard Hofstadter notes, the American public has a longstanding "dislike of specialists and experts" (Hofstadter 1963), preferring to rely on the wisdom of the "common man" to someone more high-falutin.[2] It is important to mention that in *Anti-intellectualism in American Life,* Hofstadter resists an ideological characterization of this anti-intellectualism, choosing instead to focus on the cultural rejection of specialists. He notes that Americans have historically held suspicions of mavens, not because they *were* superior but because they either acted superior or just believed themselves to be superior. He writes about the difference between humor (acceptable to the public) and wit (objectionable) in this way: "... humor is folkish, usually quite simple, and readily accessible. Wit is humor intellectualized; it is sharper; it has associations with style and sophistication, overtones of aristocracy" (Hofstadter 1963). In short, Americans have a longstanding attraction to the understandable and the relatable. As a result, many Americans still regarded the idea of higher education, those colleges filled with experts and authorities, with wariness. One might have thought that more people attending college would have had the effect of democratizing higher learning, and it is possible this democratizing happened, especially in places where college was viewed as the pathway to the middle class. At the same time, it is not surprising that resentment toward snobs on campus persisted. There is a uniquely American aspect of this as well, since we are a nation that fetishizes the self-made man. The "Horatio Alger Myth" was named for the author of many books about young men overcoming poverty and great odds to triumph over adversity. The legend of the self-made, common man popularized by American cultural mythology is especially poignant for many conservatives who like the "pull yourself up" philosophy above all.

The fear of intellectual snobbery, however, paled in comparison with the anxiety over the research that scholars produced and the classes they taught. The hottest topic of the time, both on campuses and off was communism, and much of the mid-twentieth century was rooted in its absolute rejection. Conservatives scorned any compromise of the American capitalist ideal, while liberals allowed themselves to be more relativist in their thinking. The very idea that college professors and academics were spreading the Red Menace was antithetical to those on the right, and the accusations of campus bias began to be applied with a rather broad brush, yet not entirely without merit. One sociological survey from the 1950s found "nearly half of academic social scientists scoring high on an index of 'permissive' attitudes toward communism" (Gross and Fosse 2012). The sharp contrast between a liberal arts education (it is in the name, after all) and the anti-communist movement was pronounced. In *Anti-intellectualism*, Hofstadter quotes a 1951 article from the *Freeman*, a Libertarian magazine published from 1950 to 2016:

> Our universities are the training ground for the barbarians of the future, those who, in the guise of learning, shall come forth loaded with pitchforks of ignorance and cynicism, and stab and destroy the remnant of human civilization. It will not be the subway peasants of who will tear down the walls: they will merely do the bidding of our learned brethren… who will erase individual Freedom from the ledgers of human thought.[3] (Hofstadter 1963)

Academics pushed back against this criticism with the kind of relativist regard that made the conservatives batty in the first place. Seymour Martin Lipset and Everett Carll Ladd took up the earlier study of left-leaning academics and expanded upon it in 1976, and argued that intellectualism was "a rational, critical, creative mindset linked to the Western intellectual tradition," which was important for the existence of higher learning, and they concluded this kind of creativity was "naturally at odds with most forms of conservatism" (Gross and Fosse 2012). Not surprisingly, conservatives were not mollified by this explanation, and many on the right began to protest loudly against the scholarly hotbeds of liberalism. They did so in speeches, articles, and books.

Calling itself a "major force within the conservative movement," Regnery Publishing was established in 1947 and the house published William F. Buckley's *God and Man at Yale* in 1951. Regnery remains a conservative publisher today, and in 2017 announced that it would no longer recognize the *New York Times* accounting of book sales, arguing the *Times* counting was (you guessed it) biased against conservatives (Bauder 2017). The *Times* responded: "The political views of authors have no bearing on our rankings, and the notion that we would manipulate the lists to exclude books for political reasons is simply ludicrous" (ibid.). Regnery was not placated and broke from the *Times* for good in order to maintain its conservative bona fides, after 70 years in the business. Back in 1951, when Regnery was in its publishing infancy, William F. Buckley was one of the first modern authors to publically criticize academia, and *God and Man* made a pretty big splash. Clearly an intellectual, Buckley was one of the first to call attention to liberal biases in academia and in doing so set the stage for conservative intellectuals to set themselves apart from the leftist scholars. Buckley took Yale to task for promoting a collectivism that was antithetical to conservative values. He specifically called out the textbooks and faculty[4] and wrote that his book proposed:

> ...to expose what I regard as an extraordinarily irresponsible educational attitude that, under the protective label "academic freedom," has produced one of the most extraordinary incongruities of our time: the institution that derives its moral and financial support from Christian individualists and then addresses itself to the task of persuading the sons of these supporters to be atheistic socialists. (Buckley, *God and Man at Yale* 1951)

Buckley's early aversion to academia did not subside in the following decades, since among his more famous quotes was: "I'd rather entrust the government of the United States to the first 400 people listed in the

Boston telephone directory than to the faculty of Harvard University" (Davenport 2015). But his dislike and distrust of academia went further than simple displeasure of the professorial class; in the 1955, "Publisher's Statement" that introduced the *National Review*, the conservative magazine he founded as an antidote to the liberal press,[5] Buckley wrote about the creation and dissemination of bad ideas:

> One must recently have lived on or close to a college campus to have a vivid intimation of what has happened. It is there that we see how a number of energetic social innovators, plugging their grand designs, succeeded over the years in capturing the liberal intellectual imagination. And since ideas rule the world, the ideologues, having won over the intellectual class, simply walked in and started to run things. Run just about everything. There never was an age of conformity quite like this one, or a camaraderie quite like the Liberals'. (Buckley, Publisher's Statement on Founding National Review 1955)

Buckley was not alone. Suspicion and dislike of liberal academics and intellectuals spread through the right-wing of mid-century American politics. 1952 and 1956 presidential candidate Adlai Stevenson gave the impression of embodying that elitist spirit, even as Stevenson noted himself that "not even the Messiah could have beaten Eisenhower in 1952" (Epstein 1968). In 1954, the social critic Irving Howe wrote: "Stevenson was the first of the liberal candidates in the post-Wilson era who made no effort to align himself with the plebeian tradition or with plebeian sentiments; Stevenson was the candidate whom the intellectuals, trying hard to remove plebeian stains, admired most" (Howe 1954). Distrust of snooty intellectuals gained political ground during the Nixon administration where Vice President Spiro Agnew served as the official voice against the snobs and arrogant highbrows who dominated leftist thought. Agnew wove specific hits against scholars where he could. In one 1969 speech made in Jackson, Mississippi, Agnew regionalized his dislike when he said: "For too long the South has been the punching bag for those who characterize themselves as liberal intellectuals" (Story and Laurie 2008). Later that year in Harrisburg, Pennsylvania, he spoke more broadly when he criticized the proponents of academic freedom as hypocritically intolerant and, in what could be seen as a predictor of modern free speech arguments around the country, said about college professors: "In the name of academic freedom, they destroy academic freedom.... They would have us believe that they alone know what is good for America; what is true and right and beautiful. They would have us believe that their reflective action is superior to our reflective action; that their revealed righteousness is more effective than our reason and experience" (Story and Laurie 2008). In a clap-back to the early arguments of an elitist/common man contrast, Agnew said about scholars: "I call them snobs for most of them disdain to mingle with the masses who work for a living" (Story and Laurie 2008).

In short, Spiro Agnew was the 1970s not-so-secret agent against intellectuals, and he gave good quote. Yet it is also important to see the culture in which his remarks were received since, during the protest generation, many Americans regarded universities as lawless places of demonstrations and tumult. This was for good reason. The counterculture of the 1960s was thriving on college campuses across the country, because the young are idealistic folk and they have some time on their hands. Students first protested against racial inequality and then the Vietnam War, and the dissent that grew from unrest to radicalization in places drew national media attention. Protests turned into riots at UC Berkeley, Columbia, Jackson State, and other universities around the country. Most famously at Kent State University in Ohio, National Guardsmen killed four students in an unprovoked shooting. Some of the time, news coverage fostered the idea that American universities were where students demonstrated, rioted, did drugs, had sex, and occasionally learned something from a radical professor who was preaching communism. A broadside landed very well against the institutions that not only hosted such behavior, but also seemingly encouraged it.

And so conservatives began to fight back against these intellectuals and their institutions in several ways. They continued their public attacks on the universities and their professors but they also began to engage young people and fund academic programs of their own to combat the bias they perceived. Not only did William F. Buckley rail against liberal intellectuals in *God and Man at Yale* and bring an important intellectual magazine into the culture with *The National Review*, but he also worked tirelessly to encourage a new generation of conservatives. The Young Americans for Freedom (YAF) was founded in 1960 and their first meeting was held at Buckley's Connecticut estate. The YAF "Sharon Statement" was their own opening salvo where they listed political and economic freedom as tandem goals, maintained that the sole function of government was to protect these freedoms, and wrote: "That when government ventures beyond these rightful functions, it accumulates power which tends to diminish order and liberty" (Story and Laurie 2008). The idea to culti-vate young talent (an ideological farm team, if you will) was a good one and the birth of YAF encouraged other such efforts. During the protest era of the 1960s, the Olin Foundation (which closed in 2005) concen-trated their attention on elite schools where campus protests were held. Calling it the "Beachhead Strategy," the Foundation's James Pierson headed up the effort to inject a free-market conservatism into these left-leaning campuses. The group focused first on Cornell University where, in 1969, African-American student protestors armed themselves as they aimed to occupy the school (Gibson 2016). As Jane Mayer writes in *Dark Money*, the foundation worked to infiltrate the most elite uni-versities "because they were emulated by other colleges and universities of lesser stature" (Mayer 2016). This kind of trickle-down economic lib-erty was important in the area of education because specific departments, especially those in the social sciences, were "hostile to capitalism" (Mayer 2016). This attempt to sway higher learning to the right continued into the 1980s and 1990s when the Koch brothers got into the game.

In what can be seen as a continuation of the Powell Doctrine, in 1996, Richard Fink of the Koch Foundation wrote a paper called "The Structure of Social Change," which argued for a stronger conservative/libertarian influence in universities, think tanks, and advocacy groups. The paper titled "From Ideas to Action: The Role of Universities, Think Tanks, and Activist Groups" was published in *Philanthropy* mag-azine and was based on the writings of conservative economic philos-opher Friedrich Hayek. Calling it a "talent pipeline," the Kochs paid attention to college programs and college students and this has grown in the past three decades (Kotch 2017). The higher education dona-tions, which come mostly from the Charles Koch Foundation, go toward underwriting free-market academic centers, professorships, post-doc-toral and graduate fellowships, scholarships, and course creation. Their lecture series usually features speakers who come from universities or think tanks funded by Koch. They also help fund student groups that read laissez-faire economics books, including books authored by Koch himself (Kotch 2017). This direct attention to colleges was one part of a long game that has since born fruit, as students graduate from these programs and enter the workforce as young libertarians. Dave Levinthal is a researcher at the Center for Public Integrity and has written about the Koch brothers funding colleges. In a 2015 *Atlantic* piece, Levinthal wrote that in 2013, the Kochs donated almost $20 million to 210 college campuses (Levinthal, Spreading the Free-Market Gospel 2015). That number has steadily increased in recent years, and many schools have found themselves strapped for cash and happy to accept the donations. One frequently asked question concerns the impact of these donations; the Koch organizations argue that funding academic programs help to level a biased intellectual playing field as it increases the quality of higher education. Those who push back against such donations contend that the strings attached are antithetical to higher learning. I spoke with Levinthal who made another salient point: that high school students may go to colleges without knowing or (caring who) is funding their programs (Levinthal, Senior Reporter, Center for Public Integrity 2017). Since the Kochs fund so many programs at so many different schools, it can be challenging to identify pedagogical cause and effect. This is clearly not the case for George Mason University, frequently referred to as "Koch U," but many of the other Koch-funded endowments are considerably smaller and, thus, less obvious.

There are other conservative schools that are funded by conservative donors, and in the past decade, these universities have garnered attention and prominence. Colleges like Grove City, St. Vincent's, and Hillsdale have begun to serve as conduits to bring active conservative students to DC as interns and young staffers. According to an article about Hillsdale in *The New York Times*, the school has been successful in increasing their profile around Washington thanks to their significant student population:

> In Washington, Hillsdale plays an active role in an ecosystem of conservative thought and policy. It joined with the Heritage Foundation to run a fellowship program for congressional staff members. Its D.C. outpost, the Allan P. Kirby Jr. Center for Constitutional Studies and Citizenship, runs a lecture series and serves as a base for Hillsdale undergraduates who are interning at conservative think tanks or publications. (Eckholm 2017)

Shifting the educational objective to center on a conservative perspective is one way that conservatives combat the perceived biases on campuses, but as Levinthal notes this has led to the thought that those on the right have to seek out specifically conservative universities (Levinthal, Senior Reporter, Center for Public Integrity 2017). That, in turn, adds to the antagonism toward academics that has been building for five decades, building on the notion that higher learning must be changed in order to shape ideological discourse.

Other ways to influence intellectual debate include the formation of outside groups to monitor the colleges and universities where conservatism is not so prominently featured. The primary argument for these watchdog groups is that colleges are so inherently liberal, they must be scrutinized and then outed to expose their ideological biases. One of the oldest and more established groups, Accuracy in Academia, was founded in 1985 to scrutinize colleges, faculty, and publications. A *Washington Post* article about the group's introduction described it as such:

> The idea behind AIA… is to draw attention to professors whose courses are ideologically biased by writing about them in newsletters to AIA subscribers and student representatives. Newsletters will be issued only after professors have been contacted and given an opportunity to respond to students' complaints, they said. (Muscatine 1985)

Such a group could only have launched and lasted within an existing culture of skepticism, and AIA built upon the foundation of anti-intellectualism built during the run-up to the 1980s. Interestingly, while one might assume that the Reagan administration would have supported such an organization, they did not.[6] The Education Secretary at the time was William Bennett who demurred when asked to comment on the founding of AIA. Instead, his assistant made a statement and the *Post* reported on it thusly:

> William Kristol, on leave from the faculty at Harvard University's Kennedy School of Government, said he opposes the group's tactics. 'Of course there is a bias on campus, but this kind of scrutiny by an external group isn't the way to attack it,' he said. Kristol, who teaches political philosophy and described himself as a conservative, said his colleagues at Harvard are 'predominantly liberal, but very tolerant. On the whole, professors try not to indoctrinate students'. (Muscatine 1985)

Two points are important from this *Washington Post* story. First, in 1985 a plucky, young Bill Kristol was already exercising his conservative intellectual muscles in defiance against an ideologically intemperate wing of the GOP. Second, Kristol's opposition fell on deaf ears because these groups not only endured; they have increased in number today. Another large group, the Leadership Institute, was founded in the late 1970s to train conservative activists, and in 2009 launched its own campus-monitoring offshoot project called "Campus Reform." These activist groups specifically counter liberalism on college campuses by calling out classroom biases and name-checking the scholars who are engaging in such bad behavior. David Horowitz first institutionalized this tactic in a 2006 book called *The Professors: The 101 Most Dangerous Academics in America*, which listed and chronicled the "worst" liberal instructors with whom Horowitz vehemently disagreed. Since then, the idea of outing leftist professors has moved online, and there are now Web sites dedicated to these efforts. Turning Point USA (TPUSA) is an activist group that organizes and coaches young conservatives on college campuses to promote the "principles of freedom" and economic liberty. On their Web site, TPUSA has a link for their "Professor Watchlist" which, according to the group, is supposed to "expose and document college professors who discriminate against conservative students and advance leftist propaganda in the classroom" (Turning Point USA 2018). These activist groups continue the conservative hostility toward academics and are increasingly using students as their campus foot soldiers.

This current mistrust of academia seeps into electoral politics with regularity. The 2016 Republican Party Platform included this line about higher education: "Our colleges, universities, and trade schools, large and small, public and private, form the world's greatest assemblage of learning.... Their excellence is undermined by an ideological bias deeply entrenched within the current university system" (RNC 2016). Not surprisingly, a 2017 study conducted by the Pew Research Center found that 58% of Republicans polled had a disapproving view of colleges and universities, saying that these institutions had a "negative effect on the country" (P. R. Center, Sharp Partisan Divisions in Views of National Institutions 2017). This pessimistic view of academics then leads to a shortage of conservative college professors because of the rather circular situation where conservatives believe that they are not welcome in academic ranks and thus do not apply to graduate programs in order to become academics. For that reason, there is a dearth of conservatives in academe. It is a pickle. A 2010 sociological study by Gross and Fosse showed that liberals dominate academia for several reasons, one being stereotyping. The study found that since there is an existing categorization of liberal college professors, many conservatives will not even consider "professor" as a viable job choice. The two authors argue that:

... given the way the American academic profession was institutionalized and its twentieth-century history, it has acquired such a strong reputation for liberalism and secularism that over the last 35 years few politically – or religiously – conservative students, but many liberal and secular ones, have formed an aspiration to become professors. (Gross and Fosse 2012)

This is a real drawback, especially if one considers a hallmark of higher learning to be diversity of thought. The lack of conservative voices among many professors throughout the academy is challenging, therefore, as it leads to a possible bias by faculty while at the same time it also encourages the accusations of bias that are pervasive. What it does most significantly, however, is maintain a schism between liberals and conservatives about truth, scholarship, and higher learning, which is dangerous both inside the classroom and outside of it.

Currently, a central argument against academia has shifted back again to the students, as protests against conservative speakers (and counter-protests to those protests) have cropped up on college campuses around the country. These protests were fodder for the right-wing narrative that colleges were too liberal and so they gained an incredible amount of attention, which then fed efforts to trigger more protests, which then emboldened louder criticism of universities. All of the outrages launched when so-called safe spaces began to appear on campuses where students would be free from hearing challenging or difficult ideas. Once these spaces gained national attention the debates about the First Amendment and the oversensitivity of students roared to life. In 2015, President Obama said that he disagreed with those students who wanted to be shielded from opposing thought and argued that this kind of indulgence was problematic, especially when students "have to be coddled and protected from different points of view. ... That's not the way we learn" (Arnold 2017). Obama's comments did not seem to matter: the storyline of conservative versus liberal was set, which then sparked a whole new round of fighting. Conservative groups began to invite purposely antagonistic speakers to campus which naturally drew the kinds of protests that kept the story going. Massive demonstrations at schools like UC Berkeley and the University of Wisconsin made national news, which only served to intensify the anger on both sides. This, of course, is exactly the point. The larger the hostilities and the louder the name-calling are politically profitable for those who paint with broad brushes to attract and excite a membership.

A 2018 episode of the public radio show *This American Life* was dedicated to the issue of free speech on college campuses and used an encounter between two people at the University of Nebraska at Lincoln (UNL). The segment featured reporting from Steve Kolowich of the *Chronicle of Higher Education* who wrote a lengthy piece about campus protests, and both the radio show and the *Chronicle* article highlight how ideological battles at Universities have become political lightning rods (Kolowich 2018). On one side was a 19-year-old student named Kaitlyn who was a new member of the aforementioned conservative activist group TPUSA. On the other side was Courtney, a 47-year-old graduate student and adjunct instructor who saw Katie handing out leaflets and took it upon herself to demonstrate in loud opposition (Glass 2018). This was, essentially, a protest consisting of two people but it quickly became heated. Courtney made her own sign that read "Just say NO! to neo-Fascism" and using the slang nickname for a privileged white girl, stood across from Kaitlyn's table (which displayed buttons and stickers reading "Big Government SUCKS!") and yelled: "Becky the neo-fascist, right here. Wants to destroy public schools, public universities. Hates DACA kids" (Kolowich 2018). As Kolowich states on the radio program: "Courtney knew she was playing to type, the liberal academic who cried racism. But she didn't really care. She was there to make a scene" (Glass 2018).

This specific-scene moved in sadly predictable ways, culminating in the right's outrage against politically correct "snowflakes" who cannot handle dissent or opposing thought, but a few things combined to make what should have been a smallish incident into a major conservative story. The first was that Courtney went personal and offensive in her opposition to Kaitlyn and TPUSA, saying that supporting TPUSA was akin to supporting the Ku Klux Klan (which it's not). Ramping up the language led to an escalation of tensions that included screaming, cursing, crying, and obscene gesturing, and Courtney prompted most of this. But Kaitlyn turned up the volume by sending a picture of Courtney giving her the finger to TPUSA. This had the multi-pronged effect of turning Kaitlyn into a conservative cause celeb while demonizing UNL professors, the hitch being that as a graduate student, Courtney was not a UNL professor herself. Courtney was released from her adjunct instructor duties at the university, and the whole event had become so massive Nebraska politicians put pressure on the university president to do more about curbing the liberalism on campus. Garnering national

attention, as well as the label "conservative hero," there was no motivation for Kaitlyn to tamp down her own rhetoric. She testified against a Lincoln City Council resolution affirming diversity and said: "Due to my traumatic experience on campus, I worry that I'm going to fall victim to the resolution…. Based on one person's definition of race and hate, am I going to have to fear that the police are going to come to my door, for me standing up for freedom?" (Kolowich 2018). This statement is as illogical as the comparison between TPUSA and the Klan, and all of this hyperbole only makes it hard to see another side of an argument. That is problematic.

Another problem concerns painting with a broad brush. Assuming that *all* universities are the same neglects the considerable disparities between the types and styles of American colleges. There are dissimilarities between campus cultures, which have to do with geographic location, size, degree-granting programs, and accreditation, but seldom are these differences recognized. Add the rise of specifically conservative colleges to these differences and the sweeping generalizations about college students should not work, and yet they are working quite well. The University of Nebraska is not regarded as a hotbed of political activism or a steaming cauldron of liberalism, but this specific incident happened there and so UNL became, to conservative activists, as turbulent as UC Berkeley. When TPUSA circulated the video, it added fuel to the on-going right-wing fire against leftist universities which is fueled very much on purpose, because the flames are attention getting. A *Politico* article about White House advisor Stephen Miller helps to explain how this kind of animosity has triumphed in recent years.

> Miller represents a rising generation of conservatives for whom 'melting the snowflakes' and 'triggering the libs' are first principles. You can find them on college campuses, holding 'affirmative action bake sales' or hosting rallies for alt-right figures in the name of free speech. You can see them in the new conservative media, churning out incendiary headlines for *Breitbart News* or picking bad-faith fights on Twitter. Raised on talk radio, radicalized on the web, they are a movement in open revolt against the dogmas of 'political correctness'—and their tactics could shape the culture wars for years to come. (Coppins 2018)

When conservatives overemphasize small and singular examples or rage against the college campuses with "snowflake" students, they confirm a natty stereotype to be used in an ideological battle, but they also add to the distance between students and professors, parents and collegiate expectations, university credibility and reality. The accusations of bias against liberal professors are renewed in the minds of public, even where these allegations are unwarranted, unproven, or untrue and this comes with a cost: A 2017 study by the Pew Research Center found that while Democrats gave college professors an overall "warm" rating (at 66%), only 30% of Republicans feel similarly and 43% view college professors "coldly" (Fingerhut 2017). This is a problem that extends beyond my own desire to be thought of warmly: The right-wing's rejection of colleges and professors has pitted a segment of the American public squarely against academics. As a result, in an environment where politicos use the phrase "alternative facts" with a straight face and routinely discard scientific data, anti-intellectual biases have very real consequences for policymaking.

## ANTI-GOVERNMENT

The conservative hostility toward academe bleeds into other areas, since research is used in formulating policy and in media coverage of politics. Anti-intellectualism is one-third of a conservative argument against the left and the next third of the argument concerns trust in government. In short, there is almost none. According to a 2015 Pew Research Center study, only 19% of Americans actually trust the federal government to work. The problems are obvious: The government is too big and unwieldy, and according to Pew, "frustrating and badly managed" (P. R. Center, Beyond Distrust: How Americans View Their Government 2015). Many involved in governing are surprised by the aspersions cast against a system they view as, though imperfect, strong. The problem is that these charges of inefficiency and corruption, while erroneous as a sweeping indictment of a generally admirable governmental system, are rooted in some truths. In the past century, the federal government has rather considerably grown in size. New federal agencies, departments, and programs all need bureaucrats and staffers to run them and its sheer size is formidable. With this growth in size comes an immense scope of regulation that aims to assist all Americans, but we have varying ideas about how much government we want and need. Those on the left like the idea of government oversight to protect the country from the avaricious and powerful, but those on the right take the view that a massive government exceeds its proper role as a traffic cop. Liberals believe that the federal government should help the neediest among us while conservatives argue that too much government regulation adversely harnesses business in the name of protection, interferes with individual liberty, and is generally anathematic to what the Founders intended in the first place. In addition to fights about regulation, ideological clashes concern the question of duty, so conservatives maintain that government programs designed to further social justice are both excessive and beyond the scope of the government's purpose and those on the left argue that it takes a government to level a playing field. Where you stand on these issues depends on where you sit, but if your stand is that the government infringes upon personal rights and leaves you out of the bargain in the process, then the government is to blame. In the course of all of this fighting about the size and scope of the federal government, the approval ratings for our elected officials have plummeted. Interesting debates about the role of government have devolved into blanket condemnations against politicians, and throughout the time the term "Washington establishment" has gone from being an explanation for our complicated government to a personal attack.

The seeds of governmental distrust were planted decades ago and have grown into a mighty tree of hostility. Tempting though it would be, to begin with William F. Buckley standing athwart history yelling, "stop," or fast-forwarding to the modern repeal of the regulatory state, this exploration begins with the anti-communism of the 1950s. From Joseph McCarthy to Robert Welch to Barry Goldwater, there was a direct line drawn between the threat of international communism to the danger of domestic policy collectivism that would lead to severe and punitive government intrusion in America. The 1950s were dominated by the Red Scares, which led to Blacklists and uncompromising government suspicion, and McCarthy was at the forefront of this effort. His 1950 *Lincoln Day Address* took aim at the government which, he alleged, was riddled with ComSymps, those who were not only soft on communism but also aiding the enemy. McCarthy claimed to have a list of 57 communists working in the government and blamed both the political system and a spineless public for the danger: "...one of the important reasons for the graft, the corruption, the dishonesty, the treason in high Government positions – one of the most important reasons why this continues is a lack of moral uprising on the part of the 140 million American people" (Story and Laurie 2008). It took a while to discredit McCarthy, who was able to frighten the public for so long because he played into a commonly held fear. People were so afraid of communism that most Americans simply bought what McCarthy was selling, which meant that the fear of communism continued even as McCarthy faded from prominence.

In 1953, Russell Kirk published *The Conservative Mind* and carefully defined "conservative" to be a detailed set of principles steered by an unbending underlying ethos. These included an emphasis on morality, class distinctions, and economic liberty, among a serious distaste for radicalism. Postwar conservatives felt liberalism was a serious threat to these core values because they bumped up against the ideas that supported communism. Tying moral relativism and a collectivist government to the Red Menace was both culturally frightening and politically effective. Anti-communism was a cornerstone of modern conservatism and it paired nicely with anxiety about an expanding federal government. During this time, Ronald Reagan highlighted one major problem of a big federal government: It keeps getting bigger. And Buckley quipped: "One must bear in mind that the expansion of federal activity is a form of eating for politicians." In addition to fighting communism, the conservative movement of the 1950s and 1960s became dedicated to a fight against Washington.

The tangible threat of communism is a dominating authority gone wild, and thus it was rational for mainstream conservatives to worry about a federal government that was growing in range and reach. That said, some on the fringes of conservatism took the fear of communism and extended it into far more dangerous territory, where anti-communism blended with racism, anti-Semitism, and Xenophobia. One of the most important of the fringe groups of the mid-twentieth century was the John Birch Society, founded in 1958 and dedicated to the twin-causes of anti-communism and small government. On its face, this seemed to align with the rhetoric of the Republican Party. The group's leader, Robert Welch, connected an activist government with communism when he said in 1959: "We have the cancerous disease of collectivism firmly implanted now. We have people feeling that nothing should be done by them, but everything for them by the government. Its disastrous ravages are quite far advanced..." That might have been a palatable sentiment, but the JBS moved into radicalism when it publically opposed the Civil Rights Movement and Dwight D. Eisenhower, both for having communist tendencies. William F. Buckley and Russell Kirk spoke out against Robert Welch in the early 1960s, labeling him extremist, and Kirk once said that he was "loony and should be put away" (Buckley, Goldwater, the John Birch Society, and Me 2008). As the standard bearers of the conservative intellectual movement in America, they also saw Welch as a threat to serious conservatives with good ideas, and they had a point. The discussion shifts when a fringe figure dominates a political conversation, which makes it easier to discount the important ideas. And so the Grand Old Party hip-checked the Birchers out of the tent while maintaining their fight against communism and big government. Those on the far right stayed close to the GOP, since they did not have anywhere else to go, but until recently Republican politicians took pains to distance themselves from this faction. The faction never really went away.

Barry Goldwater, the firebrand Senator from Arizona, wrote in *Conscience of a Conservative*: "The root of evil is that the government is engaged in activities in which it has no legitimate business" (Goldwater 2007). In his 1964 presidential campaign, during his Republican Convention speech, he delivered his ultimatum against communism in a line cobbed from Cicero: "I would remind you that extremism in the defense of liberty is no vice. And let me remind you also that moderation in the pursuit of justice is no virtue." While these lines garnered negative attention from most on the left and smelled a bit too much like the John Birch Society for many in the middle, the Goldwaterian beliefs in fighting communism and promoting small government remained popular among conservatives. Ronald Reagan spoke on Goldwater's behalf during the 1964 presidential race, and predicted his own campaign rhetoric to come: "This is the issue of this election: whether we believe in our capacity for self-government or whether we abandon the American revolution and confess that a little intellectual elite in a far-distant capitol can plan our lives for us better than we can plan them ourselves" (Reagan 1964).

The lasting legacy of this period is an almost inextricable connection between the perils of a Soviet-style regime and the expansion of American governmental programs. This link has not gone away, which is why even today insults against liberals include "socialist" and "communist," even when these labels do not make sense. What has also stuck is the distrust of the government, because one needn't be a virulent anti-communist in the 1970s to think that the government was defective. Lara Brown from George Washington University made a very interesting point about government distrust during this time: It was totally bipartisan. First, LBJ lied to the American public about Vietnam, and then Nixon lied to the American public about Watergate. Both Democrats and Republicans had skin in the anti-government game because nobody trusted anyone (Brown 2017). This wide-ranging doubt about the institutions of government and the national dislike of our elected officials remained steadfast. A political scientist named Arthur Miller wrote:

> A period of sustained discontent may result from a deep-seated social conflict which, for some segment of the population has been translated into negative orientation toward the political system because their sense of insufficient political influence implies a futility in bringing about desired social change or control through political efforts; hence, they feel government is generally not to be trusted because it does not function for them. (Miller 1974)

In other words, political distrust was a nonpartisan endeavor for a time.

And then it became partisan again. Reagan was elected president in 1980 and the small government outlook grew stronger and became the foundation of the modern Republican Party. Reagan's 1980 convention speech included the line: "Our federal government is overgrown and overweight. Indeed, it is time for our government to go on a diet" (Story and Laurie 2008). In his 1981 Inaugural address, he said: "It is time to check and reverse the growth of government, which shows signs of having grown beyond the consent of the governed." Gaining steam throughout the 1980s was the "devolution revolution," which aimed to move power to the states. Reagan's New Federalism intended to shift power from the federal government to the states but when the initial plan fell flat, Reagan crafted a *new* New Federalism. His 1983 State of the Union address outlined the 92-page legislative proposal that would transfer power to the states through three large federal grants. According to one Treasury official: "The real intent of this legislation is to take a major share of the Federal grant system and transform it into revenue sharing, to withdraw Federal involvement in these activities and transfer the responsibilities to states, with the least possible disruption" (Pear 1983). All of this movement away from the federal government was predicated on the idea that it was too big, bloated, and broken. In a book from 1997 called *Why People Don't Trust Government*, political scientists Joseph S. Nye, Philip Zelikow, and David King noted the change from 1964 to 1996 where public trust in government dropped from 75 to 25% (Nye et al. 1997). The authors filled an entire book with reasons for the decline in trust, to include the difficulties in governing itself because a deliberative democracy is a system designed for fairness, not speed, and changes in the "human condition" in terms of how we work, play, and live (Nye et al. 1997). The constant denunciation of the federal government in rhetoric and policy did not help build confidence. But while all of these explanations are fair, to read other accounts from the 1990s and more modern reflections on that period, the real perpetrator of modern government distrust is Newt Gingrich.

It is impressive how many scholarly and journalistic resources point to former House Speaker Newt Gingrich and his 1994 "Republican Revolution" as pivotal in the advancement of anti-government sentiment. To review this point in time: The Democrats had been in control of the US House for forty years when Gingrich, a Republican from Georgia,[7] aimed to take party control of the chamber. First, in the early 1980s he formed the "Conservative Opportunity Society," a group of young GOP House members, who for years chipped away at the Democratic leadership by highlighting their mistakes and loudly complaining about their policies. Gingrich was elected House Minority Leader and said his goal was to "build a much more aggressive, activist party" (Komarow 1989), and he was successful, in part, because the political environment was ripe for the kind of angry, anti-establishment assault that he used to gain power. He played upon the misgivings about Congress at a time when many were already feeling wary. In a 1994 article for *The Washington Post*, venerable columnist David Broder wrote about the scorn that was plaguing the Nation's Capitol at the time:

...cynicism is epidemic right now. It saps people's confidence in politics and public officials, and it erodes both the standing and standards of journalism. If the assumption is that nothing is on the level, nothing is as it seems, then citizenship becomes a game for fools and there is no point trying to stay informed. (Broder 1994)[8]

Gingrich came of political age during this time of heightened pessimism and used the mood to elevate his own standing, an ironic thought since disparaging the political system ended up giving him significant political power.

Through a highly disciplined plan that included using C-SPAN cameras to speak directly to the American public,[9] Gingrich devised a new style of political leadership that defied norms and stunned the opposition. His attack was multi-pronged: He went against House traditions and customs to act in an obstructionist way, he worked hard to nationalize House elections, and, in the process, he centralized power within the House leadership (Cottle 2016). These efforts had legs, and they have lasted well beyond Gingrich's run as Speaker. We still see the obstructionism in Congress where lawmakers simply refuse to let bills, nominations, and budgets progress. House and Senate elections are now routinely nationalized with viral ad efforts and massive fund-raising attempts that extend well beyond their district or state borders. The power in the House remains centralized among a small group of leaders, and the lessons taught by Gingrich's success as Speaker persist on the Hill.

Also enduring has been the "take no prisoners" communications style that Gingrich employed. He orchestrated a public relations offensive against the Democrats that used message discipline and tight party control. He crafted a ten-point plan called the "Contract With America" that simplified his goals to the size of a *Readers Digest* insert. He went on a media offensive to sell the contract and in doing so disparaged his opponents to a national audience. Gingrich then had House Republicans use the same words that he did, to amplify his message and to keep everyone on-point. In a memo titled "Language, a Key Mechanism of Control," Gingrich distributed a list of 64 words to use in repetition against the Democrats, including "decay, traitors, radical, sick, destroy, pathetic, corrupt and shame" (Stolberg 2012). Constantly repeating the accusations of gross mismanagement, Gingrich hammered on the idea that Congress—and by extension Washington, DC—was extraordinarily defective and the Democrats were to blame. The tactic worked, as the 1994 midterm elections ushered in 54 new House and 8 new Senate Republicans, but it was not without cost; the name-calling that was predicated on the idea that government was atrocious might have been electorally reliable, but it led to the commonplace use of governmental distrust as "a political weapon" (Fried 2012). So commonplace, in fact, that now both parties rail against Washington (the Swamp) even as they aim to be a part of the establishment.

As the 1994 Republican Revolution hit Congress, Democrats took the hint and folded this smaller government idea into their own philosophy. During the 1990s, the Clinton/Gore administration crafted their

"Reinventing Government" program to shrink the federal bureaucracy. Thus, began a series of executive efforts to streamline a government viewed as too big just as legislative efforts aimed to roll back the government programs antithetical to conservative dogma. Under President Bill Clinton, the Democrats moved centrist, and under Speaker Gingrich, the Republicans turned right and kept on moving that way through the election of George W. Bush. The emphasis on small government, individualism, and economic liberty was a constant drumbeat heard by the public from politicians, many of whom ran on the platform: "DC is wrecked so elect me to change it." Both Republicans and Democrats continue to campaign with this pitch. Hence, the American public, told for decades that the government is mightily flawed, does not like DC very much. Why would they? The people who beg for jobs that take them to Washington routinely call it a cesspool.

This anti-Washington tactic works. The 2010 midterms was another one of those elections where antagonism against Washington was on the front burner, and Republicans ushered in 63 new members to the House and six to the Senate; the largest majority swing since 1948. Calling themselves members of the Tea Party, these anti-government activists rallied in protest against the big government in general, President Obama in particular. Florida Senator Marco Rubio, who would go on to run for president in 2016, said at the time: "The Tea Party movement is a sentiment in America that government is broken… and if we don't do something soon, this exceptional country will be lost" (Cohen 2010). The current state of anti-government sentiment is perhaps most easily captured by our election of a man without any political experience to the highest political office in the land. When Donald Trump consistently disparaged politicians on the 2016 campaign trail, calling Washington, DC "the Swamp," Trump tapped into a sentiment that had been growing for decades, fed by politicians who came before him. In a 2016 *The Wall Street Journal* op-ed piece, then-candidate Trump wrote: "The only antidote to decades of ruinous rule by a small handful of elites is a bold infusion of popular will. On every major issue affecting this country, the people are right and the governing elite are wrong" (Trump 2018). Denigrating the political system for political benefit is not new, but its efficacy is not without cost: The thought of becoming a politician today is laughable because the idea of "public service" has been so thoroughly trashed in the minds of the electorate. This means that good people are dissuaded from running for office, leaving the pursuit of public service to those who are more selfishly inclined. After all, who would want to work in a swamp filled with losers and ne'er-do-wells? The underlying argument is that government is bad—and any plan for government assistance, by extension, is bad as well. Yet many run for office and continue the assault against Washington with the kind of fervor once reserved for patriotism. In doing so, they use the media which brings us to the third antagonist in modern politics.

## Media Bias

The allegations that the media are liberally biased are so constant and universal, such statements come reflexively to many without evidence or understanding. It has become so deeply rooted in our polarization that for many, actual evidence of bias is unnecessary; liberal media bias is a simple fact of conservative life. Academics and journalists fight these allegations with data and gusto, to wit the conservative response often goes along the lines of: "Why should we believe you? You're liberally biased too." And the fight continues.

What is media bias, though? Much of the time, when someone alleges bias from news organizations, they speak in terms of ideological slanting where an organization is simply out to get one side or another. But news bias, as opposed to opinion parsing seen on cable TV (and on political blogs and on talk radio), is not so easily identified, nor does it happen in such a ham-handed way. Definitions are in order.[10] First and most importantly, the word "bias" when attached to news coverage has to mean that the coverage deviates from an "ideal" (Schiffer 2018). This ideal mandates coverage that is sourced, impartial, and independent. There is much to be said about structural bias, which is when news organizations, hungry for ad revenue, highlight the dramatic in order to keep viewers. But in this case, of importance is an ideological bias which is when there is a partisan slant to the news delivered. This slant can come in different shapes.

There is "gatekeeping," which is how news organizations determine what gets covered and what does not. Bias here can come in the form of either emphasizing certain stories or ignoring others. "Framing" is how a story is covered; this is the kind of bias where the frame of a story predicts the outcome, because a frame can move an audience to feel a certain way that strays from the ideal, impartial news coverage. Ideological bias is also seen when one side of a story is offered more forcefully than

another, or when two sides of a story are offered when one side is suffi-
cient, or when the coverage lacks quality, or when the tone of a story is
purposely snarky. In short, there are myriad places to find bias—but this
does not mean that there are myriad examples of bias to be found. Most
news organizations take rigorous steps to avoid the perception and reality of partiality, since bias is a death knell for a real news organization.

There are those who do not look in any of these places to find bias
because it is easier to allege unfairness without specifics, and there is an
academic theory that describes this. It is called the "hostile media effect"
and this theory, first explored in 1985, found that partisans especially
were prone to thinking that the media were biased against them (Vallone
et al. 1985). Since then, scholars have studied these hostile effects and
Richard Perloff from Cleveland State University did a thirty-year retrospective of the theory and found that with the growth of the media,
the advent of social media, and the heightened polarization in American
politics, the hostile media effect is alive and well (Perloff 2015). This
appears at first blush to be rather self-evident, but the author offered a
counter-possibility that because partisans seek out ideological news that
reinforces their existing opinions, the hostility toward the other side
could be diminished.

While a good idea, it was not found to be true, and an interesting
article by Kevin Arceneaux, Martin Johnson, and Chad Murphy helps
to explain why. Arceneaux et al. examined the highly fragmented news
climate to find out two things about what they called the "oppositional
media hostility," the theory being that there was not only partisan media
that championed someone's political beliefs, there was also enough
media to counterbalance this. They wanted to see if the abundance of
"counter-attitudinal" media (meaning, the partisan programming that
opposes someone's beliefs) brought about strong negative reactions
about the specific stories covered and the news media in general. They
also looked to see if "selective exposure" (meaning, the one-sided media
chosen specifically to reinforce someone's beliefs) helped to moderate
the negative feelings. They determined the content with which people
disagreed did, indeed, make them angrier but also found that having
programming that confirmed their preexisting opinions helped sooth the
ruffled feathers (Arceneaux et al. 2012). I spoke with Arceneaux about
the consequences of media self-selection and he proffered an interesting
point: partisan selective exposure leads to, among other things, overconfidence (Arceneaux 2017). This makes sense; if everyone from whom

you are hearing agrees with you, then you are less likely to challenge your own ideas or listen to any idea that contradicts your belief system. In total, this means that there exists a combination of believing that the media are hostile to your side and that you are spot-on 100% of the time. No wonder people feel strongly that the media are biased. And no wonder they are hostile about that.

Much like the decades-long evolution of arguments against academics and the government, there has been a similar progression of antipathy toward the media. Historians and media scholars will remind readers that the earliest American newspapers were both partisan and rooted in entertainment because the "modern concept of 'news' – information about the world reported accurately to readers – hadn't materialized" (Uberti 2017). According to Andie Tucher, a Columbia Journalism professor who was quoted in an article on *Splinter*, during the Founding: "Editors were party functionaries. Newspapers were very clear and open about it. No one was breaking any rules, because there were no rules" (Uberti 2017). No less than Alexander Hamilton, prescient in so many ways (a Broadway star before his time), wrote prolifically and criticized opponents in many different outlets, a process he referred to as a "diffusion of information" (Uberti 2017). Our information diffusion may be far more widespread today, but the same kind of news and opinion assortment still makes for a media environment that is ripe for partisanship.

Once advertising changed the monetization of the press (see Chapter 3), the very concept of journalism changed form. During the mid-twentieth century, the idea of impartial news and journalistic norms became standard. Only when there are norms from which to deviate can there be bias; when everything is partisan, bias is the rule, not the exception. And so once the standards kicked in, so too did the allegations of ideological partiality. Nicole Hemmer traces the earliest roots of the modern conservative media back to the Progressive Era, where reforms and muckraking dominated the press, through the New Deal where FDR fought with the "press lords" who ran the newspapers, right into the mid-century period when disgruntled conservatives coalesced around anti-interventionist attitudes that were not reflected in the press (Hemmer, Messengers of the Right 2016a).[11] From there, conservative magazines and publishing houses began to grow in number. *Human Events,* the *Manion Forum,* and the aforementioned *National Review* and Regnery Publishing were created to represent an alternative to what became known as a liberal bias. The mission of *Human Events* puts it best:

In reporting the news, *Human Events* is objective; it aims for accurate representation of the facts. But it is not impartial. It looks at events through eyes that are biased in favor of limited constitutional government, local self-government, private enterprise, and individual freedom. (Hemmer 2016b)

With this new refutation to the press, a conservative counterpoint was born. The seeds of modern media criticism were planted by bright and articulate ideologues who found a niche news market within the right-wing. According to Hemmer, the creation of a conservative media was just the first step in the argument against the press. The next step was an argument against government regulation; Hemmer writes that conservatives felt that journalists were biased and the government regulators of the media, in the form of the Federal Communications Commission (FCC), were biased as well. Conservatives especially disliked the "Fairness Doctrine," the rule that mandates both sides of an argument be represented on the news. According to Hemmer:

Conservative discontent with the FCC focused on the Fairness Doctrine, a broadcast standard meant to regulate controversial issues on radio and television. Conservatives felt the Fairness Doctrine unfairly tilted the playing field against them. Though devised to encourage controversial broadcasting, in practice the doctrine often led broadcasters to avoid controversy so they wouldn't have to give away free airtime. To conservatives, avoiding controversy inevitably meant silencing right-wing voices. (Hemmer, The Conservative War on Liberal Media Has a Long History 2014)

Additionally, according to conservatives, not only did the media silence right-wing voices, they crafted what we now call "fake news," and the argument went that, liberals were not just content to broadcast their own opinions, they made up the news they reported. The sum total of all of these perceived offenses on the part of the press meant that a solid conservative argument against the news media became stabilized in the culture. On his 1964 campaign plane, Republican Presidential candidate Barry Goldwater handed out pins to the traveling pool that read "Eastern Liberal Press" (Special 1964). As the USA entered Vietnam and the counterculture began to protest ever louder, the news media's coverage of the War and the protests further contributed the allegation that the press was left-leaning. Into this fray, according to *New Yorker* columnist David Remnick, rode Spiro Agnew, the Republican pit bull against liberalism. About Agnew's attention to the press, Remnick wrote:

> [Nixon] dispatched Agnew to map out a cultural description of another enemy, the op-ed unfriendlies and the network mandarins of what was beginning to be called the media. The views of "this little group of men" who "live and work in the geographical and intellectual confines of Washington, D.C., or New York City," Agnew noted darkly, "do not represent the views of America." He inscribed himself in history, and in famous-quotation anthologies, forever, when he said, "In the United States today, we have more than our share of nattering nabobs of negativism. They have formed their own 4-H club—the hopeless, hysterical hypochondriacs of history." (Remnick 2006)

This deliciously articulated slam from Agnew (penned by conservative intellectual William Safire) was just the gravy on top of Nixon's anti-media outlook. President Nixon despised the press, once telling the Chairman of the Joint Chiefs of Staff: "The press is your enemy. Enemies. Understand that? ... Because they're trying to stick the knife right in our groin" (Press 2017). Nixon went so far as to declare "war" against public television in the early 1970s arguing that the Corporation for Public Broadcasting (CPB) was liberally biased. A White House aide named Clay Whitehead wrote a memo that said: "No matter how firm our control of CBP management, public television at the national level will always attract liberal and far-left producers, writers and commentators" (Kramer 1979). For his part, President Nixon "requested that all funds for public broadcasting be cut immediately" (Kramer 1979). They were not. But in the 1970s, the conservative revulsion against the press was palpable and it only grew stronger.

Much like the watchdog groups that monitor college campuses for bias, organizations were created to monitor the airwaves. These groups included the Committee to Combat Bias in Broadcasting and Accuracy In Media (AIM) were founded. When Accuracy in Media founder Reed Irvine died in 2004, his *New York Times* obituary stated that AIM was "dedicated to exposing, challenging and at times bullying those he accused of slanting news coverage from a liberal perspective" (Kaufman 2004). Brent Bozell, the nephew of William F. Buckley, launched the Media Research Center (MRC) in 1987 to "expose and neutralize the propaganda arm of the Left: the national news media" (Media Research

Center 2018). These groups were eventually matched by watchdog groups on the left, such as Fairness and Accuracy in Reporting (FAIR) who made the counterargument that the media was, in fact, conservatively biased, but the dominant claim was that the press was irredeemably liberal. Even during the 1980s when the Fairness Doctrine was revoked (1987) and consequently talk radio became a powerful force in conservative media circles, even after the launch of *Fox News* in 1996, even after the profusion of conservative Web sites and blogs, the liberal media bias declaration persists. Books have been written[12] to support this claim and a segment of the American public accepts a liberally biased press as fact.

There are several reasons that the accusations of bias have stuck throughout the decades, and one important one is that many reporters in the mainstream press have behaved in a way to allow the bias allegations to stick. Conservatives point to specific incidents in the past twenty years, including Dan Rather's retracted allegations against George W. Bush's National Guard duty and fawning attention to Barack Obama in the early years of his presidency, as proof that the news media are pro-Democrat or anti-Republican. Journalists argue that this contention is hogwash and that journalists consistently investigated the Obama presidency with the same kind of determined consideration they did to the Bush administration, because that is the duty of the journalist. Tracy Grant, deputy managing editor of the *Washington Post* argued:

> I think people are called to this profession sometimes have a sense of mission about shining light in dark places… but I also think that anybody who thinks that the mainstream media — the *Washington Post* — didn't make Hillary Clinton's life miserable or Barack Obama's life miserable by holding them the accountable is just not looking at the record. (Wemple 2017)

The argument also goes that shilling for one side over another is bad for the journalism industry because when a news organization loses credibility, they also lose their audience. *Fox News'* Chad Pergram is the recipient of the Edward R. Murrow and Joan Barone Awards for reporting is one of the most respected Capitol Hill reporters. He has accomplished all of this because he strictly adheres to the rules and norms of journalism. Pergram is the most followed congressional reporter on Twitter because he has never tweeted his own thoughts about anything: He tweets facts and direct quotes from lawmakers, which makes him well regarded on both sides of the aisle. This differs considerably from the opinion side of

*Fox News*, which does not adhere to journalistic norms or values. At all. But today, it is not a firing offense to be opinionated, and as conservative journalist, S. E. Cupp rightly points out: "Opinion news has become its own industry. You don't have to pretend not to have an opinion; you can make a career out of having an opinion" (Cupp, Host, S. E. Cupp Unfiltered 2017a). There is money to be made in peddling opinions, which is one reason that the political media landscape is so crowded. And so while many journalists hold the line on their reporting, so-called opinion journalists do not, and it can be confusing for the public to differentiate who is doing what.

One consistent reason for the argument of liberal media bias concerns geography, specifically the locations of the news media's headquarters and consequently the issues the mainstream press focus upon because of this placement. S. E. Cupp argues that the urban, coastal dominance of the mainstream media has left the average American behind:

Ever since the advent of "the media" as an industrial complex -- large corporate conglomerates based in coastal cities where many of the ad agencies are -- it's been a left-leaning, urban-minded, somewhat elitist outfit with a blind spot for conservative America. As the media merged with Hollywood, another bastion of cultural liberalism, it grew even bolder in its disregard for the common man -- the commuting salesman, the farmer, the churchgoer, the truck driver. From 1966's "Is God Dead?" *Time* magazine cover, to a portrayal of the returning Vietnam veteran as a ticking time bomb, to a newspaper's indiscriminate publishing of law-abiding gun owners' home addresses, the media became a decidedly secular and leftist business. (Cupp, Why Conservatives Lost Faith in Mainstream Media, 2017b)

This idea that geography plays a major role in the leanings of the news media is an influential one. Lisa George is an economist at Hunter College who studies the economics of the news media, and she made the argument that when television news became the dominant forms of news, the news became nationalized by virtue of that shift. This changed the attention of the public toward national coverage, and so when the *New York Times* began to distribute their papers around the country more easily because of satellite technology, the public's attention to national coverage was already focused.[13] On its own, the fact that the country became attentive to national news did not mandate ideological biases, but the fact that these major media companies were headquartered mostly in New York meant that their newsrooms were not exactly representative of the nation as a whole. This was acknowledged by the *New York Times* itself in 2004 when its Public Editor, Daniel Okrent, answered the question: "Is the *New York Times* a liberal paper?" Of course, it is. Okrent surveyed not the politics of the *Times* journalists, but the issues that the newspaper covered and the way they covered them. He wrote that political matters aside, it was the policies that were most illustrative:

> ...the flammable stuff that ignites the right. These are the social issues: gay rights, gun control, abortion and environmental regulation, among others. And if you think *The Times* plays it down the middle on any of them, you've been reading the paper with your eyes closed. But if you're examining the paper's coverage of these subjects from a perspective that is neither urban nor Northeastern nor culturally seen-it-all; if you are among the groups *The Times* treats as strange objects to be examined on a laboratory slide (devout Catholics, gun owners, Orthodox Jews, Texans); if your value system wouldn't wear well on a composite *New York Times* journalist, then a walk through this paper can make you feel you're traveling in a strange and forbidding world. (Okrent 2004)

The *New York Times* is not alone here. The major newspapers of record, arguably the place where most of the real shoe-leather journalism is done, are all in major metropolitan cities, most of which are dominated by Democrats. Put simply, in 2016, Hillary Clinton won Washington, DC with 91% of the vote (Wemple 2017). Conservative writer (and podcaster) Matt Lewis brought a few ideas together when he said: "I do think that the kinds of people who go into journalism and where journalism outlets tend to be based has the inevitable outcome of slanting it not even just leftward but in a cosmopolitan, secular way" (Wemple 2017).

Geographic homogeny is not the only problematic sameness. A 2013 article in the Hoover Institution's journal, Bruce Thornton argued that when more journalism was professionalized, they also became more liberal. Why? Because the professionalization was done on college campuses where (you guessed it) liberal college professors indoctrinated the would-be press before they could dirty their hands with real reporting:

> [J]ournalism became a "profession" certified by a university degree. Before then, as films like *The Front Page* and *It Happened One Night* show, journalism was a working-class trade.... Once reporters started coming out of colleges and universities, however, they were shaped by the leftist

perspective of those institutions. These perspectives, once marginal in American public discourse, became increasingly prominent in the press and television news shows. Now the old progressive view that the press should not just report facts, but mold public opinion to achieve certain political ends, served an ideology fundamentally adverse to the free-market, liberal-democratic foundations of the American Republic. (Thornton 2013)

The *Washington Post's* Erik Wemple echoed this claim, writing that the major papers mostly hired graduates from the elite universities, and this further slanted the ideology of the reporting staff (Wemple 2017).

It also does not help that a significant number of reporters self-identify as Democrats. A 1992 *New York Times* article reported that a Freedom Forum survey found in that year, 44% of reporters identified themselves as Democrats and 16% as Republicans. These numbers were far different from a previous survey taken in 1971 where surveyed reporters self-identified as 36% Democrat, 26% Republican (Glaberson 1992). A more recent update of these numbers conducted by the Indiana University School of Journalism found that in 2014, these numbers dropped to 28% Democrat, 7% Republican, with the majority reporting self-reporting to be Independents (Wemple 2017). There are two sets of explanations for this shift toward Independence. Tom Rosenstiel is the director of the American Press Institute and he says that this shift away from the two major parties reflects the broader national polarization. On the other hand, the Independent self-identification by journalists could be a facade. Tim Graham is the executive editor of *NewsBusters*, a conservative publication from the MRC that monitors the liberalism of the press. Graham argues that liberals "check the 'independent' box to avoid being properly identified" (Wemple 2017).

All of these reasons put together show that there are legitimate justifications for accusing the press of bias, but proving bias is more difficult to do because most major news organizations work extremely hard to get their facts straight and act professionally. Additionally, coming up with specific examples of bias is challenging because this takes up too much time. Figuring out the truth about the world around us is hard enough—to do media criticism at the same time is a daunting task. The complicated governing process and the details of policymaking are confusing; calling a news organization biased is comprehensible. The idea that the mainstream media is liberal or that the right-wing media is angrily hyper-partisan is an undemanding distraction from more challenging fare (Schiffer 2018).

Adding fuel to the fire, politicians and candidates (most notably President Trump) now take great joy in insulting the news media, which helps to grow the distrust and dislike. It might feel as if all politicians whine about the press, but the 2016 election brought something new. President Trump began his near-constant assault against the journalists covering him during the 2016 campaign and continued it through the start of his presidency. This sentiment has been echoed by the president's highest-ranking advisors, such as former advisor Steve Bannon, who said early in the Trump administration to the *New York Times*: "The media should be embarrassed and humiliated and keep its mouth shut and just listen for a while … I want you to quote this … The media here is the opposition party" (Grynbaum 2017). A truly bizarre hybrid of media hating from the president and a member of the press was evidenced in an interview with Fox News' Sean Hannity in 2017, where President Trump described the press as "very hostile people," and Hannity concurs:

> TRUMP: These are very hostile people. These are very angry people.
> HANNITY: But they also colluded against you in a campaign-- TRUMP:
> Yeah. HANNITY: And my question to you is-- TRUMP: Well they're very
> dishonest people. The media is very dishonest. I've been saying it. I say it
> openly. HANNITY: I said journalism's dead, so we agree. (Hannity 2017)

This kind of language helps to explain why the news media are in a defensive crouch. When the president of the USA uses the bully pulpit to call your industry dishonest, one can get a complex. In the course of the 2016 presidential elections, where the news media were excoriated more than in the past (which is saying something, given the periodic unpopularity of the press throughout American history), American trust in the media was at an historic low. Since then, trust in media has continued to drop as evidenced by polling data released in 2017, and some of the details of these polls are harrowing. According to one study from the Poynter Institute, 44% of Americans believe the news media invents stories about President Trump. 69% believe that the media favors one political side (Poynter Institute 2017). What is so concerning is that self-identified conservatives distrust the news media far more than those on the left, and the Poynter study found that Democrats with high political knowledge have the most faith in the press while highly knowledgeable Republicans are the most distrustful. This partisan imbalance was replicated in a Reuters Institute report, which also found that Republicans were more than three times more likely to distrust the media than their ideological counterparts (Bilton 2017).

This brings us to fake news. In recent years, one of the most significant causes of media distrust has been the near-constant accusation of "fake news." This term has become popularized and is used frequently, but it has two very different definitions. The folks at PolitiFact, the Pulitzer Prize winning fact checking organization, defines "fake news" as "fabricated content that internationally masquerades as news coverage of actual event" (Drobnic Holan 2017). Conversely, the term has been commandeered to mean news that disagrees with a worldview. President Trump uses the term to "describe news coverage that is unsympathetic to his administration and his performance, even when the news reports are accurate" (Drobnic Holan 2017). Both of these definitions are important to unpack, since they both have an alarming effect on the public's trust in the news media.

The real fake news is purposely distributed in order to achieve a goal, and much of this fake news began to spread on social media, which is notoriously unregulated. Fake news is generally just close enough to the truth to be believable, which is why it is effective. There are bizarre fake news stories such as the infamous "Pizzagate," where a Facebook post alleged Hillary Clinton was engaging in satanic rituals, sexually abusing children in the basement of Comet Ping Pong, a pizza restaurant in Northwest Washington, DC. The Facebook post spread virally, to Twitter, and then to the right-wing Web sites *InfoWars* and *Breitbart*. A North Carolina man believed the story enough to drive himself and an assault weapon to Comet to investigate and shoot the place up. Happily, no one was hurt, but the example serves as a ham-fisted explanation for fake news since most Americans, regardless of ideology, would not believe that Hillary Clinton was a Satanist who sexually abused children in the basement of a pizza parlor.[14] *Rolling Stone* magazine reporters uncovered the genesis and circulation of the story described the Pizzagate story in terrific detail,[15] and the entire episode involves the dark web's spread into the right-wing media bubble, Russian Internet robots, and then social media.

The convoluted path of the Pizzagate story is one reason for concern about fake news, because it involves three different components of information spread. The dark web is a term for a part of the Internet that is not indexed by search engines and can only be accessed with specific software. Much of the activity on the dark web is illegal, and so users are able to post anonymously, which has opened up some channels to extreme political conversations. These have linked to more easily accessible, but still extremist, alt-right forums such as 4Chan where users can post anonymously about conspiracies. When the right-wing Web sites InfoWars, run by the famously conspiracy-minded Alex Jones, and Breitbart ran the Pizzagate story, they moved a conspiracy from the depth of the Internet into something a bit more mainstream, which then allowed more right-wing Americans to access it. Social media picked it up as well, and the story began to bounce around Facebook and Twitter, which gave it even more exposure. And bots helped to spread the fake news story even more by sending the story around to thousands (if not many more) social media users. The combination of these elements all contributed to the Pizzagate story gaining the traction that it did. And that should be alarming for everyone, since while Pizzagate may seem ludicrous, most other fake news is far more believable, and can spread just as thoroughly and quickly.

In the 2016 election, Russians used troll farms and bots to spread fake news and propaganda across American social media platforms with the intent of inciting citizens and sowing political discord. It was estimated that 126 million Facebook users saw Russian-linked content, and 1.4 million Twitter users interacted with this content (Kirby 2018). The fake news stories that most Americans saw were not nearly as explosive and farfetched as Pizzagate, which made them all the more dangerous. Therefore, the American public has heard about and been warned of this kind of fake news because it is something to be cognizant of. That is how the actual definition of "fake news" made its way into public discourse.

The second meaning of "fake news" has to do with President Trump, who has been not only using the term to describe any media coverage he does not like; he has also taken credit for coining the phrase: "Look, the media is fake. The media is -- really, the word, I think one of the greatest of all terms I've come up with -- is fake. I guess other people have used it perhaps over the years, but I've never noticed it" (Drobnic Holan 2017). Given that he did not create this term, this statement in itself is fake news. Regardless, the American public now hears from the president himself that journalism about him is false and they hear this from him very frequently. FactCheck documented a list of 320 times the president used the term in 2017 alone (Kiely 2018). Because this tactic has been so effective for the president it has spread to other countries, and political leaders in Venezuela, Burma, the Philippines, and Syria have all adopted this term to denounce the reporting of their various genocides and atrocities (Millbank 2018).

One issue that has compounded the question of President Trump's use of the term is the current use of anonymous sources in political reporting. While always a resource, anonymous sourcing has become prevalent during the Trump administration, which is especially prone to leaks. These leaks have been the basis of some excellent reporting, but without attribution, it is easy to dismiss the news as bogus. Andrew Seaman is the ethics chair for the Society of Professional Journalists, and he said that the way to believe anonymous sourcing is to find a news source that was credible:

> While I don't like the overuse of anonymous sources, I do have confidence in stories based on those sources from most large news organizations. My advice to the public is to always consider a news organization's history and track record. The *New York Times*, *Washington Post* and others all have scandals in their pasts, but the overwhelming weight of evidence shows their journalism to be reliable and trustworthy. (Drobnic Holan 2017)

The problem is obvious: If someone does not believe the *New York Times* or *Washington Post* are credible to begin with, they will not trust the stories coming from anonymous sources there anyway. All together, these two definitions of fake news, the public hears that the news and information they are getting is not to be believed, which has an eroding effect on trust in the media.

It is evident that conservative distrust of the news media is not only pervasive, but also growing thanks to the increased hostility toward specific news outlets from partisans and politicians. The larger issue, of course, is that a democracy is reliant upon a free and trustworthy press to not only report the news, but also to hold our elected officials accountable for their actions. Vilifying the mainstream media for the last half-century has been good fodder for politicians who think that there is bias in journalism or who believe that they are getting a raw deal from the press, but there has been a serious cost to this denigration. Not only does the American public question fact and information, the idea of "alternative facts" has made its way into legitimate political discourse. Trump adviser Kellyanne Conway on NBC's *Meet the Press* first used the term in 2017 when discussing then-White House Spokesman Sean Spicer's estimation of Trump's Inaugural crowd as "alternative facts." This began an uproar as proponents of truth and opponents of Trump piled on the ludicrous statement and Conway herself. The editors of Merriam Webster's Dictionary tweeted out a definition of "fact" in the aftermath, just so there was no confusion. But Conway herself shrugged off the controversy and defended her statement to Olivia Nuzzi in *New York* magazine: "'Two plus two is four. Three plus one is four. Partly cloudy, partly sunny. Glass half-full, glass half empty. Those are alternative facts,' further defining the infamous phrase as 'additional facts and alternative information'" (Nuzzi 2017). The idea that there are two truths comes directly from the distrust in the facts reported by journalists, and this leads directly to the alternative right-wing media that exists today.

## CONCLUSIONS

Eliana Johnson from *Politico* summed this distrust up nicely when she said that it:

> [S]tarted with what was an ossified system with three networks and two newspapers. There was an elite: a journalistic elite and a government elite and judicial elite, and they were all the same people and they went in and out of each other's world.... The distrust started from people beginning to realize that there is this group of people, that's inbred, and ... these people had certain biases that they didn't share. (Johnson 2017)

The distrust sown by conservatives was persuasive, but the public still needs academics and experts to provide data and facts so that the government can craft policy. The public needs the government to run the country, and the media have to report on the government. The arguments against these institutions have an alarming effect on what is called "external efficacy," the belief that the political system is not only valuable but also responsive to the needs of the people. They also have an effect on the perceptions of truth and of the people who provide us with accurate information. The nation was founded on the idea of skepticism, and pushing our institutions to improve is important, but in the past half-century, this cynicism has grown into something more profound. According to a study from media expert Thomas Patterson of the Shorenstein Center at Harvard, there is a cost to all of this disparagement:

A healthy dose of negativity is unquestionably a good thing. There's a lot of political puffery, ineptitude, and manipulation that needs to be exposed, and journalists would be shirking their duty if they failed to expose it. Yet an incessant stream of criticism has a corrosive effect. It needlessly erodes trust in political leaders and institutions and undermines confidence in government and policy. (Patterson 2016)

This trust is further eroded when it is commonplace to personally insult members of the media, academia, and the government. President Trump consistently feeds the suspicions against these three entities with allegations that the "press is the enemy," that he "loves the uneducated," and that he believes in the "deep state." It is small wonder that this kind of disparagement encourages the cynicism that has been building for decades, leading to ideological sorting and continued destruction of institutional efficacy.

Our hyperpolarization did not begin with President Trump, but he enflamed the rage and amplified the resentment. During the 2016 presidential campaign, Trump took credit for lack of media trust. A Gallup poll at the time showed public confidence in the media at an all-time low, and Trump said:

I think I had a lot to do with that poll ... because I've exposed the media. If you look at The New York Times, and The Washington Post, and if you look at others: the level of dishonesty is enormous. It's so dishonest... Everybody is talking about the dishonesty — the total dishonesty — of some of the papers and the media generally. CNN is unbelievably dishonest. They call it the Clinton News Network. I am very proud to say that I think I had a lot to do with that poll number. (Gold 2016)

Since taking office, Trump has only increased his assault against the press. He has said: "Don't believe the crap you see from these people — the fake news. What you're seeing and what you're reading is not what's happening" (Schwartz 2018). He has tweeted: "I just cannot state strongly enough how totally dishonest much of the Media is. Truth doesn't matter to them, they only have their hatred & agenda. This includes fake books, which come out about me all the time, always anonymous sources, and are pure fiction. Enemy of the People!" (Trump 2018).

There is a military expression known as "command climate," where the tone for the unit is set at the very top of the power structure.

President Trump's attacks on the press is having a very real effect among the electorate. Although President Trump never served in the military, the expression remains relevant to his tenure in office. His behavior is setting a tone for the rest of the nation, and as a result, his disdain for what he terms "the fake news media" has deleterious effects on trust in the press and free speech. Not surprisingly, this effect is more pronounced on the right than on the left. A 2018 poll showed that 43% of self-identified Republicans said that they believed "the president should have the authority to close news outlets engaged in bad behavior," and 48% said they believed "the news media is the enemy of the American people." Seventy nine percent said that they believed "the mainstream media treats President Trump unfairly" (Stein 2018). Trump's idea of what is fake news is, clearly, news with which he disagrees. One of his tweets showed this: "91% of the Network News about me is negative (Fake)" (Keith 2018). Jay Rosen, Media Professor at New York University, writes: "In the United States the President is leading a hate movement against journalism, and with his core supporters it is succeeding. They reject the product on principle. Their leading source of information about Trump is Trump, which means an authoritarian news system is for them up and running" (Bump 2018).

Additionally, Trump's "fake news" definition has taken on international significance as well. He referenced "legitimate media and fake-news media" at meeting with NATO leaders (Wise 2018). When Trump was on a 2018 trip to Great Britain, he demonized *CNN, The New York Times* and the London tabloid newspaper *The Sun* at a press conference, prompting this report from *The New York Times*:

> Nonstop denigration of journalists has become an indelible part of the Trump presidency, so routine that it threatens to recede into the background noise of this chaotic administration, a low hum lost in the racket. But in taking his act on the road, Mr. Trump gave a fresh audience a front-row seat to his treatment of the press. The spectacle of a president bashing his nation's news organizations on foreign soil — in scenes broadcast live around the world — was a reminder of how Mr. Trump's conduct with journalists can still shock. (Grynbaum 2018)

According to Rob Mahoney, the deputy executive director of the Committee to Protect Journalists, this call of "fake news" is contagious and treacherous: "It's music to the ears of dictators and authoritarian leaders. Leaders have latched on to the term 'fake news' to undermine independent journalism and even jail reporters. Every time President Trump uses that term to dismiss critical coverage or avoid a reporter's question, it sends a terrible message" (Grynbaum 2018). According to one count, there are 15 countries where political leaders or state-run media outlets have used the term "fake news" to denounce opposition (Schwartz 2018).

This is especially dangerous when it signals that journalists are disposable, and in 2017, the Committee to Protect Journalists identified 21 journalists around the world who were jailed on charges of "fake news" (Chan 2017). The group's report stated: "President Donald Trump's nationalistic rhetoric, fixation on Islamic extremism, and insistence on labeling critical media 'fake news' serves to reinforce the framework of accusations and legal charges that allow such leaders to preside over the jailing of journalists" (Chan 2017). Authoritarian nations are particularly susceptible to destabilizing the press, as exemplified by Syria's dictator Assad claim that: "You can forge anything these days. We're living in a fake-news era." When Amnesty International identified thousands of murders by the Assad regime, Assad said the "fake news" of the killings was seeking "to demonize the Syrian government" (Friedman 2017). The authoritarian penchant for media control is more easily achieved when the press is delegitimized. Yet Trump continues the assault against the press at home and abroad, seemingly uncaring of the effects of his posturing.

When everything we hear and read is lumped together as one and people believe only their version of the truth, the nation loses perhaps the most valuable quality of our American political system: Our ability to debate serious questions and find solutions to important problems through compromise. What are we supposed to believe in when fact-finding journalism is so easily and casually characterized as "fake news," when professors who are experts are denigrated as hacks and partisans, and when the government is offhandedly maligned as fraudulent? When partisans tell half the country that these institutions are against them, the informational chasms are gigantic. This is the largest problem with the fifty-year march against the perceived liberalism of academics, government, and media. Bias should be identified and addressed, but the remedy of wholly rejecting these institutions is wrong. This rejection means constructing separate truths and realities, and we have split ourselves into squads where we will not tolerate opposing thought. We are so busy rooting for our teams, besmirching our opponents and sorting ourselves into like-minded crowds, we can no longer see the value in disagreement.

It therefore makes sense that we have an entirely separate media system, a right-wing media that is insular and self-reinforcing, and a mainstream media that is defensively trying to fight for sustainability. The next chapter examines the modern American polarization to show how this both sustains and feeds the polarized media.

## NOTES

1. Tip of the hat to Adlai Stevenson.
2. Hofstadter's *Anti-intellectualism in American Life* (Alfred Knopf 1963) is the most influential examination of this subject during this period, plus it is a wonderful read.
3. Which seems pretty cynical to me.
4. A precursor to the Powell Memorandum!
5. Buckley hit a triple against all three institutions: Intellectuals, government, and media. More on those to come.
6. At least not publically.
7. Frequently and consistently described as "brash," "bombastic," or "bombthrowing."
8. And that was back in Broder (1994)!
9. A precursor to President Trump's Twitter use, if you think about it.
10. For this section, I turn substantially and strongly recommend Adam Schiffer's excellent 2018 book *Evaluating Media Bias* (Lanham, MD, Rowman & Littlefield) which takes a thorough look and provides definitions and guidelines.
11. Hemmer's book, *Messengers of the Right* is an absolute must-read for anyone interested in the evolution of the conservative media.
12. See: Groseclose, *Left Turn: How Liberal Media Distorts the American Mind* (2012), Goldberg, *Bias: A CBS Insider Exposes How the Media Distort the News* (2014), and Bozell, *Weapons of Mass Distortion* (2005).
13. This issue of media economics is addressed more completely in Chapter 3.
14. More on conspiracy theories is covered in Chapter 5.
15. The story, written by Amanda Robb, is called "Pizzagate: Anatomy of a Fake News Scandal" from the November 16, 2017, *Rolling Stone* edition.

# WORKS CITED

Allen, Mike. 2017. *Scoop: Jeff Sessions' Culture War*, September 25. https://www.axios.com/axios-sneak-peek-2489079872.html?rebelltitem=5&utm_term=emshare#rebelltitem5.

Arceneaux, Kevin, interview by Alison Dagnes. 2017. *Professor, Political Science*, April 7.

Arceneaux, Kevin, Martin Johnson, and Chad Murphy. 2012. Polarized Political Communication, Oppositional Media Hostility, and Selective Exposure. *The Journal of Politics* 74: 174–186.

Arnold, Chelsie. 2017. *6 Conservatives Sparking Free Speech Debates on Campuses*, March 14. http://college.usatoday.com/2017/03/14/6-conservatives-sparking-protests-and-free-speech-debates-on-campuses/.

Associated Press. 2017. *Remember Nixon? There's History Behind Trump's Press Attacks*, February 17. https://www.voanews.com/a/trump-press-relationship-history/3728829.html.

Bartlett, Bruce. 2015. *How Fox News Changed American Media and Political Dynamics*, June 3. Available at SSRN: https://ssrn.com/abstract=2604679.

Bauder, David. 2017. *Conservative Publisher Wants Nothing More to Do with Times*, September 4. http://www.foxbusiness.com/markets/2017/09/04/conservative-publishers-wants-nothing-more-to-do-with-times.html.

Bilton, Ricardo. 2017. *Why Don't People Trust the News and Social Media? A New Report Lets Them Explain in Their Own Words*, November 30. http://www.niemanlab.org/2017/11/why-dont-people-trust-the-news-and-social-media-a-new-report-lets-them-explain-in-their-own-words/.

Broder, David. 1994. War on Cynicism. *The Washington Post*, July 6: Op-Ed.

Brown, Lara, interview by Alison Dagnes. 2017. *Professor, George Washington University*, August 17.

Buckley, William F. 1951. *God and Man at Yale*. New York City: Regnery.

———. 1955. Publisher's Statement on Founding National Review. *National Review*, November 19: 5.

———. 2008. *Goldwater, the John Birch Society, and Me*. Accessed May 25, 2018. https://www.commentarymagazine.com/articles/goldwater-the-john-birch-society-and-me/.

Bump, Philip. 2018. Trump Eliminates the Middleman in his War Against Journalists. *The Washington Post*, October 1. https://www.washingtonpost.com/politics/2018/10/01/trump-eliminates-middle-man-his-war-against-journalists/?utm_term=.66b1072de520.

Chan, Sewell. 2017. Number of Jailed Journalists Hits Record High, Advocacy Group Says. *The New York Times*, December 13. https://www.nytimes.com/2017/12/13/world/europe/journalists-jailed-committee-to-protect-journalists.html.

Cohen, Tom. 2010. *Tea Party: Return to Basics or Divisive Force on Right?* September 27. http://www.cnn.com/2010/POLITICS/09/26/tea.party/index.html.

Coppins, Mccay. 2018. *Trump's Right-Hand Troll*, May 28. https://www.theatlantic.com/politics/archive/2018/05/stephen-miller-trump-adviser/561317/.

Cottle, Michelle. 2016. *Newt Broke Politics—Now He Wants Back In*, July 14. https://www.theatlantic.com/politics/archive/2016/07/newt-broke-politicsnow-he-wants-back-in/491390/.

Cupp, S.E., interview by Brian Stelter. 2017a. *Host, S.E. Cupp Unfiltered*, November 21.

———. 2017b. *Why Conservatives Lost Faith in Mainstream Media*, November 21. https://www.cnn.com/2017/11/16/opinions/conservatives-and-media-distrust-opinion-cupp/index.html.

Davenport, David. 2015. *Apparently 90% of Harvard Faculty Can Agree on Something: Giving to Democrats*, May 7. Accessed September 23, 2018. https://www.forbes.com/sites/daviddavenport/2015/05/07/apparently-90-of-harvard-faculty-can-agree-on-something-giving-to-democrats/#692835451b9d.

Drobnic Holan, Angie. 2017. *The Media's Definition of Fake News vs. Donald Trump's*, October 18. http://www.politifact.com/truth-o-meter/article/2017/oct/18/deciding-whats-fake-medias-definition-fake-news-vs/.

Eckholm, Erik. 2017. *In Hillsdale College, a 'Shining City on a Hill' for Conservatives*, February 1. https://www.nytimes.com/2017/02/01/education/edlife/hillsdale-college-great-books-constitution-conservatives.html.

Edwards, Mickey. 2017. *We No Longer Have Three Branches of Government*. Accessed October 11, 2017. http://www.politico.com/magazine/story/2017/02/three-branches-government-separation-powers-executive-legislative-judicial-214812.

Epstein, Joseph. 1968. *Adlai Stevenson in Retrospect*, December 1. https://www.commentarymagazine.com/articles/adlai-stevenson-in-retrospect/.

Fingerhut, Hannah. 2017. *Republicans Much 'Colder' Than Democrats in Views of Professors*, September 17. http://www.pewresearch.org/fact-tank/2017/09/13/republicans-much-colder-than-democrats-in-views-of-professors/.

Fried, Amy. 2012. *Distrust in Government as a Political Weapon*. New York, NY: Scholar Study Network.

Friedman, Uri. 2017. The Real-World Consequences of 'Fake News'. *The Atlantic*, December 13. https://www.theatlantic.com/international/archive/2017/12/trump-world-fake-news/548888/.

Gibson, Connor. 2016. *To Charles Koch, Universities Are Propaganda Machines*, January 27. https://www.huffingtonpost.com/connor-gibson/to-charles-koch-universit_b_9090404.html.

Glaberson, William. 1992. *Increasingly, Reporters Say They're Democrats*, November 18. https://www.nytimes.com/1992/11/18/us/increasingly-reporters-say-they-re-democrats.html.

Glaister, Dan. 2008. *Tricky Dicky: Nixon Recordings Confirm Popular View*, December 3. Accessed October 3, 2018. https://www.theguardian.com/world/2008/dec/04/richard-nixon-recordings.

Glass, Ira. 2018. *My Effing First Amendment*, May 4. https://www.thisamericanlife.org/645/transcript.

Gold, Hadas. 2016. Donald Trump Takes Credit for Public Distrust of the Media. *Politico*, September 15. https://www.politico.com/blogs/on-media/2016/09/donald-trump-takes-credit-for-distrust-of-media-228221.

Goldsmith, Jack, and Adrian Vermeule. 2017. *Elite Colleges Are Making It Easy for Conservatives to Dislike Them*, November 30. https://www.washingtonpost.com/opinions/elite-colleges-are-making-it-easy-for-conservatives-to-dislike-them/2017/11/30/0d2ef31a-d52a-11e7-a986-d0a9770d9a3e_story.html?utm_term=.04e4ab80bb9d.

Goldwater, Barry. 2007. *Conscience of a Conservative*. Princeton, NJ: Princeton University Press.

Gross, Niel, and Ethan Fosse. 2012. Why Are Professors Liberal? *Theory and Society* 41: 127–168.

Grynbaum, Michael. 2017. *Trump Strategist Stephen Bannon Says Media Should 'Keep Its Mouth Shut'*, January 26. https://www.nytimes.com/2017/01/26/business/media/stephen-bannon-trump-news-media.html?_r=0.

Grynbaum, Michael. 2018. 'Fake News' Goes Global as Trump, in Britain, Rips the Press. *The New York Times*, July 13. https://www.nytimes.com/2018/07/13/business/media/trump-cnn-london.html.

Hannity, Sean. 2017. *Cable Exclusive: President Trump Sits Down with Sean Hannity at White House*, January 26. http://www.foxnews.com/transcript/2017/01/26/cable-exclusive-president-trump-sits-down-with-sean-hannity-at-white-house/.

Hemmer, Nicole. 2014. *The Conservative War on Liberal Media Has a Long History*, January 17. https://www.theatlantic.com/politics/archive/2014/01/the-conservative-war-on-liberal-media-has-a-long-history/283149/.

———. 2016a. *Messengers of the Right*. Philadelphia: University of Pennsylvania Press.

———. 2016b. *The Birth of Conservative Media as We Know It*, September 2. https://newrepublic.com/article/136390/birth-conservative-media-know.

Hofstadter, Richard. 1963. *Anti-intellectualism in American Life*. New York City: Vintage Books, Random House.

Howe, Irving. 1954. *Stevenson and the Intellectuals.* https://www.dissentmaga-zine.org/online_articles/stevenson-and-the-intellectuals-winter-1954.

Johnson, Eliana, interview by Alison Dagnes. 2017. *National Political Reporter, Politico,* May 31.

Kaufman, Michael. 2004. *Reed Irvine, 82, the Founder of a Media Criticism Group, Dies,* November 19. http://www.nytimes.com/2004/11/19/us/reed-irvine-82-the-founder-of-a-media-criticism-group-dies.html.

Keith, Tamara. 2018. President Trump's Description of What's 'Fake' Is Expanding. *NPR,* September 2. https://www.npr.org/2018/09/02/643761979/president-trumps-description-of-whats-fake-is-expanding.

Kiely, Eugene. 2018. *Trump's Phony 'Fake News' Claims,* January 16. https://www.factcheck.org/2018/01/trumps-phony-fake-news-claims/.

Kirby, Jen. 2018. *What to Know About the Russian Troll Factory Listed in Mueller's Indictment,* February 16. https://www.vox.com/2018/2/16/17020974/mueller-indictment-internet-research-agency.

Kolowich, Steve. 2018. *State of Conflict,* April 27. https://www.chronicle.com/interactives/state-of-conflict.

Komarow, Steven. 1989. *House Republicans Elect Gingrich to No. 2 Spot, Chart Battle with Democrats.* Washington, DC: Associated Press.

Kotch, Alex. 2017. *Charles Koch Ramps Up Higher Ed Funding to Fuel 'Talent Pipeline',* February 2. https://www.prwatch.org/news/2017/01/13210/charles-koch-ramps-higher-ed-funding-talent-pipeline.

Kramer, Larry. 1979. Nixon's War Against Public TV. *The Washington Post,* February 24: A12.

Lemann, Nicholas. 2005. Fear and Favor: Why Is Everyone Mad at the Mainstream Media? *The New Yorker,* February 14.

Levinthal, Dave, interview by Alison Dagnes. 2015. *Spreading the Free-Market Gospel,* October 30. https://www.theatlantic.com/education/archive/2015/10/spreading-the-free-market-gospel/413239/.

———. 2017. *Senior Reporter, Center for Public Integrity,* December 4.

Major Garrett, interview by Alison Dagnes. 2017. *White House Correspondent, CBS News,* August 13.

Mayer, Jane. 2016. *Dark Money.* New York: Doubleday.

Media Research Center. 2018. *About,* May 29. https://www.mrc.org/about.

Millbank, Dana. 2018. *Trump's 'Fake News' Mantra Becomes an Effective Weapon—Against America,* April 16. https://www.washingtonpost.com/opinions/trump-bulldozed-truth--and-not-just-in-washington/2018/04/16/0f65718c-41b2-11e8-8569-26fda6b404c7_story.html?utm_term=.b25bdb956649.

Miller, Arthur. 1974. Political Issues and Trust in Government: 1964–1970. *American Political Science Review* 68: 951–972.

Muscatine, Alison. 1985. *Group Monitoring Academia Stirs Support, Concern on Campus,* November 3. https://www.washingtonpost.com/archive/

local/1985/11/03/group-monitoring-academia-stirs-support-concern-on-campus/b676f559-a707-4cb1-b311-ba59b70473c8/?utm_term=.748 dafc8e4b7.

*New York Times Special.* 1964. Goldwater Bestows Pins on Reporters Who Ride His Plane, September 20. http://www.nytimes.com/1964/09/20/goldwater-bestows-pins-on-reporters-who-ride-his-plane.html?_r=0.

Nuzzi, Olivia. 2017. *Kellyanne Conway Is a Star*, March 18. "Two plus two is four. Three plus one is four. Partly cloudy, partly sunny. Glass half full, glass half empty. Those are alternative facts," she said, further defining the infamous phrase as "additional facts and alternative information".

Nye, Joseph S., Philip Zelikow, and David King (eds.). 1997. *Why People Don't Trust Government.* Cambridge, MA: Harvard University Press.

Okrent, Daniel. 2004. *THE PUBLIC EDITOR; Is the New York Times a Liberal Newspaper?* July 25. https://www.nytimes.com/2004/07/25/opinion/the-public-editor-is-the-new-york-times-a-liberal-newspaper.html?pagewanted=all&src=pm&_r=0.

Patterson, Thomas. 2016. *News Coverage of the 2016 General Election: How the Press Failed the Voters.* Cambridge, MA: Harvard Kennedy School.

Pear, Robert. 1983. *Reagan Modifies 'New Federalism' Plan*, January 26. http://www.nytimes.com/1983/01/26/us/reagan-modifies-new-federalism-plan.html.

Perloff, Rochard. 2015. A Three-Decade Retrospective on the Hostile Media Effect. *Mass Communication and Society* 18: 701–729.

Pew Research Center. 2014. *Political Polarization in the American Public.* Washington, DC: Pew Research Center.

———. 2015. *Beyond Distrust: How Americans View Their Government*, November 23. http://www.people-press.org/2015/11/23/beyond-distrust-how-americans-view-their-government/.

———. 2017. *Sharp Partisan Divisions in Views of National Institutions*, July 10. http://www.people-press.org/2017/07/10/sharp-partisan-divisions-in-views-of-national-institutions/.

Powell, Lewis. 1971. *Attack on American Free Enterprise System.* Richmond, VA: N/A.

Poynter Institute. 2017. *Poynter Releases New Study Examining Trust in the Media*, December 4. https://www.poynter.org/news/poynter-releases-new-study-examining-trust-media.

Reagan, Ronald. 1964. A Time for Choosing. *The Heritage Foundation*, October 27. http://www.heritage.org/initiatives/first-principles/primary-sources/a-time-for-choosing-ronald-reagan-enters-the-political-stage.

Remnick, David. 2006. *Nattering Nabobs*, July 10. https://www.newyorker.com/magazine/2006/07/10/nattering-nabobs.

Riffkin, Rebecca. 2015. *Americans' Trust in Media Remains at Historical Low*, September 28. http://www.gallup.com/poll/185927/americans-trust-media-

remains-historical-low.aspx?g_source=TrustinMedia&g_medium=search&g_
campaign=tiles.
RNC. 2016. *Great American Families, Education, Healthcare, and Criminal
Justice*, July. https://gop.com/platform/renewing-american-values/.
Schiffer, Adam. 2018. *Evaluating Media Bias*. Lanham, MD: Rowman &
Littlefield.
Schwartz, Jason. 2018. *Trump's 'Fake News' Mantra a Hit with Despots*,
December 8. Accessed October 11, 2018. https://www.politico.com/
story/2017/12/08/trump-fake-news-despots-287129.
Shapiro, Ari. 2010. Distrusting Government: As American as Apple Pie.
*NPR.org*, April 19. http://www.npr.org/templates/story/story.
php?storyId=126028106.
Statista. 2017. *Educational Attainment Distribution in the United States from
1960 to 2016*. https://www.statista.com/statistics/184260/educational-
attainment-in-the-us/.
Stein, Sam. 2018. New Poll: 43% of Republicans Want to Give Trump the Power
to Shut Down Media. *Daily Beast*, August 7. https://www.thedailybeast.
com/new-poll-43-of-republicans-want-to-give-trump-the-power-to-shut-
down-media?via=twitter_page.
Stolberg, Sheryl Gay. 2012. *Gingrich Stuck to Caustic Path in Ethics Battles*,
January 26. http://www.nytimes.com/2012/01/27/us/politics/the-long-
run-gingrich-stuck-to-caustic-path-in-ethics-battles.html.
Story, Ronald, and Bruce Laurie. 2008. *The Rise of Conservatism in America,
1945–2000*. Boston: Bedford/St. Martin's Press.
Thornton, Bruce. 2013. *A Brief History of Media Bias*, June 12. https://www.
hoover.org/research/brief-history-media-bias.
Trump, Donald. 2018. *Let Me Ask America a Question*, April 14. https://www.
wsj.com/articles/let-me-ask-america-a-question-1460675882.
Turning Point USA. 2018. *Professor Watchlist*, May 24. https://www.professor-
watchlist.org/about-us/.
Uberti, Peter. 2017. *Fake News and Partisan Blowhards Were Invented in the
1800s*, October 8. https://splinternews.com/fake-news-and-partisan-blow
hards-were-invented-in-the-1-1819219085.
Vallone, R. P., Lee Ross, and Mark R. Lepper. 1985. The Hostile Media
Phenomenon: Biased Perception and Perceptions of Media Bias in Coverage of
the Beirut Massacre. *Journal of Personality and Social Psychology* 49: 577–585.
Wemple, Eric. 2017. *Dear Mainstream Media: Why So Liberal?* January 27.
https://www.washingtonpost.com/blogs/erik-wemple/wp/2017/01/27/
dear-mainstream-media-why-so-liberal/?utm_term=.db72ab9caa14.
Wise, Justin. 2018. Trump References 'Legitimate Media and Fake-news Media'
at Meeting with NATO Leader. *The Hill*, July 11. https://thehill.com/pol
icy/international/396463-trump-begins-nato-press-conference-by-referenc-
ing-legitimate-media-and.

# CHAPTER 3

# Money + Tech = Problems: Technological Development, Financial Imperatives, and the Ensuing Media Landscape

The news media have ninety-nine problems, and their financial imperatives seem to touch all of them. New and developing technologies influence how much money can be made and must be spent by media organizations. Much of the media are struggling to stay afloat in a world of evolving platforms, where content is either free or easily pirated and where the competition is fierce and expanding. Rapidly developing technology mandates one set of adjustments for news organizations while the very real and critical question of paying for these adjustments baffles those in the industry. News outlets are struggling to monetize their product, which now must be produced and distributed in different ways, and at the same time, they have to attract and maintain an audience. The move of all content online—print, radio television—has put everything in competition with everything else, and the fight for dominance has encouraged playing to the worst of the audience's impulses. While there are outstanding sources of information and analysis, the current technological environment rewards speed, volume, and emotion. This new news climate mandates a very different kind of journalism than had previously existed, one that is rooted in the concept of "more": Journalists are being asked to do more than just reporting, there are more outlets providing political media content, the public has more options, and there are more politicos vying for attention.

There is much at stake when addressing the questions of how the media are developing and how news organizations can remain financially viable. Today the public is super connected: Most Americans have

© The Author(s) 2019
A. Dagnes, *Super Mad at Everything All the Time*,
https://doi.org/10.1007/978-3-030-06131-9_3

smartphones that bring with them instant information, constant connectivity, and cameras allowing everyone to share and receive unceasing information. This powerfully affects how citizens will get their news, but even more it shapes the kind of news that is produced. With so much competition for an audience, news organizations have to fight against one another, forcing them to make journalism and punditry more interesting and easier to access across varying platforms. This affects the way journalists work as they try to break the news first, racing against other outlets, social media, and regular Americans who have tiny personal computers and video cameras in their pockets. News organizations have to produce more with fewer resources, add more splash to stories to attract an audience, and increase commentary because talk is cheap and facts are expensive. Competition pits news outlets against media forms that were not in existence two decades ago and companies who have been around for centuries. Private citizens now have a very public voice, politicos have a dazzling array of communication options, and with so many voices competing for attention the volume is high. The shifting landscape requires revenue streams in areas that have heretofore been free, changing the ways we get and pay for the news. Legacy outlets play catchup to organizations that have a leg up on technology but have no understanding of traditional journalism. The standard funding sources of ad revenue and subscriptions have shape-shifted and are becoming obsolete without a much-needed replacement.

This shambolic media climate is one reason for the polarized news system that we have today. Amidst all of the clutter and the innumerable places to get information, the public tries to sort through their options to find reliable sources of information or analysis that explains the massive amount of data in front of us. Many try to find news that simply reinforces their existing attitudes and beliefs because this kind of validation is comforting in a noisy political world. There are so many information providers with varying levels of credibility, and it can be difficult to distinguish fact from opinion, truth from lies, and spin from reality. In the course of these challenges, the press struggles for legitimacy and solvency against criticism that there are unworthy (or worse). Yet even though some of the American public says that they hate the news industry, it remains a lucrative industry and a vital one for American democracy. To understand the political media climate of today, this chapter examines the technology that brings us our information, the financial imperatives of the media that end up driving the formation of the news, and the final product, densely populated with politicos, that transpires because of these two factors. The combination of easy access to information, profitability of new media structures and outlets, and a heightened capacity for immediate gratification have fused to help create the partisan news system we have today.

## Problems from a Changing Media System

Remember the old days, way back in the twentieth century, before Al Gore invented the Internet? Financing the news was far more linear then. News outlets have always had to commodify their product in order to be sustainable, but it used to be easier to follow the money. Newsgathering has dependably rested on two major costs: Money has to go to the actual media form itself (meaning producing broadcasts or printing papers) and journalists (plus editors, photographers, techies, etc.) who supply the content. Those two expenditures can be pricey as journalism can be quite expensive. The work of foreign correspondents or investigative reporters is impressive, time-consuming, and costly; in order to do their jobs, these journalists have to conduct research, travel for interviews, and gather data, and they also need time to write. There must be cameras, editors, and satellites to bring those stories home, and in total, quality newsgathering requires a commitment of resources. The news media have a long history of trying to remain afloat in trying economic times because monetizing the news has never been stress-free.

Legacy media, meaning outlets from the newspaper and broadcast industries, had a relatively simple equation in terms of financial necessity and constraints. Sara Fischer of *Axios* told me about the transition in media economics once the Internet was developed. Pre-Internet most of the traditional media spending went to the people who staffed the news outlet. The requirements for the actual media machinery of print and broadcast have historically remained static: A newspaper needed a printing press and supplies, radio broadcast mandated telegraph and wire mechanics, and then television expanded on those structural requirements for broadcast transmission. Moving from print to broadcast was certainly more costly, but it also was predictable, and much of the real money went to the editors, journalists, and staff who produced the news. At the larger outlets, big-name journalists and editors were paid big-time salaries, but arguably, these major news organizations had more subscriptions and ad revenue to cover these costs. All of this changed with the digital shift and the move online up-ended the financial structures of the news media. As Fischer notes, the digital migration swung the cost from people to technology, and so those in the legacy media have been playing catch up to the new tech giants who came to journalism with the technology already established (Fischer, Media Trends Reporter 2017b). For a newspaper to move from print to digital, the financial costs and learning curves have been enormous.

For digitally native outlets, those news sites born on the web, the challenges are different. Digital news may come to the political media with their tech structures in place, but since they cannot operate in the same manner as the legacy outlets, they have to be more innovative. Additionally, because new sites and apps launch every day, they have the double-edged dilemma of thick competition and the need for name recognition. Throughout the entire political media system, the fight for solvency and survival is consistent, even as the specific challenges vary by medium and organization.

## PROBLEMS FROM THE START

One can only assume that someone stood next to Gutenberg and said, "You know, we could make some money from this Bible." In America, even during the time before the Founding, pamphlets were printed slowly and infrequently, and as printing press equipment advanced, so too did the newspaper industry. Those early years after the Founding saw the first blushes of party control of the newspapers, which swelled further during the Partisan Era (approximately 1840–1890) when technology increased the number of papers mass-produced at one time. In the peak of this Partisan Era, the political parties had their own papers to disseminate information according to their biases and party positions, and when Alexis de Tocqueville wrote *Democracy in America*, he accurately referred to the USA as a "nation of newspapers." The political parties relied on the newspapers as their official house communication organs, and the public relied on the news and opinion that these papers delivered. When modern media critics argue that our current partisan media climate is nothing new, this is what they mean.

One important point to note is that during the original Partisan Era, editors and writers had absolutely no independence because the newspapers were financially reliant upon the parties. When the technology advanced again, allowing increased newspaper production, the papers were able to break with the parties and sustain themselves through ad revenue. Media economist Maria Petrova wrote about the effect of this shift from a partisan press to one that was privately funded and found that advertising revenue dramatically altered the shape and form of the news (Petrova 2011). Free from the confines of party control, newspapers were able to forge their own path and produce the kind of journalism that they wanted to pursue. It also meant that they had to raise their own funding, but conversely, they could reap economic rewards if they hit on a strategy that was profitable. Once there was a direct correlation between the independence of a newspaper and higher ad revenue, many newspapers found freedom from partisan shackles to be valuable (Petrova 2011). Since there was money to be made away from the political parties, the nation entered a new era of independent journalism. It would be nice to think that this was the result of high-minded discussions about truth and justice, but really, it was all about money. This is going to be a common theme in this chapter.

As a predictor of our current cutthroat media climate, newspapers found freedom in their independence but also struggled with competition and fought for audience share. While under party control there was a built-in readership for a paper, so when editors and writers gained their freedom, they also lost a big chunk of their audience. Smaller, local papers were hit especially hard since they had fewer readers in the first place. The larger the ad market, the more independent the newspaper and the smaller the market, more reliant the paper was upon the party for financing (Petrova 2011). This was yet another precursor of our modern partisan news environment; you could always guarantee an audience by appealing to a specific political team, but the larger papers moved away from that model. Liberation from the political parties had an important effect on journalism, which was a new standard of objectivity and impartiality, but it had a financial result as well. Newspapers became more centralized, and, according to media economist Lisa George, big newspapers flourished in major cities. It was, says George, a simple matter of scale because it all came down to "moving paper around": When one could deliver newspapers easily around a city to loads of readers, they made more money (George 2017). This kind of centrist-based model drove the type of news that was covered, since city papers would naturally cover the news that was most immediate to them. The major cities around the country began to teem with new residents and grow with industrialization, and they had newspapers that were massively popular and important in the Progressive movement; many newspaper and magazine reporters of this era were at the forefront of the anti-corruption efforts against the sleaze in government and big business. This kind of investigation was good for the news business because coverage of scandal and corruption sold papers. According to one description of these stories: "They sought out crime, scandal and salacious detail. Facts that got in the way of a gripping story could be left out. Imaginary details could be added. Any excuse to include an image of a scantily-clad woman was welcome" (Woolfe 2016). This was the logical consequence of for-profit journalism, which became decidedly lucrative by attracting an audience with astonishing reports (and images of scantily clad women). The emphasis on reporting that was shocking and attention grabbing never went away and in fact only grew worse as the media grew in size and reach. There was an upside to this kind of explosive journalism, which was that intrepid reporters uncovered all kinds of corruption and fraud in their stories. That was a good thing. The emphasis on the negative, however, was perceived problematic, and this is how Theodore Roosevelt coined the term "Muckrakers." He gave a speech in 1906 and said:

> In Bunyan's Pilgrim's Progress you may recall the description of the Man with the Muck-rake, the man who could look no way but downward with the muck-rake in his hands; Who was offered a celestial crown for his muck-rake, but who would neither look up nor regard the crown he was offered, but continued to rake to himself the filth of the floor. (Howard 2009)

TR had mixed feelings about the press, but he saw that they were an unbreakable force in the early twentieth century. Newspapers continued to dominate cities, which kept the primary focus of the news on urban areas, especially those that were centers of politics and commerce. Elsewhere around the country, Americans read their local newspapers which focused on their town or region and heard about national news when it was important enough to pierce their local bubble. The growing emphasis on entertaining news was felt at both the national and local levels, and the new norm of journalism included highlighting the dramatic. When broadcast television debuted, it expanded the prominence of spectacular content while it also stretched the ability of average Americans to get national news with ease. Instead of merely reading about their local news in the papers, Americans were able to watch the national news on TV. Television quickly became wildly popular, and it shifted people's attention to national news while it also changed the financial model of the industry.

The three broadcast networks (*ABC, CBS, and NBC*) competed against one another for audience share, and this meant that their singular goal was to get the largest audience possible. While broadcast news journalists may have wanted to appear as unbiased and trustworthy reporters, the organizations that employed them simply wanted to appeal to the most people to garner the largest possible viewing audience. This meant maintaining a non-partisan approach to increase the audience size, since once a news organization takes a political stand in their reporting, they lose half of their viewers. Because of this, the ideal of independent newsgathering continued and prospered in the twentieth century and became the standard by which we judge modern journalism. We fell in love with the idea that news would be impartial with professional norms applied to the journalistic process, and it became the new normal, but really, the journalistic objectivity of the twentieth century was financially driven. And the norm of objectivity was a temporary condition.

## PROBLEMS FROM SATELLITES

Another technological expansion transformed two different media forms at once and in doing so revolutionized the way we get and absorb the news. Satellite technology[1] directly led to news decentralization, which exacerbated audience fragmentation. Satellite changed everything in two important ways, the first having to do with newspaper distribution and the second having to do with cable television. Media economist Lisa George studied the national distribution of *The New York Times* which began in the 1980s thanks to satellite technology. Satellites first transmitted pages to a Chicago printing plant where papers were then distributed by trucks. According to George, this new circulation changed the way we think about the news because more Americans around the country were able to read the *New York Times,* and as they did so, they began to compare it to their own local newspapers (George 2017). This is a seemingly unfair comparison on a good day, and it swung a good number of newspaper readers away from their local papers to the larger, more prestigious *New York Times.* This then served the purpose of separating those who preferred a more cosmopolitan news source from those who favored the hometown fare. This division led to an ideological separation between the readers of the left-coast elitist *Times* from those who stuck with the local daily. Readers who dropped local papers and paid more attention to national and international news trended liberal, while conservatives paid attention to local (George 2017). The effects of this readership turn to the *New York Times* were an increase in news nationalization and a perceived partisan difference in source selection, all at once.

Satellite technology also led to the cable television boon of the 1980s and 1990s. Cable initially expanded the number of television channels from 3 to 14, and then to dozens, and then to hundreds. The expansive number of channels available meant that programming became specialized, and this kind of niche programming ran counter to the broadcasting of old. Smaller networks were not fighting for half of the country—they were forging new ground in their content area, trying to microtarget segments of the population who were unilaterally interested in sports (*ESPN*), real estate (*HGTV*), "Law and Order SVU" (*USA*), or real housewives (*A&E*). *C-SPAN* launched the idea of 24-hour public affairs programming in 1979 and a year later *CNN* debuted with 24 hours of current events, and cable consumers were able to devote their entire viewing experience to the news.[2] *C-SPAN*, the cable network that broadcasts the US House of Representatives (*C-SPAN I*) and the US Senate (*C-SPAN II*) in its entirety, has a very different mission than those who copied the idea; *C-SPAN* is a just-the-facts, unedited broadcast of the governmental system at work. The network's funding comes from the cable and satellite providers who deliver content to their subscribers. In other words, *C-SPAN* does not do ratings because there is no need; the cable and satellite companies that fund them will do so regardless of their popularity. *C-SPAN* founder Brian Lamb points out that this allows *C-SPAN* to stay true to its mission as a public service at the same time that it poses an existential threat to the network. As Lamb told me in 2018: "Our whole revenue stream comes from people who buy either satellite or cable, and when that's gone, we have no money" (Lamb 2018). This perfectly exemplifies the larger economic crisis in American journalism. *C-SPAN* is the gold standard of information presentation because there is no embellishment added. Yet while this makes *C-SPAN* an invaluable democratic resource, it also makes it rather unexciting. Audiences clamor for excitement, which means *C-SPAN* could not exist as it is without funding from the cable industry (or another outside source). The other 24-hour news networks who copied *C-SPAN's* basic premise but did so with a profit motive, and in trying to attract a sizable audience, developed different styles and emphasis. Lisa George observed that the technological expansion into cable happened around the same time that the *New York Times* began to circulate nationally as well, which culminated in a two-pronged effect: Americans had more options for news; at the same time, they were able to start selecting the type of news they consumed.

Being able to pick between styles of news led to audience segmentation by issue area and also by ideology. The ideological divide between readers of the *New York Times* and the readers of local papers was exacerbated by the popularity and intensification of cable news. Cable news was designed to attract a particular audience to begin with, but the audiences became even more specified as the cable news networks became partisan. *CNN* launched in 1980 to have 24-hour news. *Fox News* launched in 1996 to provide 24 hours of a conservative alternative to the so-called liberal media. Those are two *very* different ideas for cable news channels. One reason for the divided news media landscape we have today is this kind of separation that grew from the shifts in technology in the 1980s, and as with most of the media changes, there were financial benefits for this separation. A partisan news organization breeds loyalty, which attracts a specific and dedicated audience. This harkens back to the Partisan Era when the political parties controlled the press; when you champion one political team, you get a segment of the population who are ready to put on their jerseys. That kind of reflexive audience is attractive to a network looking for viewership and ratings, and so when *Fox News* introduced the idea of a purposely right-leaning 24-hour news network onto the cable lineup, they could sell advertisers the notion that about half of the voting public would be interested in their content. Partisan news networks are, by dint and virtue of partisanship, passionate and noisy. This can be entertaining, and entertaining can be profitable. Case in point: *Fox News Channel* is peerless in its success.[3]

It is not all profit and rainbows, however, and there are drawbacks to the financial models of partisan cable news. Even though there is a guaranteed audience segment who will support a network's ideological bend, an opposing segment will never tune in. Additionally, there is a growing distrust of partisan news channels, which has a deleterious effect on new trust writ large. In a study from 2008, Joel Turner found that reception of a story was influenced by identifying the presenting news outlet as either *CNN* or *Fox News*. Once someone heard that *CNN* or *Fox* was the source of a story, they would (or would not) not believe the story to be true (Turner 2007). What this means for money is clear: someone who does not believe *Fox News* content will never watch *Fox News*—so that audience segment is lost forever and forever stretches a long way.

Another potential financial pitfall for partisan news channels concerns how highly politicized everything is today which can lead to advertising and consumer boycotts. The angrier we are about politics, the angrier we are about everything touched by politics. As *Politico's* Eliana Johnson said in an interview: "The space between culture and politics has collapsed" (Johnson 2017). We are so polarized; we sort ourselves in the food we eat and the restaurants we go to (Wilson 2016). We sort ourselves by the clothing we wear from the designers with whom we politically side (Brown 2017). And we sort ourselves by the news we watch. This means that everything that touches a network, either through advertising sponsorship or story coverage, is subject to the network's partisanship and is thus also subject to the fealty toward or hostility against that ideology. Accordingly, the more partisan the channel, the more likely they are to become entangled in national boycotts when something highly polarizing hits the zeitgeist.[4]

The financial hazards of partisan news are offset by the money that can be made from all the hostility. As the American political climate has become more polarized, the news media writ large is seeing an increased interest to current affairs and, accordingly, they are seeing higher ratings and subscription rates as well. The technology that puts a tiny computer in your phone helps because as with all media, cable news has shifted online. Some have lamented that the current climate is overwhelming, because it can feel like we are drowning in information with breathless updates and alerts reaching us constantly. This is a fair lament, but as *Fox News* anchor Brett Baier said in an interview with *Variety*, this is a new normal, thanks to the technological shifts that have made the American public highly attentive:

> We are just working at a different pace now.... It's not just this administration but our society. People are now used to absorbing things in a nanosecond, and they expect their 24-hour cable news to be as fast as they are. (Steinberg and Littleton 2017)

This speed imperative goes for all of the news media. Being first to report something has a certain kind of appeal in a climate where people get constant notifications, and as a result, news orgs push that speed imperative as Americans reach for their phones for instant news updates. In addition to a faster speed of delivery, news organizations now are doubling down on the emotion, because, as OnMessage's Guy Harrison noted: "It's not about fact. It's about emotion" (Harrison 2017). This emotional emphasis has always been present in politics, and as Harrison notes, political advertising has been universally devoid of fact throughout history. But the technological development of the media has increased the emotional quotient significantly, since the Internet is rooted in reaction. To keep up with our reactions and to feed them at the same time, news outlets have been working to examine the emotional impact of their stories in order to provide more content that makes us feel more. (Fischer, Psych Economy: News Companies Using Your Emotions 2018). As a result, the public is now accustomed to partisan news that gallops toward an audience at full speed, breathing anger and emotion into their programming. This approach appears to be working, as Americans are gripped by the news, marking record ratings for many large, national organizations.

The way that television channels monetize their content involves the age-old notion of ratings and audience share. The math is straightforward: The more people who watch a TV program, the higher the ratings; the higher the ratings, the more a network can charge for advertising. In 1980, before the cable news surge, the three evening news programs on broadcast television brought in a little more than 50 million viewers per night. In 2016, according to the Pew Research Center, the three broadcast news programs had a combined audience of 24 million (Pew Research Center 2016). While this indicates a significant drop in audience numbers, compare this audience to that of *Fox News*, the highest rated channel (news or otherwise) on cable television: 2.5 million (Katz 2017). Broadcast news may have lost half of its audience when the cable news industry expanded and selectively appropriated their viewers, but the big three evening newscasts are still a dominant force in TV news today.

Television remains the dominant medium, although its domination varies generationally. Democratic political consultant Julian Mulvey told me that older Americans watch an amazing number of television hours: "TV is the 600 pound gorilla in the room, but it's losing weight. If you want to move numbers quickly it's the best thing you've got, particularly with older audiences. When you look at viewing numbers, the average American over the age of 65 watches 222 hours a month. It is a full time job. It *is* their job" (Mulvey 2017). That is a tremendous amount of television, proving Americans remained glued to its content.

Broadcast TV content is not just for broadcast televisions anymore, as many networks, both broadcast and cable, are looking to "cut their cords" and move to streaming services. This is known in the business as "Over the Top" (OTT) programming, and apparently, this wave of the future is crashing down on our shores at present. According to Sara Fischer of *Axios*, people still watch TV, just not from traditional content providers, not only on computers but also on traditional televisions using up-to-the-minute technology: "We watch a lot of video content – more people are using streaming services than paid television" (Fischer, We're Watching More Video, Just Not on TV 2017a). There are several ways to watch content now on computers, phones, iPads, or on TVs because of streaming services. All of these ways afford networks challenges and opportunities.

The challenges come from the loss of a potential audience and a funding guarantee. When Americans sign up for cable, most sign up for the whole line up; when someone subscribes to Comcast, they get everything from *ESPN* to the *Cooking Channel*, all at once. This has kept the major cable providers fat and happy for decades as it has helped to support niche cable channels. Very popular networks, like *Fox News* (#1) and *ESPN* (#3), are expensive and help pay for the lesser-watched networks like *The Tennis Channel* (#89) and *Justice Central* (#102). While this has sustained the cable providers, cable subscribers are less than thrilled. Americans hate their cable bills for good reason: The cost of cable television is borderline-offensive. According to an article in the *Los Angeles Times*: "...average cable bills have risen nearly four times faster than the inflation rate in recent years, and there's no sign of that changing. If anything, pay-TV companies will reach even deeper into subscribers' pockets to make up for the growing number of people cutting the cord" (Lazarus 2017). And the number of cutters is, indeed, growing. The idea of so-called skinny bundles where customers can select just a handful of channels is both new and underutilized, although this is changing. The five largest pay-TV companies are all testing different kinds of bundles for their subscribers who want to hand-select channels to watch. Cord cutting led to a 3.3% decline of cable subscriptions in 2017, which at the time was predicted to be 4% in 2018: Consumers were moving off cable to different services at a fast clip (Frankel 2017). As a result, media companies, already facing the external threats from new technology and heightened competition, are facing threats from inside their own houses as well. *Axios'* Fischer wrote of this: "These companies are getting whacked by digitalization and rapidly changing consumer habits and expectations" (Fischer, The Skinny Revolution 2017d). Even *C-SPAN* tweaked their funding model a tiny bit in 2014 because of the changing nature of cable viewing. In order to access *C-SPAN* content on the web, Americans now have to authenticate that they are cable subscribers. This move made some consumer activists howl in protest. John Wonderlich, policy director at the Sunlight Foundation, articulated these concerns: "C-SPAN describes itself as a public service, so you have to be concerned about what their definition of public is, when they start to restrict their offerings to cable subscribers" (Hattem 2014). The problem is that eventually, if Americans get cable content from the web without paying for a cable subscription, there will not be a cable industry any more—and then *C-SPAN* goes away as well. *C-SPAN* has to pay for their staff and infrastructure somehow, as do the rest of the news media.

As Americans continue to look for ways to get more content with less cost, they are finding innovative ways to avoid a hefty cable bill, all of which means the cable media have to adjust to new platforms and shifting audiences. Another challenge of the movement away from linear television concerns the devices to which we are moving. When someone streams content on a screen, it can approximate the display of a television set. This is not the case for the tiny-screened smartphones, and so video content on cell phones is not easy to watch, since most video is produced with TVs and computers in mind. This can change the form of the content, according to Republican ad consultant Guy Harrison. He's a partner at OnMessage, and when I asked him about the shift to cell phone use from bigger screens, he made two interesting observations: First, Harrison noted that content changes form when it shifts to smaller screens; it has to be simple and short, the graphics have to be larger, and the sound has to be clearer. He also noted that the shift to producing content with smartphones in mind was not a substantial trend. The people who were watching content on tiny screens tended to be younger, those infamous "Millennials" who seem to be glued to their phones (my words, not his). Harrison noted that older people bought bigger televisions, and since TVs are increasingly less expensive, even if people cut their cords, they still watch most content on larger monitors (Harrison 2017). The fight, according to Harrison, is to attract and audience regardless of how people will watch television content—either by cord cutting and streaming or through another mechanism. This presents a real challenge for content providers.

Another threat comes from the sheer number of viewing options available, because between network streaming, *Netflix* and *Amazon*, there is simply far more programming available for consumers. In 2017, there were 487 original scripted programs produced, which both heats up the competition for an audience as it places pressure on traditional television companies to pony up new shows. John Langraf, the CEO of the cable channel FX, who wins an award for understatement: "There's no question that streaming services are putting an enormous amount of pressure on the business model" (Koblin 2018). This extends beyond entertainment programming to the news, and, as *C-SPAN* founder Brian Lamb noted, while this allows more freedom for the audience, at the same time it provides too many options (Lamb 2018).

Yet despite these challenges, there are substantial financial opportunities for the TV industry as well. *Axios'* Sara Fischer addressed the shift from "programmatic" TV advertising (advertisements that are scheduled and air when the TV programs air) to digital ads (the ads that are placed during on-demand or streaming content). She described it as such: "For decades, TV has had a fixed amount of ad inventory (there's only 24 hours of programming in a day), but on-demand programming will create an infinite demand for ads, shifting the power balance from the seller to the buyer" (Fischer, TV Ads Are Going Digital, Slowly 2017f). This profit incentive has inspired networks and content providers to experiment with different ways to deliver the goods. Major media companies are all announcing their shifts toward OTT—to include *ESPN, HBO, CBS*—in order to grab an exclusive audience, and this means that many are also pulling out of broader streaming services in order to keep their audience to themselves (Tsukayama and Radu 2017).

In order to be heard above the competition and maintain an audience that has every incentive to be fickle, cable news channels now feature actual news and commentary that serves as a political cage match. The divide between the news and editorial sides of cable news channels is growing increasingly wide, as exemplified by the pundit class of *Fox News* which operates in stark contrast to the journalistic side. In 2018, several *Fox News* reporters left the network citing the network's emphasis on pro-Trump punditry over fact-finding journalism. The *Fox* audience prefers the pro-Trump commentary, which is why the network provides it in abundance, and this one way that the network maintains its high ratings and its profitability. Additionally, it is not only lucrative to produce popular political theater, it is less expensive than producing the news. Asked about the departures from *Fox News* amidst criticism that the network is doing less real journalism than before, former *Fox* anchor Greta Van Susteren said: "News gathering is very expensive. Talking in a studio is very inexpensive. And as long as the ratings are high when they're talking in the studio, you're going to get more of that" (Schwartz 2018). Thus, cable news set into motion the niche programming and the emotional programming that have become mainstays of the modern political media landscape. This became even worse when everything moved online.

## PROBLEMS FROM THE INTERNET

Although digitally native media organizations have proliferated in recent years, most online news content originates from offline sources. Newspapers, magazines, broadcast, and cable television channels all have significant (and growing) online presences which combine video, flash animation, data-heavy charts, and copy. The legacy and traditional news outlets that have moved online have the disadvantage of having to improve and advance their production to meet the new web component while digital natives do not have as much of a learning curve or infrastructure ramp-up with which to contend. Yet all Internet news organizations face the same set of problems that have to do with the considerable competition. To stay solvent, Web sites need revenue which they get from running ads or charging for subscriptions. In order to get people to visit a Web site, news organizations have to contend with the so-called duopoly of the Internet: the two-headed monster that is Facebook and Google. The way that the public finds news rests largely on the shoulders of the duopoly. News consumers will Google a question about a person or an event, and the search engine provides the news about it. People share stories on Facebook allowing their friends to consume the content as well. In the summer of 2017, the Pew Center released a study that showed 67% of Americans got some of their news from social media (Shearer and Gottfried 2017). Add to that the fact that Google is both a noun and a verb, and one can see how the influence of the duopoly should not be underestimated. Hence, a news organization trying to attract and build a loyal audience must make sure that their content is interesting (flashy, exciting, or infuriating), and it hits an emotional chord with a reader. This is where algorithms come in.

An algorithm is computer language that analyzes the way a user consumes a site. It looks at the kinds of things someone will click on, how long someone spends on an article or a posting, and then those algorithms predict the kind of material a user might want to see. If an online company knows your interests, it can target ads and content to you much more effectively, which is why I see a great deal of content about American politics, the media, and ads for dresses from Title Nine and Ann Taylor. Social media algorithms tend to be based on emotion and not fact; hence, something that makes a reader feel strongly will get a larger push from the algorithm than something dry and technical. In this way, algorithms have a function similar to structural bias in that they look for entertaining fare, something spicy to seize attention. Social media algorithms are especially powerful since these sites sort through a tremendous amount of content to match content to user. An article from *Slate* addressed how the Facebook algorithm works:

> It doesn't just predict whether you'll actually hit the like button on a post based on your past behavior. It also predicts whether you'll click, comment, share, or hide it, or even mark it as spam. It will predict each of these outcomes, and others, with a certain degree of confidence, then combine them all to produce a single relevancy score that's specific to both you and that post. Once every possible post in your feed has received its relevancy score, the sorting algorithm can put them in the order that you'll see them on the screen. The post you see at the top of your feed, then, has been chosen over thousands of others as the one most likely to make you laugh, cry, smile, click, like, share, or comment. (Oremus 2016)

Social media algorithms all operate this way, and they need to in order to capture and keep their users. This is where the problems come for online news sites: News organizations need the traffic provided by social media in order to maintain their own ad revenue, and so they try to accommodate the different algorithms of varying social media platforms. But as news orgs try to find stories that will accommodate a specific algorithm, sometimes that algorithm will change. Additionally, if a news organization is trying to fit their content into a particular algorithm, it changes the nature of the news itself. Said one former editorial staff at Mic.com:

> It provides an opportunity where people think there is a system to play, a game to play. You start designing stories to play into an algorithm.... Then you start picking stories based on what will do well on Facebook. People start to focus on that and not the news itself. (Levine and Burch 2017)

Playing into the hands of an algorithm may feel manipulative, but for news organizations, this is honestly about survival. In order to maintain solvency, a news site has to have enough readers to see their ads or subscribe to their content.

In 2018, President Trump expanded his assault on the press to include a broadside against Google. Charging the search engine with a liberal bias, Trump alleged Google's algorithm discriminated against conservatives, himself especially. Pointing to a flawed report on *PJ Media*, Trump alleged 97% of Google searches came up with liberal news sources. This stemmed from a study published in the journal *Computers in Human Behavior*. The research found that there was homogeneity in search results during the 2016 campaign when participants of varied demographics and ideologies ran searches on Hillary Clinton and Donald Trump (Owen 2018). An impressive consistency was found when 79% of top news results went to only 14 organizations:

> Across the four searches, fourteen news organizations ranked in the top five: *CNN, Politico, Fortune, The Chicago Tribune, Business Insider, The New York Times, The Wall Street Journal, The Washington Post, CNBC, ABC, Time, The Los Angeles Times, HuffPost,* and *USA Today.* Together, these outlets made up 79 percent of the total number of news recommendations suggested to searchers.

> The number of recommendations was unevenly distributed among these organizations as well, with the five most prominent outlets — *The New York Times, CNN, Politico, The Washington Post* and *HuffPost* — making up half (49 percent) of the 1653 total recommended links. In other words, while Google News indexes many thousands of English-language news sources, every time our participants searched for news, they had a 49% chance of being directed to one of these five outlets. (Owen 2018)

However, the study further found that this kind of siloing had less to do with ideology than with a Google algorithm preference for national news organizations:

> There is some degree of diversity among the fourteen news organizations that occupied the top spots in the two experiments. Some are legacy print media, some are digital-native, and others are television networks and magazines. Some are general interest outlets, and others are focused on the political world. But almost all of them are large national organizations, and 79 percent of them are based in only two metro areas: New York City and Washington, D.C. (with the exceptions headquartered in the Atlanta,

Chicago, and Los Angeles areas). These findings indicate that more than dissecting the public conversation into fragmented silos, digital distribution of news might narrow the conversation around a small set of national outlets.

To conservatives, this is tantamount to liberal bias. Since the right-wing media outlets are not among these top fourteen, Americans would not be directed to them in a Google search. Google maintained that its algorithm emphasized original reporting and fact-gathering journalism, but regardless the study supported the claims of bias that grew from the divide between national and local news already addressed. The narrative of even more liberal bias by information providers was picked up by the right-wing media and spread, as it underscored an existing (and growing) narrative of unfair treatment and ideological discrimination.

It is vital for online outlets to increase their audience size, which is why Google searches are so important. Howard Polskin releases a daily tipsheet called *TheRighting* that aggregates the top stories on the leading right-wing media circle Web sites, and when President Trump began his assault against Google, Polskin wrote an article about the power and reach of these Web sites where he argued that, contrary to the president's claims, conservative outlets were not hurting for traffic. Quite the contrary, Polskin found that these sites frequently exceeded the web traffic of the mainstream media outlets:

> When I first began analyzing conservative websites, not only was I knocked back on my heels by the sheer daily editorial output coming from the right, I was also astonished by the size of the audiences for the sites I studied. I don't want to diminish the power of cable's Fox News or right-wing talk radio, but the vast breadth of right-wing websites combined with their ability to attract large audiences – with many attracting anywhere from 10 to 70 million audience visits a month – make them impossible to ignore when considering their influence over a large part of the voting population. (Polskin, Right-Wing Sites Not Being Left Behind by Mainstream Ones 2018b)

So the right-wing outlets are incredibly popular, but what do these clicks mean? Most of all, it means that these outlets are extremely profitable.

The key to ad-based revenue rests on popularity, but unlike TV ratings, online use is measured in several different ways. According to Brent Merritt of Metric Communications, the two measurements are exposure and engagement. Merritt defines "exposure" as: "who was listening, for how long, and how often." "Engagement" is "how involved people were in a broadcast" (Merritt 2017). Exposure models are the ones that are tied to the old-school standards of news media monetization, the idea being that the most eyeballs that see (or ears that hear) the news being offered, the better. Engagement, however, determines whether readers or listeners stick with the platform long enough to connect with the content in a meaningful way, the theory being that if the audience is involved with the Web site, they will return regularly and (perhaps) with frequency. These are the kinds of viewers that Web sites like the best, mostly because people are creatures of habit, and if their habit involves your Web site, you can sell more stuff to them through ads. It is not a bad argument.

Exposure remains the dominant school of measurement, and to determine exposure, a Web site generally quantifies the number of times someone visits them. Once they know how many visitors they have to their site, they can then construct rates to charge advertisers. This rests on the traditional relationship between popularity and money; the larger the audience, the higher the ad rate. With the Internet, the most common way to charge an advertiser is by producing a rate based on the "CPM," the cost per thousand impressions, or the cost of reaching a thousand people. Another way to charge is the "cost per click," or "CPC." One can imagine that these models generate conversations that sound like this: "We have 5 gazillion hits per month, so we can charge a thousand dollars for an ad," or something like that. Many newspapers who have moved their content online rely on these click models to calculate their readership, and in the newsrooms of *The Washington Post* and *The Baltimore Sun,* there are gigantic monitors that list the articles being run each day and post the number of hits each article receives, constantly updating in real time. Paul Farhi from the *Washington Post* told me that when editors to move stories around their site in order to goose the numbers (my words, not his), it can be beneficial to a reporter whose work is in the paper. For example, Farhi told me that he is less concerned now if his work is featured in the Style section, instead of the front section:

> ... [H]ow much does it matter if my story is on E16, D1 or A1? A1 certainly holds some prestige and symbolically shows the reader of the newspaper that this story is more important than some other stories.... But I no longer have to fight the battles of display. Before the internet, there was

this fierce competition to get on A1.... This makes all that a shrug, because the number of people who are going to read that story are not going to read that in the physical Style section, or even in the physical paper itself. They're going to read it.... Having linked to it somewhere, having seen it somewhere, on Facebook, Twitter, whatever it might be. (Farhi 2017)

Also along those lines, David Zurawik from *The Baltimore Sun* told me that seeing the number of hits on his article brought out a sense of competition in him and he found himself keeping a sharp eye on those traffic monitors (Zurawik 2017).[5]

Even though the benefit of stories moving around a webpage means that readers can access more content, there are two negative consequences as well. The first is that the loss of an A1 position disregards the cues about story importance; the second is the way story skimming and outlet hopping further shrink our attention spans. Both of these phenomena contribute to the deleterious media ecosystem. The first problem is what CBS News' John Dickerson calls "flattening," when all stories are deemed important and are given equal weight. The public is bombarded with push-notifications and urgent updates that announce the vital significance of so many events that it all runs the risk of becoming insignificant, and we do not even have the old-style prompts to help us determine rank. The more traditional news formats were built to give information and also give cues about their importance. If a story ran in a newspaper above the fold, it was clearly important; if it ran on page 13, it had less weight. If a news story aired first on the Evening News, it had significant meaning; if it was buried between traffic and weather, then it had less standing (Dickerson 2016). Media scholars refer to this idea as "gatekeeping," where news organizations not only select what is important but also indicate an order of consequence. This worked in a linear media environment organized by chronology or significance. However, when articles are run online, there is very little to distinguish rank and weight, since stories so frequently link to other stories and are constantly updated and reorganized. When you layer in the hyperbole used to sell a story, it sometimes feels like all news items online are of equal value, even when there is no false equivalency at play. Put together, the equal coverage of disparate subjects and the dearth of signals to indicate meaning can lead to a rather confused audience who are overwhelmed by content.

The second negative effect concerns engagement or a lack thereof. Suhail Doshi, founder of the analytics company Mixpanel, has called the measurements of new users or page views or hits "bullshit metrics." Doshi recommends that different sites establish what he refers to as their "one key metric," user engagement that is fundamental to the mission of the site. For political news outlets, that key metric may be how deeply a patron reads an article. Not only would a consumer benefit from a complete understanding of a piece of journalism, the outlet would benefit from greater user engagement. In an ideal world, news consumers absorb and analyze material thoroughly, but our world at present is less than ideal. Even though Twitter doubled their character limit to 280, American attention spans are increasingly shrinking. This has dramatic implications for news consumers who may be easily sidetracked by frivolous, amusing, or confirmation bias-producing content. The emphasis on traffic encourages journalists and editors to write and run stories that are exciting and provocative, because the more people read a story, the more a news organization can charge for advertising. Yet the simple act of clicking on a story does not mean a reader understands the topic or its significance with actual clarity. Since hits to a Web site are an important part of monetization models, what is known as "clickbait" is quite valuable to a news organization. Clickbait refers to stories with attention-grabbing headlines or shorthands that seem to exist only to get attention and distract us from the real news.[6] Because there is so much content available and because we are easily distracted, Americans are lulled into clickbait stories which they quickly abandon, and this leads to even less engagement with online content. Academic studies have shown that we are becoming more comfortable with the habit of shallow reading. Scholars from Columbia University and the French National Institute found that people are increasingly sharing articles without reading them, which makes click-bating headlines even more powerful and dangerous (Dewey 2016). Worse, researchers at Notre Dame University found that on Reddit: "84% of participants interacted with content in less than 50% of their pageloads" which is especially bad because Reddit is a forum for people supposedly interested in the content on their feeds (Byrne 2017). If readers do not take the time to examine the content within the links, they are sharing carelessly, without fully understanding what they are reading. This is how fake news spreads so quickly: It hits on our biases, and we do not take pains to ascertain its veracity.

Engagement encourages more time spent with material, arguably more comprehension as well. This kind of measurement is tied to another form of content monetization which are subscription models. Since most of the Internet was born (and spent its infancy) as a free source of content, consumers grew accustomed to site-hopping without cost. Americans are loath to pay for something they used to get gratis, and so the idea of paying for online content is *very* annoying to most people. Because there are so many digital news options, all of which allow consumers an abundance of choice, it is easy for a consumer to click away from a webpage when they are told that they have to pay for it. This is the biggest hurdle for news organizations that want to rely on subscription models for their funding.

Subscriptions come in the form of paywalls are currently seen most frequently from print journalism that has migrated to the web, and different news sites have varying rules for accessing their content. Some sort their news by "premium" and non-premium stories; some allow a specific number of features to be accessed each month. The overarching idea is to get the news-interested public to pay for the journalism they enjoy, a concept that was tried and accepted when people paid for newspapers. Yet although the concept of paying for content is proven, it is increasingly difficult to operationalize since there are so many stand-alone news outlets, many of which offer free access, all of which need funding. There are basically two types of media consumers: those who pay for content and those who don't. In addition to the subscription fees for streaming services, online news sites, and legacy media sources, there are also "free" sources that require donations to stay afloat. For those who do pay, the list of payments can be impressive, and those who fund the media sources are essentially carrying the water for the pirates among us. My own personal list of media expenditures is lengthy, and I shocked myself when I sat down to list them, as the sum total equals roughly twice of Donald Trump's net worth.[7] Kidding aside, the point stands. Media organizations need funding or they cannot exist. Remember *C-SPAN*?

While many people say they are willing to pay for subscriptions and content, the actual number of Americans who pony up the monthly subscription fees remains relatively small, even with the surge of newspaper subscriptions seen in the Trump Era. As a result, news organizations have been tinkering with different types of subscription models in order to lure readers to the automatic payment page. News sites have toyed with an iTunes-style model where people pay per article, or they demand that readers pay for a specific number of articles within a period. In doing so, news companies try to directly attract and keep an audience. Additionally, outside companies are developing models for news consumers and in doing so illustrate the complications of this proposition. A new company called Scroll created a site where subscribers pay $5 per month to access all sorts of content without ads. Scroll incentivizes readers to subscribe, and these subscriptions are the enticement for publishers to join the service. A program called LaterPay allows publishers to price individual articles and then charges a reader later on, when they have consumed a specific number of this premium content. LaterPay has a multi-pronged effect of not only getting money for content, but also striving for the goal of audience retention. A bit like the military's psychological operations, this tactic aims to change people's behavior: They want site visits to become habitual and indispensable, which will in turn boost subscriptions. Both Scroll and LaterPay try to attract new readers in order to turn them into full subscribers. There are also media companies that try to shift the emphasis from ad revenue to subscriptions, based on the idea that since ads are so irritating consumers will pay to stop them. A company called Invisibly offers readers a choice. With Invisibly, readers can either abide by the existing paywall rules (meaning, readers can access a specific number of free articles per month or purchase a day or week pass), or they can watch a video ad that will unlock content for a specific amount of time (Doctor, Can Startup Invisibly Be the New Revenue Stream Publishers Dream Of? 2017b). This is attractive to both a news audience who benefits from a concentrated but limited ad push, and the ad buyers who want the public to be actively involved in the ad they are paying for. All of these new ideas, from Scroll, LaterPay, and Invisibly, are evidence that monetizing online news is (a) crucial; (b) challenging; and (c) completely unsettled. As news outlets tinker with new ways to fund their journalism, some find their financial woes more severe than others.

This is highlighted by the divide in profitability between national and local newspapers. Only 2% of news consumers actually have subscriptions to their newspapers of choice, and much of the time their choice is either *The New York Times* with a US monthly audience of 97 million or *The Washington Post* with 92 million (Doctor, Newsonomics: Our Peggy Lee Moment: Is That All There Is to Reader Revenue? 2017a). Large national outlets have seen what is referred to as the "Trump Bump," an increase in subscriptions for the news organizations that break news about the administration. This growth, however, is not felt by smaller local and regional papers. At a 2018 Berkshire Hathaway meeting, Warren Buffet predicted: "No one except the *Wall Street Journal, The New York Times* and now probably the *Washington Post* has come up with a digital product that really in any significant way will replace the revenue that is being lost as print newspapers lose both circulation and advertising" (Levine 2018). Even with the "Trump Bump" of increased news audiences, trying to turn something once free into something with a price tag is a challenge. There is a significant divide between the larger, established national news organizations and the smaller, regional and local outlets who are struggling to survive at a time when the competition is fierce. The burden on local papers is especially heavy, since these are the information sources that matter the most for smaller areas. Al Cross, director of the Institute for Rural Journalism and Community Issues, was quoted in a report from the *Columbia Journalism Review* about local news and said:

> The kinds of things people get from a local newspaper are the kinds of things that people will continue to want one hundred years from now. What's going on within my locality? What's happening with my school system? What's happening with my taxes? What's happening with planning and zoning? What kind of businesses or jobs might we get? It's only the local newspaper that is likely to be the consistently reliable source of that information. (Ali and Radcliffe 2017a)

Local papers accomplish a number of important democratic goals. They monitor the town council and reporting on the school system, they encourage political participation among the citizens of a town with their reporting on "average" people, and they provide a check on our elected officials. Since one hallmark of a free press is holding politicians accountable, there needs to be a free press to do the accounting. Spectrum News Editor Errol Louis noted on *CNN* that if there are no local journalists on site to investigate, elected officials are "going to get away with murder" (Stelter 2017). Because national news organizations rely on smaller outlets for original reporting, there can be a trickle-up effect when there is no local coverage on which to base larger, significant investigations. When local newsrooms fail, lost also is the information they gather and provide to the public. Put together, this means that the problems facing local news outlets in terms of monetizing their content and shifting to new technologies are essential to solve.

The *Columbia Journalism Review* published a report in 2017 outlining the challenges occurring at once for local papers. Local outlets suffer from the same pressures as national ones, but seem to be hit twice as hard thanks to the overall cultural shifts that come from our increasing reliance on cell phones and the Internet. At the same time that Americans move online to get their news, they are also moving online to go shopping and this has changed the local consumer experience and the advertising placed by those smaller independent stores (Ali and Radcliffe 2017a). Accordingly, local news entities have to be even more creative than their national counterparts since the ad revenue streams are drying up on several fronts. The CJR report notes that most local papers are experimenting with varying and multiple revenue models, including "paywalls, increasing the cost of print subscriptions, the creation of spin-off media service companies, sponsored content, membership programs, and live events" (Ali and Radcliffe 2017a). Yet even as local news outlets try innovative ways to bring in more revenue, most have to cut costs by reducing resources and as a result, more than 20,000 newsroom jobs have disappeared (Ali and Radcliffe 2017a).

In this precarious economic climate, it is not hyperbole to write that the survival of the news remains in question. There have been "white knights" who have swept into save a dying news organization with an infusion of cash. Laurene Powell Jobs is a majority investor in *The Atlantic* and is also an investor in *Axios*. Tech billionaires have stepped in as well, like Marc Benioff who bought *Time* Magazine, and Patrick Soon-Shiong bought *The Los Angeles Times*. Amazon founder Jeff Bezos bought *The Washington Post* in 2013 and saved the paper from the financial devastation that threatened it, and this is seen as a success story. But the *Washington Post* is a national paper and a national institution: This is the paper that brought down Nixon and was staffed by Robert Redford and Dustin Hoffman. Other examples prove that the white knight scenario is not always as effective, and in the past decade, wealthy backers have purchased both legacy and digitally native outlets only to realize how difficult such a purchase can be. Millionaire Joe Ricketts shut down the New York City Web sites *DNAInfo* and *Gothamist* when workers at the publications tried to unionize. *The New Republic* was purchased in 2012 by Chris Hughes, a former Facebook executive who sold the magazine four years later after ending its print run and decimating its editorial staff. Amidst the carnage left behind at *TNR*, Hughes wrote in a letter announcing his intent to sell the magazine that he: "underestimated the difficulty of transitioning an old and traditional institution into a digital media company in today's quickly evolving climate" (Somaiya 2016). Local news orgs are especially vulnerable, since they lack the audience size, name recognition, and prestige of the national outlets. Derek Thompson writes in *The Atlantic:*

> National reporting might be stronger than ever, but the combination of print's demise, digital advertising's duopolistic concentration, and the geographical sorting of journalists has gutted local newspapers. Like the slow demise of print advertising itself, it is the sort of story that news organizations might be structurally designed to miss. The opposite of a sudden and shocking calamity exhaustively covered by every media organization, it is, rather, a thousand local disappearances, with nobody left to report on what has gone away. (Thompson 2016a)

The only remedy for the dire economic condition of the press today is for Americans to support the news they need and reinforce the institutions that maintain the values of our free press. In less lofty terms, this means that consumers have to pay for content. There is simply no other way for the press to survive, and it has become increasingly evident that a free press is vital to our American democracy. Columbia University Professor Tim Wu wrote *The Attention Merchants* (2016) about the advertising business. In an interview about the book, Dr. Wu prescribed the cure for the suffering media, and it rests in the hands of the public: "We have to get over our addiction to free stuff. Suck it up and pay". (Thompson, Does Advertising Ruin Everything? 2016a)

## PROBLEMS FROM SOCIAL MEDIA

One might think that local news sites would benefit from a large-scale shift to the web because more people are getting their news online, but it does not work that way. Most people, being creatures of habit with varying degrees of cell phone addiction, go to two places most frequently: Facebook and Google (the duopoly, once more). As cell phones become smarter, faster, and more agile, there has been a correlated shift from desktop computers to mobile, which means that the duopoly dominates. According to a 2017 *Atlantic Monthly* article (accessed online, for what it's worth):

The theory of digital publishing has long been that because people are spending more time reading and watching stories on the internet than other places, eventually the ad revenue would follow them from other media types. People now spend more than 5.5 hours a day with digital media, including three hours on their phones alone. The theory wasn't wrong. Ad dollars have followed eyeballs. In 2016, internet-ad revenue grew to almost $75 billion, pretty evenly split between ads that run on computers (desktop) and ads that run on phones (mobile). But advertising to people on computers is roughly at the level it was in 2013. That is to say, *all* the recent growth has been on mobile devices. And on mobile, Facebook and Google have eaten almost all that new pie. These two companies are making more and more money. Everyone else is trying to survive. (Madrigal 2017)

As more Americans get their news from these two tech giants, the duopoly squeezes the rest of the online news industry, even as the news media experiment with new revenue streams. According to most estimates, the duopoly is earning between 84 and 89% of new online ad revenue, which means that every other Web site (on the whole Internet) is sharing the remaining 11–16% of the ad revenue (Ritson 2017). As *Axios'* Sara Fischer wrote in 2017: "Google's ad revenue is roughly the same as all print ad revenue globally and Facebook's ad revenue nearly topples all radio ad revenue globally" (Fischer, Tech Giants Eating the Advertising World 2017c).

Duopoly domination leads to problems beyond the fact that Facebook and Google are eating up almost all of the online advertising profits. One important concern stems from the fact that the tech giants are currently under-regulated by the government (the Federal Communications Commission or the Justice Department), which leaves the companies to regulate themselves. Thus far, this self-rule has had mixed results.[8] Social media executives are consistently brought in front of Congress to answer questions about data breaches, foreign interference in the 2016 presidential campaign, hate speech, fake news, and the over-sized influence of technology in our everyday lives. As more Americans get their news from tech companies, and as tech companies refuse to admit they are media companies, these problems will continue. Tech executives walk a very thin line between acquiescing to demands to remove offensive content and First Amendment questions about censorship, and they are loath to lean into plans for more governmental oversight. In recent years, Google spent more money on lobbying in Washington than any other company, an indication that it sees the regulatory writing on the wall and is working hard to get in front of it (Bach 2018).

The greatest consequence of the duopoly's vague status is that they do not come to journalism with the same mission as legacy outlets. *The Baltimore Sun's* David Zurawik noted that established press outlets maintained a commitment to the public interest because that was engrained in their undertaking. Speaking about the gatekeepers of the news media, Zurawik said: "before you became the people in the *CBS* newsroom deciding what's going to be on the *CBS Evening News*, you were socialized to a sense of a media platform, in this case a network, functioning at least to some extent in the public interest. They had some sense of social responsibility because it was codified in a law, the 1934 Communications Act." This government regulation mandated that news organizations had to air public interest shows in order to keep their licenses, and the Federal Communications Commission regulated these outlets (Zurawik 2017). With the duopoly, none of that regulation is in place, which means the commitment to the public interest is not in place either. Case in point: During the 2016 campaign, Facebook did not include identifiers at the end of most political ads because by law they did not have to. These are the statements at the end of political ads that say "Paid for by…" Russian Internet trolls placed political ads on Facebook, which reached more than 126 million Facebook users, and Facebook has promised to change their rules for future elections. The point is that when a company that peddles in news does not call itself a news company, the result falls short of the journalistic ideal.

The combination of social media popularity and the tech giant's algorithms leads to another issue concerning intellectual isolation. Algorithms are designed to steer us toward what the tech companies *think* we want versus something challenging or divergent from our existing belief system. Sorting the news with the purpose of maintaining an audience can lead the public into what are known as "filter bubbles." Filter bubbles encourage a seclusion where citizens only receive and share content with which they already agree. People live in intellectual bubbles of their own making, and social media algorithms encourage this. Finding content that matches our interests is one natural way for media companies to seek and keep an audience, and so outlets of all kinds are trying to personalize their content for their users. Eli Pariser has written extensively about filter bubbles and in a Ted Talk on this subject addressed the scope of the problem:

There are a whole host of companies that are doing this kind of personalization. Yahoo News, the biggest news site on the Internet, is now personalized – different people get different things. *Huffington Post*, the *Washington Post*, the *New York Times* – all flirting with personalization in various ways. And this moves us very quickly toward a world in which the Internet is showing us what it thinks we want to see, but not necessarily what we need to see. (Pariser 2011)

The tighter our bubbles, the less we are exposed to opposing thought or ideas that are difficult but important. *CBS News* Chief White House correspondent Major Garrett has worked in Washington for years as a journalist and spent eight years at *Fox News*. In an interview, Garrett told me: "If from the time you wake up until the time you go to sleep at night all the news you consume that day makes you comfortable and happy, you're doing it the wrong way" (Garrett 2017). To support this point, Pariser argued that the public has to make an effort to go beyond what the algorithms feed us and that those algorithms should change:

...if algorithms are going to curate the world for us, if they're going to decide what we get to see and what we don't get to see, then we need to make sure that they're not just keyed to relevance. We need to make sure that they also show us things that are uncomfortable or challenging or important... other points of view. (Pariser 2011)

While information diversity is important, it is challenging to accomplish. People are unlikely to try something new or challenging given the combination of abundant media options, partisan selective exposure, and our social media assisted filter bubbles. Most news audiences prefer the familiar and the comfortable, which translates to a cyclical relationship between media consumers, algorithm suggestions, and political media outlets that double down on the reinforcing (and popular) content.

Niche programming grew as cable television provided entire channels targeted to specific tastes, and this trend toward the individualized only grew once the Internet expanded the media landscape to include everything. This has led to the bifurcated results of a highly accessible and personalized communication system that encourages an audience to seek out comfortable and familiar fare. Our technology is specifically geared toward solipsism; iPhones and iPads provide the exact content that we want, hence the "i." We never have to listen to a song we do not like or hear an opinion that disagrees with ours. At the same time, with so many options available, many return to the songs, programs, and news perspective that they already know and value. The advancements that have produced revolutionary technology and made unfathomable amounts of money for some also serve to separate us while financially threatening an entire industry. Many scholarly papers, literary think pieces, and entire books have and will be dedicated to the influence of social media on our politics, but it is important to remember that this influence rests on a long history of making money from making media. All of these changes in form and the financial growth that accompanied them have made for a crowded political media environment.

## THE PROBLEMS WITH A VERY CROWDED MEDIA LANDSCAPE

The technological growth that has forced platform multiplication on most major news outlets has resulted in two major changes to the landscape. First, journalists are forced to take on more duties than just reporting, because not only are they in demand to analyze the news they break, they also need to publicize themselves and their news outlet. Second, there is now an almost infinite space to fill with politicos, and so more voices are being heard from a wide variety of places. New political actors are on hand to add their expertise and advertise their party, their policy position, or their brand.

With less money to spend but more work to do, many journalists are tasked with multiple duties, producing content on different platforms. Sometimes these are known as "bridge roles" where responsibilities span from traditional journalistic and editorial functions to technical data production and engineering. In 2017, the *Post* added three newsroom management jobs including operations, product, and project editors to "allow the newsroom to partner better with the engineering team" (Cherubini 2017). These new jobs are another indication of the constant progression of technology, and the demands put upon news organizations just to keep up with the changing media landscape. Zurawik noted that younger journalists today were required to report, film, and edit their own content; they have so many more responsibilities in their work today (Zurawik 2017).

The double and triple duty extends well beyond the tasks assigned by editors; journalists are also required to stay relevant and known within an expanding industry. Most news staffers today not only report on their platform, they also podcast, blog, and take to social media with frequency. One reason for this is what *Politico's* Eliana Johnson described as the necessity of fame for journalists today. Johnson told me that someone gave her the advice to first become famous, and good journalism positions would follow (Johnson 2017). With so many outlets available, so many media forms on which to appear, this fame imperative is not as difficult to achieve as it once had been (although it clearly takes talent). Johnson left our interview to tape an appearance on NBC's *Meet the Press*, and the following weekend I heard her on *Politico's* podcast "The Political Nerdcast." She is, in fact, famous. Most reporters today have a wider wingspan than they had in the past, because being well known is an advantage in a highly competitive journalism environment. According to a *Buzzfeed* article that was titled "It's a Good Time to Be a Reporter Covering Trump If You Like Money and Going on TV," reporters say that especially with a president who seemingly only watches television, being on TV is a good way to increase their status at the White House (Perlberg 2018). In this highly competitive news environment, cable news networks have begun to sign journalists from other news organizations as paid contributors, especially print journalists who do much of the daily reporting on the Trump administration. Paid contributors to *CNN* include reporters from *The New York Times, The Washington Post, Politico, Time Magazine,* and *Bloomberg News,* while MSNBC has signed journalists from all of those outlets plus *Daily Beast, Vanity Fair,* and *Axios.* The increase in journalists shifting roles from investigators to personalities and the financial reward for such a shift prompted comedian Michelle Wolf to make this joke at the 2018 White House Correspondent's Dinner:

> I think what no one in this room wants to admit is that Trump has helped all of you. He couldn't sell steaks or vodka or water or college or ties or Eric, but he has helped you. He's helped you sell your papers and your books and your TV. You helped create this monster, and now you're profiting off of him. If you're going to profit off of Trump, you should at least give him some money, because he doesn't have any. (Perlberg 2018)

Another reason that journalists are doing compound duty is that news organizations are diversifying their platforms, and they need their own people to do more. Stand-alone news outlets are rare: It is difficult to think of a news organization that is contained on only one medium. Cable news channels have not only Web sites, but have also launched web radio channels. The success of the *Fox News Channel* has been replicated online, and the *Fox News* Web site frequently draws more traffic than *The New York Times* website, with upwards of 350 million audience visits per month (Polskin 2018a). The success of the *Fox News* Web site has inspired *Fox* to launch a new streaming service for what it calls "superfans."

In the endless technological development, there have been "pivots" to different platforms, including podcasting and video which has directed companies to innovate and diversify. For example, *The New York Times* now has a series of podcasts they produce, including the top-rated "Daily" podcast hosted by Michael Barbaro. The *Times* opened their newsroom for a Showtime documentary called "The Fourth Estate," and their column "Diagnosis" has been developed into a Netflix series. *Buzzfeed, Vox,* and *Fusion* also have deals with Netflix. Even if journalists are unable to snag lucrative deals as regular contributors on television networks, they will undoubtedly have many more opportunities to appear on different platforms in varying ways and do more. This is now part for their survival, and they are not alone in their clamor for the camera. Not only are there a growing number of media outlets available for the public to enjoy, and not only are journalists doing double and triple duty, there is a need to fill all of that air and Internet space with experts and entertaining influencers.

Politicians have always had to use the media as they run for office or fight for policy, because the media provide the most accessible outlets for reaching the voting public. As the media grew in size and scope during the 1990s and 2000s, so too did the number of press staff on Capitol Hill. Members used to have one staffer to handle the press, and then some House leadership members and Senators began to add press staff for their district offices as well. By the time the Internet came around, almost every lawmaker had at least one press assistant, many had two, and then social media inspired some lawmakers to bring on young staffers to simply deal with these platforms alone. Today, politicians have to be media savvy in new ways and have had to keep up with emerging technologies while they also keep up with their press-hungry colleagues.

At the same time, with abundant space to fill, bookers for cable, broadcast, and radio are busy finding enough suitable people to fill all of that space while digital news orgs look for expert opinions to add heft and splash to their pages. Joining politicians on these screens is an increasing number of political professionals who clamor for exposure in order to advocate and to increase their brand, their reach, and their bank accounts. New additions to the political media landscape include representatives from interest groups, activist groups, and think tanks, plus partisans, political professionals, and now "surrogates" who advo- cate on behalf of a candidate. All of these voices heard and read belong to "pundits," someone expert or experienced enough to provide com- mentary and opinion to a discussion. It is always good to get an expert and informed opinion about weighty matters. When that proves to be too challenging, a simple judgment will suffice. While pundits provide commentary on air and in print, cable news is the real mother ship for punditry. An article from the *Washington Post* helps to classify types of pundits seen and heard on cable news.

| | |
|---|---|
| News Analyst | Someone salaried or on contract to provide analysis on cable news shows. |
| Contributor | An expert who is paid for each appearance. |
| Commentator/Strategist | A partisan who carves out time to appear and opine. |
| Guests | Unpaid, sporadic contributors[9] (Farhi, We Have Reached Peak Punditry 2016). |

For the cable news networks, having a multitude of voices allows the net- work to deny ideological bias: "We have a ____ on our show to prove that we don't hate ____." Additionally, there is now an entire pundit class in Washington because of this large, mutually beneficial system. Cable news and talk radio programs, blogs, news sites, and social media outlets need to keep things fresh and entertaining, and they afford a plat- form for politicos across all parties and job descriptions. Technology and money have combined to create a massive political media with airtime to fill, clicks to earn, and subscriptions to sell which is now necessarily chock-full of people trying to wrestle the spotlight on to themselves. The political media are crowded and angry.

New types of political figures are coming to cable and digit screens with frequency. Political scientists refer to the unelected people who push for policy or campaign of a candidate as "outside actors," because these people have not been elected or appointed within the political system.[10] Today these groups are not very "outside" at all. In many cases, advocacy groups are the ones crafting policy, promoting it nationally, and then holding lawmakers accountable for their responses and their votes. Outside actors can be the most important players in American politics since, with increasing frequency, they drive the political conversations, policy goals, and ideological narratives. Although it might be easy to lump all of these groups together into one big advocacy ball, in truth these groups are different from one another in both form and function. There are, essentially, three general varieties: interest groups, politically active nonprofits, and think thanks.

Interest groups are the most well-known and understood type of faction[11] since these organizations promote one single issue or one set of relating issues, and issues are easy things to understand. The workings of government are complicated and demand knowledge, but opinions about issues are easier to come by. Lobbyists and interest group representatives hit the airwaves and reach out on social media to excite their members while they also make their case to the public. Interest group spokespersons are championing their cause. Conversely, politically active nonprofits are championing a creed. These types of activist groups differ from interest groups in that they organize along ideological lines and let the issues come and go according to the news cycles. Because ideology and philosophical devotion matter more than issue salience, an active membership can be alerted to different subjects and mobilized accordingly. Many of these groups are nonprofits classified by their IRS tax status, and because of this designation, they are not supposed to spend the majority of their time politically advocating. These are known as "politically active non profits," but are better known in Washington as 501(c) groups, and recently, there has been a bumper crop of them joining the discussion. There are 29 different types of 501(c) groups, ranging from churches (501(c)3s) to unions (501(c)6s) to cemetery companies (501(c)13s), but the primary kind for politicking is the 501(c)4, a "social welfare organization." 501(c)4s are legally allowed to engage in politics, as long as said politicking is not the group's "primary" purpose, and while there are certainly 501(c)4s that do not engage in advocacy, there are many who do. Political organizations such as interest groups and think tanks are increasingly adding 501(c)s to their corporate structures. These encourage extra donations and offer different ways to advocate. Since Americans are so polarized in their politics, advocacy groups are polarized as well, and the growth in numbers of these politically active nonprofits increases the number of people yelling about politics. Some say the advocacy groups feed the polarization or are the reason for it. Regardless, politically active nonprofits thrive on members who swim in the waters of angry and determined politics; these kinds of political advocacy groups attract a slice of the very attentive public who are dyed-in-the-wool ideologues.

Speaking of think tanks, this is where to go if you are looking for statistics, data, and more staid policy fare, there are think tanks. If politically active nonprofits are fixes for ideological junkies, think tanks are the excel spreadsheets of the policy wonks. These are organizations that are staffed with academics, statisticians, economists, sociologists, and policy nerds who dive deep into the waters of data. The original idea was that think tanks hired scholars to do research in a policy area, which was then made available to policymakers. In today's media environment, journalists also use think tank experts to explain a subject or an event. The studies produced by these organizations continue to be used as evidence in the policy wars. What is relatively new, however, is the think tank presence in political media, because they are increasingly visible in political media. All put together, the public hears from interest group lobbyists, politically active nonprofits, and think tank scholars more now than ever. They add expertise, opinion, and volume to political discussions about issues.

Different from policy advocates are the people who promote the election of specific candidates or political parties. Policy battles occur in between election cycles, but as the campaign seasons increasingly blur together, the public hears more from those advocating for a particular political candidate. The types of political promoters are partisans, political professionals, and surrogates. Partisans are those who represent a political party, and even with the weakened party system, partisans play an important role in political communications. They are the faces of the parties, and so they represent the two-way fights between red and blue. They are the champions of their teams in battles for policy or elections. Political professionals are the hired guns of politics, those who specialize in strategy, ad creation, and voter mobilization. They appear in political media not to advocate for a candidate, but to provide context in a campaign and advertise their own political abilities. Most of the time, political professionals are championing themselves. Finally, and new to the media landscape, are "surrogates." The 2016 election saw these candidate supporters added to cable news lineups to keep Hillary Clinton and Donald Trump "equally" represented. In order to dodge claims of bias,[12] cable news producers booked surrogates who simply shelled for one candidate or another. They not necessarily on the campaign rolls of either one; they are there to champion their candidate and themselves.

Because elections are the bread and butter of American politics, and because our election seasons have extended so far as to blur together, the politically attentive public hears from political professionals frequently. There is a relatively new phenomenon in American politics called "the invisible primary," which is the period before the actual presidential primaries begin. In 1976, Arthur Hadley wrote a book that addressed the confluence of primaries, campaign finance, and media and in doing so first addressed the idea of the invisible primary. Today, the invisible primary period is said to begin the day after a presidential election, although that too is expanding. Politicians with their eye the White House will write books, give policy speeches in New Hampshire and Iowa, and travel abroad to combat zones in order to get their names into the public discussion. This process leads to better fund-raising because name recognition matters. The invisible primary period relies on the kind of political media system that currently exists, one with space to fill with the breathless guessing game of "who will run?"

All of these politicos are now fighting for airtime against one another, sharing space with the journalists who are jockeying for position, trying to be heard over the competition. It is a congested and noisy political media system, and the public has to sort through all of this to get facts, analysis, and information vital for a democracy. Transformative technology at one time delivers the promise of possibility and innovation while it also serves up an existential threat and massive competition. Competition in the news is not a new phenomenon, but the structures around the current competition are different and untested. It is unsurprising that with all of the profit potential, an alternative right-wing media system developed and thrived. Outside of the right-wing media bubble, however, the rest of the mainstream media struggles to stay solvent and successful in a fluctuating news climate.

## CONCLUSIONS

Few will argue that advances in media technology are entirely negative. We are now able to communicate easily and with alacrity; we can get and share important news, we can give voice to our opinions without filter, and we can connect globally. These are all net positives. There are, however, some serious costs to these advances and our culture wrestles with them. The Internet is still an emerging medium, and it remains largely unregulated and unfinished. The uncertainty of the Internet drives questions about funding, which then influences news and content production, which then affects the public's news consumption. These consequences, which result from advancing technologies that shift the media landscape, are major contributors to the divided political media we have today.

To help the audience choose their channel or site in this overwhelming, crowded media landscape, news companies are engaging in two different kinds of biases; the first is structural bias. This is where organizations produce shorter stories, those that are digested easily and perhaps more entertaining, stories that are more attractive to an audience. Here, outlets are giving the public what they think the public already wants, and when the public seems to follow this lead, the news companies continue to water down their journalism to make it more appealing. This can lead to the second kind of bias, which is ideological. Media economist Lisa George notes that with so much competition, the economic equation defaults to the demand side, where the audience is in the driver's seat and gets what they want (George 2017). Apparently, the public wants polarizing news content, because the partisan news system we have today is wildly popular. Because partisan news comes full of opinion, it is less expensive to produce than investigative journalism, and this is another bonus for ideological news outlets. But mostly it is about anger (profitable) and shade-throwing (entertaining), all of which are good for business but bad for deliberation and democratic debate.

As long as the public devours the polarizing content it is offered, the partisan media will continue to offer it because it makes money. The media structure today is such that one does not need the kind of audience once attracted by the three major broadcast networks—a cable news network, a Web site, a podcast only needs several million people (out of a country of 315 million) to remain profitable. And thus, the most significant consequence of the financial imperatives of the media is that our news content will grow louder and more partisan as the competition grows. This is dangerous because it is a reinforcing cycle of cynicism and anger that earns profits, which then feeds more fury and polarization. In the course of this cycle, we dehumanize our political opponents and give up compromise. We distrust our institutions and sort ourselves even more than we are sorted already. Thus, the financial constraints and technological advancement of the news media are two reasons for our political discord. The next chapter examines exactly how that manifests in the partisan news system that we have today.

## Notes

1. Satellite: "An earth-orbiting communication spacecraft designed to send and receive data from other satellites or earth stations. This data may carry voice, audio, video, or other information. It is the basis for satellite television certain kinds of internet access and cell phone use" (Umar 2013).
2. At least, something like the news.
3. *Fox News* is perpetually #1 in the ratings, which mean that they can charge expensive ad rates. By 2018, *Fox News Channel* was the most-watched cable news network for more than 200 consecutive months (Katz 2017).
4. More on political polarization and the boycotts that result is examined in Chapter 4.
5. Occasionally, he watches his numbers too closely, obsessively walking by the monitors, much to the amusement of his *Baltimore Sun* editor.
6. On the *Post* Web site at this moment is a two-word clickbait header above the fold: "Toddler's Kidney." Another one was simply "Pythons."
7. Estimated: Still haven't seen his tax returns.
8. That is a generous assessment.
9. To be transparent, I have appeared as a guest on several cable news programs. These are unpaid appearances where a producer books me because of my Ph.D., my expertise, and my publications. I get my hair and makeup done by a professional.
10. This would make them the "real insiders."
11. Tip of the hat to James Madison who, in *Federalist No. 10* defined factions as "a number of citizens, whether amounting to a majority or a minority of the whole, who are united and actuated by some common impulse of passion, or of interest, adversed to the rights of other citizens, or to the permanent and aggregate interests of the community."
12. This did not work at all, hence the continued "CNN sucks" screaming at Trump rallies.

# WORKS CITED

Ali, Christopher and Damian Radcliffe. 2017a. New Research: Small-Market Newspapers in the Digital Age. *Columbia Journalism Review*, New York, NY.

Ali, Chrstopher, and Damian Radcliffe. 2017b. *8 Strategies for Saving Local Newsrooms*, November 6. https://www.cjr.org/tow_center/8-strategies-saving-local-newsrooms.php.

Allen, Mike. 2017. *Scoop: Steve Brill's New Start-Up*, November 3. https://www.axios.com/axios-am-2505788801.html?rebelltitem=8&utm_term=emshare#rebelltitem8.

Atkinson, Claire. 2017. *Sinclair's Growing Conservative TV Network Gets FCC Help*, November 16. https://www.nbcnews.com/news/us-news/sinclair-s-growing-conservative-tv-network-gets-fcc-help-n821346.

Bach, Natasha. 2018. *Google Outspent Every Other Company on Washington Lobbying Last Year*, January 24. http://fortune.com/2018/01/24/google-facebook-amazon-apple-lobbying-efforts/. Accessed September 4, 2018.

Bartlett, Bruce. 2017. *The Truth Matters*. New York: 10 Speed Press.

Brown, Calin. 2017. *The Politics of Your Clothes*, October 18. https://www.opensecrets.org/news/2017/10/politics-of-clothes/.

Byrne, Michael. 2017. *New Study Finds That Most Redditors Don't Actually Read the Articles They Vote On*, November 30. https://motherboard.vice.com/en_us/article/vbz49j/new-study-finds-that-most-redditors-dont-actually-read-the-articles-they-vote-on.

Cherubini, Federica. 2017. *The Rise of Bridge Roles in News Organizations*, December. http://www.niemanlab.org/2017/12/the-rise-of-bridge-roles-in-news-organizations/.

Davies, Pete. 2013. *Medium's Metric That Matters: Total Time Reading*, November 21. https://medium.com/data-lab/mediums-metric-that-matters-total-time-reading-86c4970837d5.

Dewey, Caitlin. 2016. *6 in 10 of You Will Share This Link Without Reading It, a New, Depressing Study Says*, June 16. https://www.washingtonpost.com/news/the-intersect/wp/2016/06/16/six-in-10-of-you-will-share-this-link-without-reading-it-according-to-a-new-and-depressing-study/?utm_term=.711e4fe3416b.

Dickerson, John. 2016. *Slate Political Gabfest*. Washington, DC, December 14.

Doctor, Ken. 2017a. *Newsonomics: Our Peggy Lee moment: Is That All There Is to Reader Revenue?* September 26. http://www.niemanlab.org/2017/09/newsonomics-our-peggy-lee-moment-is-that-all-there-is-to-reader-revenue/.

———. 2017b. *Can Startup Invisibly Be the New Revenue Stream Publishers Dream Of?* October 25. http://www.niemanlab.org/2017/10/newsonomics-can-startup-invisibly-be-the-new-revenue-stream-publishers-dream-of/.

————. 2017c. *Newsonomics: These Are the 3 Fault Lines Redrawing the U.S. Media Business,* December 10. http://newsonomics.com/newsonomics-these-are-the-3-fault-lines-redrawing-the-u-s-media-business/.

Farhi, Paul. 2016. *We Have Reached Peak Punditry,* June 2. https://www.washingtonpost.com/sf/style/2016/06/02/pundits/?utm_term=.99fb-b9198a1d. Accessed September 4, 2018.

Farhi, Paul, interview by Alison Dagnes. 2017. *Media Reporter, Washington Post,* July 19.

Fischer, Sara. 2018. *Facebook to Prioritize Local News in News Feed,* January 29. https://www.axios.com/facebook-to-prioritize-local-news-in-news-feed-1517258545-f4b20fdf-6f6d-4511-abec-d5bf334ebca1.html.

Fischer, Sara, interview by Alison Dagnes. 2017a. *We're Watching More Video, Just Not on TV,* March 7. https://www.axios.com/video-plummets-on-tv-desktop-2303352092.html.

————. 2017b. *Media Trends Reporter,* June 15.

————. 2017c. *Tech Giants Eating the Advertising World,* June 27. https://www.axios.com/tech-giants-eating-the-advertising-world-1513303257-450d4cea-49d1-46e3-83f1-66a7c7d8978b.html.

————. 2017d. *The Skinny Revolution,* July 4. https://www.axios.com/axios-media-trends-2452667718.html.

————. 2017e. *The War for Attention,* August 22. C:\Users\ADDagn\AppData\Local\Microsoft\Windows\INetCache\Content.Outlook\W1R1E418\email.mht.

————. 2017f. *TV Ads Are Going Digital, Slowly,* October 18. https://www.axios.com/axios-media-trends-2497131964.html?rebelltitem=14&utm_term=twsocialshare.

————. 2018. *Psych Economy: News Companies Using Your Emotions,* June 12. https://www.axios.com/news-companies-emotion-advertising-journalism-espn-cnn-nyt-3e34bcdb-1d81-4239-94c4-cfe292dd6cd0.html. Accessed October 7, 2018.

Folkenflik. 2016. *Fake Bylines Reveal Hideen Costs of Local News,* September 20. http://www.npr.org/2012/07/06/156311078/fake-bylines-reveal-true-costs-of-local-news.

Frankel, David. 2017. *Customer Losses Due to Cord Cutting to Surpass 1M in Q2, Analyst Predicts,* June 12. http://www.fiercecable.com/cable/cord-cutting-to-surpass-1-million-customers-q2-analyst-predicts.

Garrett, Major, interview by Alison Dagnes. 2017. *CBS News Chief White House Correspondent,* August 21.

George, Lisa, interview by Alison Dagnes. *Associate Professor,* June 1, 2017.

Grieco, Elizabeth. 2017. *More Americans Are Turning to Multiple Social Media Sites for News,* November 2. http://www.pewresearch.org/fact-tank/2017/11/02/more-americans-are-turning-to-multiple-social-media-sites-for-news/.

Harrison, Guy, interview by Alison Dagnes. 2017. *Partner, OnMessage*, May 31, 2017.

Hattem, Julian. 2014. *C-SPAN Limiting Access to Its Online Channels*, July 29. http://thehill.com/policy/technology/213714-c-span-limiting-access-to-its-online-channels. Accessed September 16, 2018.

Howard, Alex. 2009. *Teddy Roosevelt: The Man Who Coined the "Muckraker"*, December 2. http://historyofjournalism.onmason.com/2009/12/02/teddy-roosevelt-the-man-who-coined-the-muckraker/.

Johnson, Eliana, interview by Alison Dagnes. 2017. *White House Reporter, Politico*, May 31.

Katz, A.J. 2017. *Fox News, MSNBC Are Top 5 Cable Networks*, June 28. http://www.adweek.com/tvnewser/cable-network-ranker-week-of-june-19/333681.

Kauffman, Johnny. 2017. *Ad War Means Local TV Stations Win Big in Georgia's Special Election*, May 21. http://www.npr.org/2017/05/21/529006698/ad-war-means-local-tv-stations-win-big-in-georgia-s-record-breaking-election.

Koblin, John. 2018. With More TV Shows Than Ever Vying for Eyeballs, It's Harder to Break Through. *The New York Times*, January 8: B3.

Lamb, Brian, interview by Alison Dagnes. 2018. *Founder, C-SPAN*, January 8.

Lazarus, David. 2017. *Disney Streaming Venture Could Make Bloated Pay-TV Bundles Obsolete*, August 11. http://www.latimes.com/business/lazarus/la-fi-lazarus-disney-espn-streaming-20170811-story.html.

Levine, Jon. 2018. *Warren Buffett Says All but 3 American Newspapers Are Doomed*, May 7. https://www.yahoo.com/entertainment/warren-buffett-says-3-american-newspapers-doomed-video-135731374.html.

Levine, Jon, and Sean Burch. 2017. *What's the Cure for Ailing Mashable, BuzzFeed and Other Online News Sites?* December 6. https://www.thewrap.com/mashable-buzzfeed-online-news-upstarts-ailing-are-missing-the-mark/.

Madrigal, Alexis. 2017. *Prepare for the New Paywall Era*, November 30. https://www.theatlantic.com/technology/archive/2017/11/the-big-unanswered-questions-about-paywalls/547091/.

McCabe, David, and Sara Fischer. 2018. *Sinclair Deal Spooks Liberals Ahead of 2020 Presidential Race*, January 9. https://www.axios.com/the-2020-effect-of-sinclairs-broadcast-merger-1515448302-2e997b99-86b8-444a-96cb-161ddaa58c39.html?source=sidebar.

Merritt, Brent. 2017. *A Brief History of Media Measurement*, September 26. https://medium.com/@brentmerritt/a-brief-history-of-media-measurement-f1f28aa807ce.

Moses, Lucia. 2018. *In the Post-Facebook Era, Publishers See Increase in Direct Traffic*, May 29. https://digiday.com/media/post-facebook-era-publishers-see-increase-direct-traffic/.

Mulvey, Julian, interview by Alison Dagnes. 2017. *Devine Mulvey Longabaugh, Partner*, June 1.

Nielsen. 2017. *TV Ratings*. http://www.nielsen.com/us/en/solutions/measurement/television.html.

Oremus, Mike. 2016. *Who Controls Your Facebook Feed*, January 3. http://www.slate.com/articles/technology/cover_story/2016/01/how_facebook_s_news_feed_algorithm_works.html.

Owen, Lauren Hazard. 2018. *Does Your Google News Change Based on Whether You're Conservative or Liberal?* August 17. http://www.niemanlab.org/2018/08/does-your-google-news-change-based-on-whether-youre-conservative-or-liberal/. Accessed September 10, 2018.

Pariser, Eli. 2011. Bewarde Online "Filter Bubles". *TED.com*, March. https://www.ted.com/talks/eli_pariser_beware_online_filter_bubbles?language=en.

Perez, Sarah. 2018. *Google Experiments in Local News with an App Called Bulletin*, January 26. https://techcrunch.com/2018/01/26/google-experiments-in-local-news-with-an-app-called-bulletin/.

Perlberg, Steven. 2018. *It's a Good Time to Be a Reporter Covering Trump If You Like Money and Going on TV*, May 14. https://www.buzzfeed.com/stevenperlberg/white-house-reporters-tv?utm_term=.pvqEoL7EM#.tvRjowrjR.

Petrova, Maria. 2011. Newspapers and Parties: How Advertising Revenues Created an Independent Press. *American Political Science Review* 105 (4): 790–808.

Pew Research Center. 2016. *Network News Fact Sheet*, June 16. http://www.journalism.org/fact-sheet/network-news/.

Polskin, Howard. 2018a. *Metrics*, August 30. https://www.therighting.com/july-2018-conservative-website-traffic/.

———. 2018b. *Right-Wing Sites Not Being Left Behind by Mainstream Ones*, September 4. https://www.mediapost.com/publications/article/324545/right-wing-sites-not-being-left-behind-by-mainstre.html. Accessed September 17, 2018.

Rashidian, Nushin. 2017. *Publishers Seek Ad Dollar Alternatives*, December 14. http://www.niemanlab.org/2017/12/publishers-seek-ad-dollar-alternatives/.

Ritson, Mark. 2017. *Mark Ritson: Why You Should Fear the 'Digital Duopoly' in 2018*, December 5. https://www.marketingweek.com/2017/12/05/ritson-digital-duopoly-2018/.

Schwartz, Jason. 2018. *Second Fox News Reporter Leaves Amid Objections to Network*, August 23. https://www.politico.com/story/2018/08/23/fox-news-reporters-opinion-network-adam-housley-795278. Accessed September 3, 2018.

Shearer, Elisa, and Jeffrey Gottfried. 2017. *News Use Across Social Media Platforms 2017*, September 7. http://www.journalism.org/2017/09/07/news-use-across-social-media-platforms-2017/.

Slefo, George. 2017. *Desktop and Mobile Ad Revenue Surpasses TV for the First Time*, April 26. http://adage.com/article/digital/digital-ad-revenue-surpasses-tv-desktop-iab/308808/.

Somaiya, Ravi. 2016. *The New Republic Is Sold*, February 16. https://www.nytimes.com/2016/02/27/business/media/the-new-republic-is-sold.html. Accessed September 3, 2018.

Steinberg, Brian. 2017. *Nielsen Strikes Out-of-Home Measurement Pact with CNN, Turner Sports*, July 26. http://variety.com/2017/tv/news/nielsens-out-of-home-measurement-cnn-turner-sports-1202507448/.

Steinberg, Brian, and Cynthia Littleton. 2017. *Cable News Wars: Inside the Unprecedented Battle for Viewers in Trump Era*, June 13. http://variety.com/2017/tv/features/cable-news-wars-cnn-msnbc-fox-news-1202462928/.

Stelter, Brian. 2017. *What Happens When Local Newsrooms Wither*, November 5.   https://www.cnn.com/videos/us/2017/11/05/local-newsrooms-decline-reliable.cnn.

Techopedia. n.d. *Filter Bubbles*. https://www.techopedia.com/definition/28556/filter-bubble.

Thompson, Derek. 2016a. *Does Advertising Ruin Everything?* October 19. https://www.theatlantic.com/business/archive/2016/10/tim-wu/504623/. Accessed September 4, 2018.

———. 2016b. *The Print Apocalypse and How to Survive It*, November 3. https://www.theatlantic.com/business/archive/2016/11/the-print-apocalypse-and-how-to-survive-it/506429/. Accessed September 4, 2018.

*The New York Times*. 2017. Our History, September 18. https://www.nytco.com/who-we-are/culture/our-history/.

Tsukayama, Haley, and Sintia Radu. 2017. *Freedom from Cable Isn't Free: Flood of Streaming Services Will Make Cutting the Cord More Complicated*, August 11.   https://www.washingtonpost.com/business/economy/freedom-from-cable-isnt-free-flood-of-streaming-services-will-make-cutting-the-cord-more-complicated/2017/08/11/01f9ade0-7d1f-11e7-a669-b400c5c7e1cc_story.html?utm_term=.e41c909a47c5.

Turner, Joel. 2007. The Messenger Overwhelming the Message: Ideological Cues and Perceptions of Bias in Television News. *Political Behavior* 29 (4): 441–464.

Umar, Bitrus. 2013. Development of Satellite Technology and Its Impact on Social Life. *Journal of Information Engineering and Application* 3 (10): 13–17.

Vogt, Nancy, and Amy Mitchell. 2016. *Crowdfunded Journalism: A Small but Growing Addition to Publicly Driven Journalism*, January 20. http://www.journalism.org/2016/01/20/crowdfunded-journalism/.

Wilson, Chris. 2016. *Do You Eat Like a Republican or a Democrat?* July 18. http://time.com/4400706/republican-democrat-foods/.

Woolfe, Christopher. 2016. *Back in the 1890s, Fake News Helped Start a War*, December 8. https://www.pri.org/stories/2016-12-08/long-and-tawdry-history-yellow-journalism-america.

Zurawik, David, interview by Alison Dagnes. 2017. *Baltimore Sun, Media Critic*, October 6.

# CHAPTER 4

# Us vs. Them: Political Polarization and the Politicization of Everything

Rosanne Barr was a stand-up comedian and had an eponymous television show about a working-class family that ran from 1988 to 1997. The program was standard family comedy fare with a minor twist: *Roseanne* represented a slice of America that rarely made it onto prime-time TV. Unlike most broadcast programming which featured pretty and affluent people, aesthetically pleasing backgrounds, and milquetoast story lines, the show centered on the white working class. The most popular television show at the time was *The Cosby Show*, which was about an African-American family comprised of a doctor married to a lawyer and both shows were created by the same team, Marcy Carsey and Tom Werner. Unlike the affluent New York City brownstone setting of the *Cosby Show*, the set of *Roseanne* was purposely ordinary, the story lines conveyed concerns and themes relevant to "average Americans." It was a popular show, garnering both critical respect and solid ratings numbers, but there was a cultural contrast between the sentiments of the critics and the audience that produced the high ratings. Barbara Ehrenreich, in a 1990 *New Republic* article titled "The wretched of the hearth: The undainty feminism of Roseanne Barr," wrote that the actress's character represented "the hopeless underclass of the female sex: polyester-clad, overweight occupants of the slow track; fast-food waitresses, factory workers, housewives, members of the invisible pink-collar army; the despised, the jilted, the underpaid" (Ehrenreich 1990). While perhaps an accurate description of the show and the comedian, this one sentence sums up the yawning gap between those who related to the show and those who wrote about those who related to it.

© The Author(s) 2019
A. Dagnes, *Super Mad at Everything All the Time*,
https://doi.org/10.1007/978-3-030-06131-9_4

*Roseanne* had a good run, lasting nine seasons and earning Barr a slew of awards, to include an Emmy, a Golden Globe, and three American Comedy Awards. The show went off the air and the cast moved on to varying projects, Barr herself appearing in movies and television shows, and in 2018 ABC had the idea that they would reboot *Roseanne* in the era of Donald Trump. After all, the titular actor and her character were Trump supporters and in this period of souped-up anger and hyperpolarization, the show would tap into the audience who voted for Trump in the first place. Barr agreed with this zeitgeist-y concept, remarking at a press tour event that the show was "realistic" and that the audience who related to the show would enjoy the fresh take on politics because, after all: "it was working class people who elected Trump." She later tweeted: "J edgar comey, millions of 'feminists' marching in support of women's subordination, & leftys opposing Russia? gr8 time 4my new/old tv show!" (Ohlheiser 2018). When the show re-launched, many conservatives hailed it as a win for the Trump supporters whom the coastal elites had previously neglected. It appeared that there was a new diversity on television, one that conservatives could stand behind. *Breitbart* ran an article headlined "Pro-Trump Roseanne Thanks God for Making America Great Again," and *Newsmax* ran back-to-back articles after the launch titled "Roseanne Roars Back" and "Roseanne Returns, Garners Massive Audience." *Fox News* reported "Roseanne Reboot Strikes a Chord." An op-ed in the *Washington Times* hailed the show as evidence that the elite and effete were ignorant of real Americans. Many of the show's story lines bent toward that narrative with subplots about snowflake Millennials, angry feminists, and shrill liberals. President Trump tweeted after her show premiered: "Wow amazing. Congrats @therealroseanne. If you're not too busy already maybe work in a late night show too… seems there's some demand for an alternate viewpoint. #Rosanne." He then called Barr personally to congratulate her on the highly rated reboot premier, and in a rally shortly after the first new episode the president bragged to his cheering fans that the show was "about us."

What could possibly go wrong?

What went wrong was that just as the reboot was renewed for a second season after high ratings and impressive ad revenue, and just as the right was doing a cultural victory lap, Roseanne Barr went to Twitter and posted a racist tweet about former Obama advisor Valerie Jarrett, an African-American woman. Barr tweeted that if the "muslim brotherhood & planet of the apes had a baby=vj." She later apologized, but *ABC* immediately canceled the show, and *ABC*'s entertainment president Channing Dungey released a statement saying: "Roseanne's Twitter statement is abhorrent, repugnant and inconsistent with our values" (Kolbin 2018).

It should not have been shocking that Roseanne Barr had tweeted something offensive: Her social media feeds were chock full of conspiracy theories about undocumented citizens voting in the 2016 election and the murder of DNC staffer Seth Rich. She consistently referenced the conspiracy protagonist QAnon and retweeted postings from fringe groups. Right before the premier of her show's reboot, Barr fed into an odd fringe conspiracy theory about pedophile sex trafficking when she tweeted: "President Trump has freed so many children held in bondage to pimps all over this world. Hundreds each month. He has broken up trafficking rings in high places everywhere" (Weill 2018). Beyond social media, Barr was well known for outrageous behavior, from screeching an off-key national anthem before grabbing her crotch to dressing as Hitler eating "Jew cookies." In other words, when conservatives put their money on Roseanne, they probably should have seen it was an unsafe bet.

But in the aftermath of the 2016 presidential election, the question that dominated the pundit class was: "how the heck did Donald Trump beat Hillary Clinton in the presidential election?" Answers fell into, essentially, two camps. The first camp argued that there was a powerfully racist backlash against the Obama years. The second camp argued that the white working class of "real" Americans in flyover country were ignored by the coastal elites who ran everything. Tired of being snubbed, on Election Day these "real" Americans pulled the lever for the guy who said he hated the Washington establishment just as much as they did. Because the election results came as such a shock to most people, much time was spent and many think pieces were written trying to explain the unexplainable. When the dust settled, it was far easier to say: "the cultural and coastal elites left out 'real' America" than it was "Americans are still very messed up about race and we need to figure this out." Thus, *Roseanne* came back to appeal to a specific segment of the country with the idea that it had once portrayed the "real" Americans whom Hollywood were increasingly neglecting. The entire idea of a *Roseanne* reboot was rooted in political polarization, where our political divisions are powerful, omnipresent, and a source of entertainment.

For a broadcast network, tapping into the sentiments of the American public who voted for Donald Trump was good business because it appealed to a wide audience segment. At the same time, the move underscored how incredibly out of sync we are with one another in this country. The whole idea of a television program based on a family torn by partisanship and issue disputes is one of those "funny not funny" ideas, but viewers went bananas for the show, each political side seeing the show and its demise as vindication of their existing beliefs. Conservatives hailed it as a long-awaited respite from the liberals who run the media and when the show was canceled, the *Daily Caller* posted an article titled: "It's Not About Roseanne, Conservatives Are Just Sick of the Damn Double Standard in Our Culture." Liberals took the opportunity to point to Roseanne Barr and say "See? Trump supporters *are* racist." In short, the *Roseanne* reboot was a symbol of our disunion.

We are a nation deeply divided. This is evident in many ways and found in myriad places, even on a television sitcom. Political polarization is no longer contained only within American politics, and it seeps into our larger national culture through the media. Even the majority of the public who tries to avoid politics cannot escape the hot rage of our polarity, because it is seemingly everywhere. How did we get to a place in time when a B-level television star and her second-rate show becomes something to passionately argue about?

The answer to this question is complicated and has a great deal to do with the way we elect people today, because in the past several decades elections have turned into vicious individual battles in a much larger partisan war. There are political, ideological, and financial victories to be claimed in these clashes and with this much at stake, the battles are intensifying. Additionally, the fights about candidates or issue positions are simplified in order to be understandable, which make them ideal for media coverage. Hence, our polarization is lucrative for the media and politically beneficial for those who fight well, which is why we hear about our divisions so frequently and with such intensity. It is also one reason for the current partisan news we have today. Our divided news media could not have emerged without the fifty years of hostility toward the media, government, and intellectualism, or without the technological advancements of the media and the ensuing financial rewards from such an expansion. It certainly could not have succeeded as it has without the angry, combative political climate that embraces the messaging.

This chapter examines our political polarization, how it has spread well beyond politics, and what this means for our broader culture.

## Polarization

People regularly confuse political parties with ideologies, and for good reason: In modern America, the Democrats are generally liberal and the Republicans are basically conservative. But party and ideology are different beasts, and today there is a growing disconnect between the two. Parties are the organizations that provide the structure for our politics, offering voters a team to root for; partisans are the people who feel strongly about the political parties. Someone is a partisan if, like Guy Harrison from the Republican advertising firm OnMessage, they "wake up every morning thinking of how to beat the Democrats" (Harrison 2017). Ideologies are ideas about a set of principles, and these beliefs help to define what the parties stand for. Ideologues are people who believe in specific worldviews which then influences their policy stands. Since people are complicated creatures with varying tastes and opinions, sometimes political parties and individual ideologies conflict. The disconnect within the Republican Party now is one example of this. The party that is supposed to be rooted in free trade and antipathy toward Russia is not supporting a tariff-leveling Putin supporter as its leader. While many Americans scratch their heads in wonder at this turn of events, the reason for this disconnect has to do with polarization.

The term polarization is used broadly to discuss our political differences, and academics who study polarization look at both ideological polarization and partisan polarization separately. Ideological polarization is the distance between policy preferences, and here most studies examine the elites (policymakers and politicos) who lead the American political system. When these elites strongly disagree on the issues, academics question if this translates into political action among the electorate, and that debate is not yet settled.[1] Another way to look at polarization concerns how members of the political parties feel about one another and how this translates to electoral behavior, and the term for this is affective polarization. Stanford University scholar Shanto Iyengar defines the modern incarnation of affective polarization as the condition where: "Democrats and Republicans both say that the other party's members are hypocritical, selfish, and closed-minded, and they are unwilling to socialize across party lines, or even to partner with opponents in a variety of other activities" (Iyengar et al. 2018). In other words, affective polarization examines the relationship between political party members and, in sum, today this relationship is terrible.

This began several decades ago and has grown worse ever since. In 2012, social scientists Jonathan Haidt[2] and Marc Hetherington[3] examined the divide between the political parties using data from the American National Election Studies (ANES). They traced the polarity back to the 1980s when the parties began to carve their identities around specific issues and, thus, blocks of voters. They examined the ANES feelings thermometer and found that while a growing polarization begins several decades prior, the public's feelings toward the opposing party took a major hit when President Obama came into office. Americans began the polarization process around Reagan, and by the time George W. Bush left town the public despised their political opponents. Polling by Gallup in 2015 and Pew in 2016 back this up; presidential support for Obama by Democrats was high, support for Obama by Republicans was low, and the political feelings toward the "other guys" more generally were cooling. As Philip Bump wrote in *The Washington Post*: "Welcome to the new era of party-polarized presidential approval" (Bump 2015). The Gallup organization's Jeffrey Jones was quoted in this 2015 article that the distrust of the president from the GOP rests (at least partially) on the political context of the time:

> These increasingly partisan views of presidents may have as much to do with the environment in which these presidents have governed as with their policies, given 24-hour news coverage of what they do and increasingly partisan news and opinion sources on television, in print and online. (Bump 2015)

And that was *before* Donald Trump was elected. This sharp partisan divide grew even more severe when the feelings for and against Trump became another building block in our polarization, as evidenced by the impressive delta between presidential approval and disapproval polling numbers. By mid-2018, the president had an 85% approval rating among Republicans and a 9% approval rating among Democrats (Gallup 2018). Americans increasingly look across the political aisle and wonder: "What on earth are you people thinking?" The power of out-party animosity leads Americans to support politicians whom they may not fully embrace, simply because such support is thumb in the eye of the opposing political party. It also leads to a tribalism that translates into pure hatred for a political rival.

In our current political climate, the percentage of Americans who have positive feelings about *both* political parties is the lowest measured since 1978, according to data from the American National Election Studies (ANES). ANES data taken in 2016 also show the following phenomena:

- Despite mixed feeling about the parties themselves, Americans remain loyal to their own parties and use partisanship as the dominant voting cue.
- Americans still support their parties even though when they do not love their own party's presidential candidate.
- Feeling measurement for an opposing party dropped like a stone.
- Dislike for the opposing party's presidential nominee was shockingly low: "well over half of Democratic and Republican voters gave the opposing party's nominee a rating of zero on the feeling thermometer which is the lowest possible score." (Abramowitz and Webster 2018)

All of these point to the rise of "negative partisanship," where citizens base their votes on their opposition to another party rather than wholly supporting their own. Americans are increasingly using political parties in their own personal identities, and in doing the growing dislike for a person from the other political side is viewed as suspect—or worse. A study by Iyengar and Krupenkin supported this:

[W]e show that polarization has altered the motivational underpinnings of political behavior in the United States. Prior to the era of polarization, ingroup favoritism, that is, partisans' enthusiasm for their party or candidate, was the driving force behind political participation. More recently, however, it is hostility toward the out-party that makes people more inclined to participate. (Iyengar and Krupenkin 2018)

American voters may not be wild about their own party, but they sure know that their own party is better than the losers on the opposing side.

Partisanship has grown increasingly polarized for several reasons, the first concerning "social identity theory." This sociological theory argues that people sort themselves informally and then identify themselves according to their group, which gives them a sense of belonging. Humans group ourselves so frequently and with such ease, we might not even be aware of it. This clustering extends from our political, cultural, and political identities to our consumer choices and social preferences. When it comes to politics, we have sorted ourselves into alliances and disparaged our opponents for a very long time. As Madison wrote in *Federalist 10*:

> The latent causes of faction are thus sown in the nature of man; and we see them everywhere brought into different degrees of activity, according to the different circumstances of civil society. A zeal for different opinions concerning religion, concerning government, and many other points, as well of speculation as of practice; an attachment to different leaders ambitiously contending for pre-eminence and power; or to persons of other descriptions whose fortunes have been interesting to the human passions, have, in turn, divided mankind into parties, inflamed them with mutual animosity, and rendered them much more disposed to vex and oppress each other than to co-operate for their common good. So strong is this propensity of mankind to fall into mutual animosities, that where no substantial occasion presents itself, the most frivolous and fanciful distinctions have been sufficient to kindle their unfriendly passions and excite their most violent conflicts. (Madison 1787)

Madison goes on to write that democracy is the best form of government to control for the natural clustering of man, because allowing everyone to speak their mind helps release our political steam. In today's polarized political climate, however, our differences are not debated until resolution, but instead are used as evidence of malevolence. Our political steam is not released, but rather continues to build.

Madison predicted this side-taking because of a natural propensity to do so. The human inclination to group ourselves makes us cliquish and distrusting of others. Accordingly, social identity theory also states that when people sort themselves against others in a different unit, they will use these categories to find non-members objectionable. In other words, once people find comfort among the like-minded, they quickly disparage those with whom they disagree: "group members of an in-group will seek to find negative aspects of an out-group, thus enhancing their self-image" (McLeod 2008). The pioneer of this theory, a Polish social psychologist named Henri Tajfel, wrote extensively about this in the 1970s (Billig and Tajfel 1973), and proved that it was ingrained in the human spirit to group and rival. Two decades later, a political scientist named Steven Greene expanded on social identity theory to examine the effects of partisanship on attitudes of an out-group. Greene found that "most American citizens do have social identifications with political parties and that these identifications substantially affect their political perceptions and partisan behavior" (Greene 1999). And because people tend to think in terms of "us and them," Greene also found that the more partisan someone was, the more they differentiated between political opponents. Worse, the more politically active and interested a person, the more likely they were to take a strong stand. When the ANES data show that negative partisanship is extremely strong today, it is evidence that our party affiliations have become powerful parts of our identities.

Political scientist Lilliana Mason concurred with this assessment in her 2018 book called *Uncivil Agreement*.[4] Mason argues that the personal and political identities of Americans have become inextricably enmeshed, and as a result we are increasingly hostile toward our political opponents. She examines the cultural battles and identity politics of the last fifty years to illustrate that Americans began to closely identify themselves according to racial, religious, and cultural issues. This had a profound effect on the parties, which sought out specific groups of people as members, and this in turn made the parties more homogenous. The confluence of identity politics and party homogenization increased our divisions, leading to the "sorting of our identities into partisan camps," which drives politics to be more personal and more emotional. Both of these things discourage any kind of compromise, and it supports the idea of negative partisanship:

> ... American partisans are working hard to participate in politics, but the ones who are most active tend to be those who cannot be convinced to change their minds. They react to threat, anger, and the strength of a whole cohort of identities that increasingly harmonized. When individuals participate in politics driven by team spirit or anger, the responsiveness of the electorate is impaired. If their own party – linked with their race and religion – does something undesirable, they are less likely to seriously consider changing their vote in the ballot booth. (Mason 2018)

Americans are politically sorting themselves by identities and issues, and these are the two areas of modern politics that cause people to freak out. Issue positions have become simplified talking points to use in our own political identities and are just as easily used against opponents. Two political scientists, Steven Webster and Alan Abramowitz, looked at contentious social welfare topics from the ANES surveys to show that issues are central to our political discord. The authors argued that if the issues were less significant, then Americans could end the polarization by highlighting the areas where they agree, but if polarization were rooted in major policy disagreements, the distance between the two sides will be more difficult to bridge. Webster and Abramowitz found that issue ideology had a profound effect on how voters chose partisan sides, and that policy disagreement drove much of the decision-making process:

> These findings show that when it comes to politics, reason and emotion are almost inseparable.... Democrats and Republicans dislike each other today because they disagree with each other about many issues and especially about the fundamental question of the role of government in American society. It is very hard to disagree without being disagreeable when there are so many issues on which we disagree and the disagreements on many of these issues are so deep. (Webster and Abramoqitz 2017)

This is the concept of ideological polarization, where the elites drive the divide by taking extreme stands on issues. Supporting this theory, Haidt and Hetherington argued that our current crop of political leaders are Baby Boomers who were raised on political conflict which then shapes the way they lead. These elites came of age when politics was "more akin to a civil war, a divisive struggle over a handful of issues that we are still fighting about today." The issues they listed included "race, abortion and women's rights, respect for authority and protection of the environment," all of which continue to sharply divide us (Haidt and Hetherington 2012). Since these issues have been the topic of debate and argued for decades, Americans are well versed in the disagreements and not only speak about them with ease, but increasingly use these policy stands as parts of their personal identities.

Not only are our divisions becoming more pronounced, but also these divisions force Americans to dig in on their opinions. Today citizens increasingly reject their political rivals because they see them as existential threats, people who want to take away the most important aspects of someone's identity. The idea that a political opponent is personally threatening to an American voter is now a constant in American politics. What began with Charlton Heston holding a rifle over his head saying "You can take my gun when you pry it from my cold, dead hands" has evolved into the President of the USA telling a group of Evangelical Christians: "If Democrats win they will overturn everything that we've done and they'll do it quickly and violently." When voters are con-sistently told that their very lives are at stake, why wouldn't they feel threatened by people who disagree with them? This "us versus them" mentality is one of the driving forces of the polarized media system we have today and, not surprisingly, the topics that most divide us also drive the news cycle. We hear much more about the issues upon which we dis-agree than those upon which we have common ground. Disagreement is tantalizing, fighting and conflict are more interesting than concord, and since the public understands most hot-button issues, they are easy to discuss. The predominant qualities of partisan media are simplicity and emotion, and so we see, hear, and read about these conflicts often. Adding to this noise, politicians stand out by taking sharp stands on top-ics to attract attention from the rich donor class and the active support-ers on the wings of the parties. It becomes easier to see why the two ends of the spectrum are pulling apart.

## EXACERBATING THE POLARIZATION

Polarization fuels the partisan media and, as discussed in Chapter 3, there is an abundance of media space to fill with activists. Our divisions have become all-encompassing and deeply personal; this emotional response is exactly what activists aim for, because emotional responses drive action. The cacophony of voices does not begin and end with the screaming on cable news. Most lobbyists and activists are just using the available resources, trying to join the conversation, influence public opin-ion, and remain relevant. This is their job, after all, and an increasingly important one in a mediated age. It is not that these politicos are doing anything wrong, it's just that there are so many of them engaged and seeking attention. Most of the lobbyists and activists with whom I spoke acknowledged the importance of keeping the public involved.

The best way to keep the public's attention is to provoke emotional responses, and modern activism is specifically geared toward that end. In order to reach a membership base with passionate interests, an advocacy group's communication must be fervent and rather unrelenting. These groups can reach out to their membership narrowly or to the broader public, and both ways exemplify the way technology has increased polit-ical activism. When advocates really want to inflame the passions of their members, they have a number of weapons in their arsenals with varied purposes; some are to raise money, some are to raise awareness, some are to advertise, and some are to inspire action. All are linked by a common principle, connected by an overarching determination to win a policy battle. Unfailingly, the keys to modern political messaging are speed and fervor. Advocacy groups of all kinds have to convince policymakers that there will be consequences for actions, either positive or negative. In order to do this, they must reach their members quickly and communicate in the strongest terms possible:

- E-mailed Newsletters: Updates on the efforts by the group, on the issues at stake, and on the movement itself.
- Morning Updates: Daily briefings on developments and activities.
- Direct Mail: An oldie but still useful, fliers sent through the actual mail to membership and affected citizens.
- Action Alerts: When groups implore members to take action and work on behalf of the issue or the organization.
- Key Vote Alerts: Notifying constituents on how their members voted on something currently important.
- Scorecards: A grade list of how lawmakers voted on a particular issue.
- Pledge Signing: A lawmaker swears in writing that he/she will uphold a voting vow.
- Social Media: Facebook, Twitter, Snapchat, Instagram.

Technology has made it affordable, easy, and feasible to reach a large audience by targeting it narrowly and specifically. For example, in order to advance their policies, NARAL Pro-Choice America relies on the help of their 2 million "member activists" who are spread around the country and have signed up to be the groups most dedicated supporters. These members subscribe to e-mail notification, sign petitions, participate in door knocking, make phone calls, and share articles and information on social media. Communications Director Kaylie Hanson Long says that their membership is the "army that supports our work and powers it forward" (Hanson-Long 2017). As a result, the work that the NARAL Communications office does is a mixture of reaching out to the public as both a reaction to local, state, and national events and as a preemptive action to mobilize the association.

The Urban Institute is a policy think tank and they know that their primary audience consists of scholars doing research and policymakers working on programs. But the larger public is still important since today there is an abundance of data-heavy journalism in the mix. Large news organizations have added accessible academic research to their offerings, and the *Washington Post* has "Monkey Cage" while *The New York Times* has "The Upshot." The politically interested public has options, which increases the reach and visibility of think tanks because now their audience has expanded. The staff at Urban uses social media to get the word out. According to Bridget Lowell, "the tiniest Tweet will have the biggest audience" and like most think tanks, interest groups, and activist organizations they craft their own content as well. Here, humor is important: "You need personality, it makes something real. You can't just have an organizational Twitter account pumping out your own content. Nobody is going to follow you. You have to be seen as an interesting aggregator of content" (Lowell 2017). To that end, Lowell says that they are making strides to personalize their content and show connectivity between their research and real life. She used an example of research from the Urban Institute about housing programs:

> Deepening our work in storytelling and narrative, go to real places and telling real stories and marrying that with the evidence. It's not just about the math and the tool and the feature and the dashboard and the forecaster where you select your variables and do your own microsimulation modeling. But it's about this woman who is trying to get off meth and doesn't have a place to live with her daughter, and what being in a stable housing program has done to help her stay clean and what her struggle has been like. (Lowell 2017)

This kind of connection between research and practice is important for Urban to show their members and the public the significance of their work. It also is a great way to engage an audience, especially those who might not be policy experts, but who are policy interested. Using the political media to target engaged Americans is a smart way to stay connected and relevant, and social media is one good area for such connections.

The fast, cheap, and easy technology that is available keeps citizens connected to the interest groups that represent them in issue areas and think tanks that are conducting important policy research. At the same time, this is also one of the reasons for our current polarization. Harkening back to Madison, being *too* connected has its dangers as well. Madison noted that an important safeguard against the mischief of factions was geographical distance. The technology that connects us undermines that protection.

Another tactic includes using the news media to focus on the public outside the Beltway who do not read *The Washington Post* or *The New York Times*. This is important because, despite what many in DC believe, they far outnumber those who are fully invested in the policymaking process. Khristine Brookes is the Communications Director of The Cato Institute, a libertarian think tank in Washington. She told me that when she travels to her home state of Idaho, she watches the local news to see how they are covering the issues and events of the day. The local news is short and it has to fit in a great deal of content: sports, weather, traffic, restaurant openings, etc. Says Brookes: "The small window [the local news has] for covering national news, I'm very curious to find out what they think it important. We do a lot of work with broadcasters in DC who feed those local networks, and it's a pretty short window that they have. We have to be able to communicate messages very simply, concisely for an audience that isn't steeped in the politics every single day" (Brookes 2017).

National news audiences are also crucial, which is why cable news channels provide the kind of wide coverage that activists desire. Before she moved to Cato, Brookes worked at The Heritage Foundation and she began there just as *Fox News Channel* was ascending in the early 2000s. It was fortunate as she had scholars at Heritage who needed to hone their media skills just as *Fox* had airtime to fill. She told me that she had a hard time getting them on *CNN* because the network was, at the time, the biggest game in town. As an up and coming channel with time to fill and few options, *Fox News* was willing to put think tank people on the air:

> I had guests on *Fox News* all the time. And it worked for us because their membership was conservative. I could send out emails to lots of conservatives around town and say: 'Hey, at 11 o'clock today watch us on the *Fox News Channel*.' So *Fox* tuned into that because, at the time, Heritage's membership was over 100,000. They knew that we had a network and that we were telling people to watch *Fox News Channel* because our scholars were going to be on. So it worked for them and it worked for us. (Brookes 2017)

Cable news channels and think tank reps solidified their relationship, and the public began to hear from these policy wonks and advocates more frequently. The relationship is symbiotic and successful, as Brookes says, because "it's easy to [book] think tank people. We want to be on TV

because that's our free advertising" (Brookes 2017). This is beneficial for the cable news channels because not only is there time to fill,
they have a built-in DC audience who want to see think tank scholars.
During the daytime hours on weekdays, the think tank staffers and policy
wonks inside the Beltway have their televisions on news all day long, and
according to Brookes, these insiders want to see the people on TV who
do the actual analysis. At the same time, the exposure helps to sell the
brand of the think tank.

The increasing presence of think tank scholars and activists on cable
news programs was perhaps inevitable as think tanks became politicized and cable news became partisan. The fulminating style of an
activist works well within what political scientists Jeffrey Berry and Sara
Sobieraj have termed the "Outrage Industry," which is also the title of
their book on the topic.[5] Berry and Sobieraj argue that partisan media
are (1) specifically triggering emotional (and thus irrational) responses
from American audiences because (2) the outrage industry is effective,
successful, and profitable. To meet the needs of the outrage industry,
politicos have to up their own outrage, which adds fuel to the fires of
polarization. Berry and Sobieraj measured what they termed "modes of
outrage" that included various types of insults and slights, varying from
name calling to character assassination to obscene language (Berry and
Sobieraj 2014). Because there are so many outside actors on the media
today, this has led to a condition that writer Paul Waldman called "perpetually outraged, perpetually outrageous" (Waldman 2016). In order to
be heard above everyone else, the language must be more aggressive and
louder, the complaints more egregious. As Berry and Sobieraj write, this
communication is specifically designed to "provoke emotional responses
(e.g., anger, fear, moral indignation) from the audience through the use
of overgeneralizations, sensationalism, misleading or patently inaccurate
information, ad hominem attacks, and belittling ridicule of opponents"
(Berry and Sobieraj 2014). This gives the American public the impression that politics is a blood sport and that in order to engage, one should
probably wear protective gear.

According to political scientist Diana Mutz, who wrote *In Your Face
Politics*,[6] this is precisely the point. Mutz maintains that political television is incessantly argumentative, has deleterious effects on our national
civility, and is wildly popular because it is entertaining. But, Mutz notes,
this characterization of politics as something akin to a gladiator match may
be popular to some, but in the main it is disliked: "Although conflict is

an essential part of the democratic process, Americans tend not to react favorably to conflict" (Mutz 2015). This is one reason that Americans are increasingly avoiding politics; for fear that a simple disagreement about policy will end up as a screaming match. Both of these books underscore the relationship between the glut of cable news airtime, the increasing number of politicos on air, and the amplified anger and volume of our political discourse. Nuance does not bring home the attention nor rally the base of support needed to be an ideological advocate in Washington today, and as a result, the messaging from interest and activist groups is pointed and filled with rage. The tweets, postings, chats, TV appearances, and blog missives are nectar.

Much of modern political advocacy has shifted from directly persuading politicians to convincing their constituents to put the pressure on instead. This comes in the form of running ads or mobilizing the voting public to make office calls and yell at their representatives themselves. It is simply good strategy to focus on the lawmakers who are movable on an issue, or those who are in danger of losing a close election, and so policy advocates run lots of television ads that target specific members or they encourage their members to go to Town Hall meetings, or flood the Capitol Hill switchboard with phone calls.

The most money spent in political campaigns is spent on ads because they can be emotional, memorable, and incredibly effective. Additionally, when an ad hits the perfect audience, its efficacy expands, which means that ad designers are increasingly attentive to specific groups of voters. This ties in with the idea of selective targets; since there are so few moveable voters in today's polarized political climate, it is vital to direct advertising toward these persuadable voters. Modern technology allows for some very innovative and creative ad creation and placement. Republican ad professional Brad Todd explained how tech helps him to use specific issues to match particular voters with candidates. This is not a new concept: For decades, political operatives sent direct mail fliers to targeted homes, and they directed specific mail pieces toward households with relevancy. If a household included children, a direct mail piece about education would arrive, a military member received pieces including pictures of soldiers in uniform, older Americans saw mail about Social Security. What technology allows now, according to Todd, is even more specificity and focus. For example, if traffic is an issue in an election, says Todd, he can find data from cell phones that move daily from suburb to city in order to reach voters specifically affected by traffic (Todd 2018). That is some serious specificity.

The polarization seen in the electorate is magnified by the polarization among the elites. This is evidenced most clearly as advocates figure out which lawmakers are persuadable. As the issues have become more politicized and because so few politicians take a nuanced view of anything, trying to find people who might change their mind on an issue position or an important vote is difficult. The Environmental Defense Action Fund President Joe Bonfiglio explained that one of the biggest challenges for a lobbyist or a communications director in this kind of political climate is finding the moveable House and Senate members: There just are not many of those. He joked that if you were to get a tattoo with the names of Senators who were flexible on environmental issues: "It wouldn't have to be a very big tattoo" (Bonfiglio 2017). There are few moderate members of congress today, and most lawmakers have their issue positions etched in stone. The ideological polarization does not help this at all: "…we are aiming all of our Comms efforts at voices or policymakers who we see as potentially getable or moveable. So we are, in many ways ignoring the fringes of both parties. And this is pretty big. If you think about a fringe being at the end of something, this is 80 to 90% of lawmakers on both parties that we are effectively ignoring for the most part over the course of a policy fight" (Bonfiglio 2017). Put into the perspective of the Environmental Defense Fund, this means they have a specific list of ardent supporters and a different list of hostile opponents, neither of whom are the target of their attention. Bonfiglio says there is a "huge swath of the House who we totally ignore on both sides"; because they're either already in the tank of the EDF or they will never be on their side. He continued:

> You're occasionally going to have a champ or two, people that you rely on to carry the water or carry the fight, and you support your allies who are close to you the best you can. That may be five. In this case, five Democrats in the United States Senate who are going to be your policy champs. You ignore the 38 other Democrats who are going to vote with you 95% of the time, you work the five that maybe I have missed on the Republican side, you ignore 47 Republicans and focus on maybe five. You're actually talking to ten members of the United States Senate. And all of the effort is focused on all that. (Bonfiglio 2017)

It is evident in modern political culture that the politicians are the real persuasion targets and using the media to goose the public into action is the most effective method of influence. With so many outside actors vying for media time, it follows that in the process they benefit from the polarization, which then encourages polarization's reinforcement. Technology connects the public more immediately with the like-minded or the opposition. As politics becomes a contact sport, it then spreads into other areas of our lives and this is where the concept of "lifestyle politics" comes in.

## SORTING

A group of Sociologists (DellaPosta et al.) published a wonderfully titled paper in 2015 called "Why Do Liberals Drink Lattes?" that examined political polarization from a sociological perspective. I do not speak Sociology fluently, but I enjoyed this research even as it took me several hours to understand the postmodern lingo. DellaPosta et al. used survey data to examine how our lifestyles have become politicized. The authors found that we are both shaped by the actions of others (the Sociology term for this is "social influence") while we try to stay among our own kind of people (called "homophily"[7] which, contrary to my initial impression, does not mean "one Philadelphia"):

> Homophily and influence become self-reinforcing when the attraction to those who are similar and differentiation from those who are dissimilar entail greater openness to influence. The result is network autocorrelation – the tendency for people to resemble their network neighbors. (DellaPosta et al. 2015)

The sociological idea that "birds of a feather flock together" is similar to a current theory bouncing around political science called "The Big Sort." This was first popularized by a Texas journalist named Bill Bishop who made the argument that Americans have become politically polarized in the past two decades, and this has translated to more ideologically homogenous communities. We are, according to Bishop, voting with our ballots *and* our feet and we are moving to places where people think and act like us.[8] In doing so, we are segregating ourselves from opposition, cocooning ourselves in bubbles of like-minded neighbors. Bishop studied national election results and contrasted these with county results to find that while national elections grew closer, results by counties grew larger

(Bishop and Cushing 2008). Bishop ascribed the increasing geographical segregation not to people purposely moving to be with their own kind, but because cultural and economic forces moved people to areas that increasingly catered to their vocations and interests. Bishop extends this argument about grouping to other areas of social settings, such as churches, and argues: "There is... a remarkable confluence of social, political, and economic trends – which began in the 1970s and continued on through 2004 – that have tended to cause like-minded people to cluster and to exclude others who are different" (Bishop and Cushing 2008). He also addressed cultural divisions around lifestyle preferences such as "Books, Beer, Bikes, and Birkenstocks," to explain why people moved to places to find and enjoy specific social elements of life.

As with most academic concepts, there are Big Sort deniers, most notably political scientists Samuel Abrams and Morris Fiorina. Abrams and Fiorina argue that while partisan sorting has indeed occurred, "geographical political sorting has little or nothing to do with that development" (Abrams and Fiorina 2012). Using the wonderful term "ideological inbreeding," Abrams and Fiorina agree that Americans are becoming more polarized and less tolerant of others. That said, they maintain that even if Americans are moving to be closer to those more similar to themselves, this would have little impact on their political behavior: "A Texas Democrat surrounded by 'drill, baby, dill' Republicans can still sit down in the privacy of his living room and write a check to the Environmental Defense Fund" (Abrams and Fiorina 2012).

Additionally, Abrams and Fiorina argue that a preponderance of data shows most Americans are not plugged into their neighborhoods the way they once had been and that neighbors who do talk to one another almost never speak about politics. Accordingly, the authors argue that the kind of sorting Bishop implies does not have the resulting effect on polarization. At the same time, perhaps something more akin to a soft sorting is going on. When people want to move to new neighborhoods, they tend to check them out first and political cues can be subtle things. An *Economist* article from 2008 included this prescient observation:

> Americans move house often, usually for practical reasons. Before choosing a new neighbourhood, they drive around it. They notice whether it has gun shops, evangelical churches and "W" bumper stickers, or yoga classes and organic fruit shops. Perhaps unconsciously, they are drawn to places where they expect to fit in. (Editors 2008)

Abrams and Fiorina may be arguing that politics does not insert itself into our everyday lives, yet it increasingly feels as if it does. As the afore-mentioned Sociologists noted, we now use lifestyle choices as indicators of our ideologies and our politics drives our lifestyle choices. This can be viewed most clearly in two supposedly non-political areas of our lives, consumer culture and entertainment.

## POLARIZATION BEYOND POLITICS

It has been argued that the dominant American ideology is neither con-servative nor liberal, but capitalistic. Americans love to buy stuff and feel strongly that (a) they should be able to buy what they want and (b) the strongest power they have is through their purses. As the Internet opened shopping to an endless extent, companies and corporations have pursued the American buyer, and the buyers have responded enthusi-astically to the wooing. Americans are more closely connected to con-sumer culture now because not only do they have more buying options, but also because online reviews give buyers more power and influence. Because we are besieged by constant news and information, because we are so polarized, and because politics stretches into everything today, Americans are more frequently hearing about corporate decisions that are politically charged. This takes several different forms: Companies now use branding to identify themselves both culturally and politically; consumers now call for boycotts of companies that engage in political and cultural behavior they find offensive; and the heads of these compa-nies take it upon themselves to steer their business into the political skid to combine commerce and activism.

In a hyperpolarized climate, Americans today increasingly extend their political beliefs onto products and the companies that sell them. There are contradictory data about this. Consumer survey research conducted in 2018 by Morning Consult showed that most Americans (60%) believe that "corporations should stick to what they do, and generally not get involved in political or cultural matters" (Consult 2018). Yet an Earned Brand Study by Edelman found that "67% of consumers would buy a brand for the first time based solely on its position on a controversial topic" (Fischer 2018). An important consideration is that some issues are more polarizing than others. Back to the Morning Consult data, researchers there found that three issues "aren't very controversial: civil rights, criminal justice reforms, and LGBTQ rights." Conversely, the most polarizing issues were "abortion, anthem protesting, and immigration" (Consult 2018). These two lists are seemingly contradictory for two reasons: The first, anthem protesting actually is about civil rights; the second is Chick-Fil-A.

Chick-Fil-A is an uncompromisingly Christian outlet that closes on Sundays so workers can attend church. While selling fried chicken sandwiches generally has nothing to do with the culture wars, Chick-Fil-A president and COO Dan Cathy announced in a 2012 interview that the company was supportive of "the biblical definition of the family unit" (Severson 2012). And after that, all hell broke loose. A woman in New York responded to the interview by organizing a same-sex kiss-in at all 1600 Chick-Fil-A stores, which prompted former Arkansas Governor Mike Huckabee to pronounce August 1, 2012, "Chick-Fil-A Appreciation Day." This then provoked the Jim Henson company, creator of the Muppets, to announce that they would pull all of their Muppet toys from the restaurant's kids meals, which then inspired Chick-Fil-A to announce a "voluntary recall" of all of the kids meal Muppet toys, claiming children's fingers became "stuck in the Muppet holes" (Severson 2012).

The Chick-Fil-A uproar is illustrative of how quickly we rise to anger, and how easily our buying habits are affected by the spread of politics. A fast-food chain became the epicenter of the culture wars and thus guaranteed one political side of the country as its faithful (no pun intended) audience base, while ensuring the other side of the political spectrum would never eat their chicken biscuit again. The obvious problem of blending politics and business goes back to the affective polarization discussed earlier. According to one branding expert: "All things politics have become so confrontational that you have to question whether your marketing message will even get through in this type of environment and whether it will be suitable for your brand" (Fischer 2018). This form of confrontational politicking is exacerbated by the way Americans increasingly use political issues as shorthand identity cues. This was seen in 2018 when Nike leaned into the controversy surrounding NFL protests of the national anthem by selecting Colin Kaepernick, the player who began the protest movement, to be the new face of an ad campaign. This moved in predictable directions. Some took to social media to call for boycotts of the company and others posted videos showing the destruction of Nike gear. One opponent tweeted: "Nike must realize that they cannot support this type of disrespect to our country without repercussions!" President Trump, a loud critic of the protests, also condemned Nike via tweet. Yet following the announcement of the endorsement deal and after the first airing of a Kaepernick ad during a football game, Nike posted a 31% sales increase, seemingly belying the outrage posted against it (Martinez 2018).

Corporate boycotts have occurred since the popularization of advertising, but social media has made it painless for citizens and activist groups to launch boycotts against corporations with whom they disagree politically. Take, for example, the 2017 consumer boycott of the coffee-maker Keurig after the company pulled advertising from the *Fox News Channel's* prime-time pundit show "Hannity." Those protesting against Keurig did so by posting videos of people smashing the coffee machines with hammers, arguably to provide video evidence of their frustration with the brand.[9] Boycotts can be an effective way of garnering attention for an issue or smearing an opponent and they are increasing in frequency, even spawning numerous Twitter movements.[10] According to Maurice Schweitzer, a professor at the Wharton School at the University of Pennsylvania, most boycotts lose steam fairly quickly but can steal the spotlight: "In practice, most boycotts achieve the more modest goal of attracting media attention" (Livingston 2018). This may be a modest goal, but the media attention of corporate boycotts is one of the reasons Americans feel they are incessantly bombarded with politics.

Another space feeling the merger between commerce and politics are online review sites, such as Yelp or Trip Advisor. When politics reaches restaurants or hotels, online communities react *en masse* to destroy the offending businesses. For example, in 2018 White House Press Secretary Sarah Huckabee Sanders was refused service by a Virginia restaurant called The Red Hen. Once she tweeted about this event, the story became the very definition of "viral":

> ...[N]egative reviews began flooding the Red Hen's Yelp page. First came the comments skewering the restaurant for political bias and underwhelming ambiance, and then — because this is the internet — came the user-uploaded images of swastikas. Within 24 hours, the number of reviews tripled from 5,000 to over 15,000, and by Sunday evening, the restaurant's aggregate star rating had dropped from close to five stars to just two. (Warzel 2018)

Businesses that rely on user reviews are especially vulnerable to this kind of online flooding, but in truth the owner of the Red Hen should have known this kind of attack was likely given the culture. As *Buzzfeed's* Charlie Warzel wrote about the event, these kinds of events are all too common:

> ...[O]ne consequence of a never-ending information war is that everyone is already well versed in their specific roles. And across the internet, it appears that technology platforms, both big and small, must grapple with the reality that they are now powerful instruments in an increasingly toxic political and cultural battle. (Warzel 2018)

These heretofore-mundane decisions about shopping and buying have turned very political, and this on its own extends the reach of polarization into our personal lives. Since it has become routine for businesses to wade into politics, more companies are doing so:

> As e-commerce opens up seemingly infinite options to customers, experts say that corporate values are playing an increasingly large role in customers' shopping decisions. Tying a brand to certain values and political beliefs is one way to beat out rivals, especially for brands attempting to establish a higher-end image. As a result, companies are expected to take sides on certain political issues. (Taylor 2018)

This side-taking begins at the top, which is why Aaron Chatterji, a business professor at Duke University, researches "CEO activism." This is where business execs lean forward to take public stands on highly politicized issues (Chatterji and Toffel 2018). Chatterji has written about CEO activism for the *Harvard Business Review*, and in an interview with Public Radio International explained why CEOs are becoming more vocal about political issues:

> We've documented this political polarization that's gripping the United States of America ... and we're seeing much more ideological sorting.... We're all kind of retreating to our own camps and our own echo chambers. In that kind of world, everything becomes political. And so, companies are being forced to respond to the hot-button issue of the day and they're feeling a lot like our politicians in Washington. (Filippino 2018)

Corporate responses come in two primary forms: either making public statements to raise awareness or putting financial pressure on states or organizations to push for change (Chatterji and Toffel 2018). While both ways have the potential to cause backlash, making public statements is easier to do and because of this are now fairly common. Examples include a case in 2015 when the CEOs of 14 major food companies cosigned an open letter about climate change just before the United Nations held the Paris talks on the topic (Chatterji and Toffel 2018) and when the CEO of Merck resigned from President Trump's Manufacturing Jobs Initiative after the racist events in Charlottesville, VA in 2017. Putting corporate pressure to encourage political change is less common because it involves a bigger swing. When North Carolina passed anti-LGBT laws, different corporations threatened economic sanctions that led to an estimated $3.76 billion in lost business over a dozen years (Chatterji and Toffel 2018). The driving force behind CEO activism, according to Chatterji, is that increasingly people "don't just buy with their heads; they buy with their hearts, too" (Filippino 2018). Not surprisingly, there is a generational difference and younger Americans are open to more CEO activism. A 2017 study cited in the *Harvard Business Review* found that: "twice as many Millennials said they would feel increased loyalty (rather than decreased loyalty) toward their own CEO, if he or she took a stand on a hotly debated issue (44% vs. 19%, respectively)" (Gaines-Ross 2017).

Thanks to consumer boycotts of media outlets, corporate sponsorship of events or denunciations of interest groups, and a big slew of political donations made by billionaires with myriad business interests, polarization has spread from the ballot box into our private lives. Today, political acts include making a cup of coffee, buying a cup of coffee, or doing a load of laundry.[11] As much as we pay attention to consumer culture, however, politics spills into our entertainment even more.

## POLITICS AND POP CULTURE

President Donald Trump's election to office without any political experience but with a high Q rating is but one indication of our national devotion to celebrity. A 2017 *USA Today* article noted "entertainment and politics are now synonymous," and that Trump's election was evidence that TV viewers took him seriously:

A poll conducted in 2015 by AMG found that 62% of Republican "Apprentice" viewers had a favorable view of Trump, while only 37% of non-viewers viewed him favorably. Evidently people thought that being tough with the lead singer of '80s band Poison translated into being tough with Vladimir Putin — a guy who literally poisons people. (Schneider 2017)

This is one reason that politics has bled into the world of entertainment. Another reason is that politics is dominating the overall national conversation, thanks mostly to President Trump's successful media command. In an article on *The Hive*, writer Peter Hamby argues that Trump's domination of media coverage is so intense, it "blocks out the sun":

...we live on a planet where Trump comes at us from every angle. In Trump's world, you see something about Trump on television, while a push alert about Trump surfaces on your phone, prompting you to text your friends about Trump and post something about whatever happened on your chosen social-media account. Trump has mastered attention capture. (Hamby 2018)

Thus, Americans are getting a ton of politics now, more than ever before, because of a combination of mass media technology and the commander in chief. It is not surprising that political content has blended so seamlessly with our entertainment, but when our politics are so divided so too then is our entertainment.

In the past, when politicians used popular culture to reach an audience, or when entertainers used politics as a structure for humor, the public knew that there remained a separation between the two. Nixon asking "sock it to me?" on *Laugh In* was not an indication of his actual interest in comedy. The audience knew he was there for a specific reason, which was to be a politician trying to be funny. And that's what made it humorous. Tevi Troy wrote a book about politics and popular culture called *What Jefferson Read, Ike Watched, and Obama Tweeted*, and in an interview with the *Washington Post*, explained why entertainment was important in the political world: "Politicians need to care about popular culture because it is one of the common bonds that tie increasingly segmented Americans together" (Rubin 2013). Yet today, the bonds of popular culture are breaking under the weight of our political divide. Popular culture is one more place where Americans feel political divisions and this is highly problematic because entertainment is supposed to be fun.

Politics slowly spread into broader pop culture as media forms evolved
and more Americans were consuming more entertainment. This opened
the door for politicians to reach a broader audience by appearing on television shows. There are two main types of political appearance: guest
spots on scripted shows or appearances on live interview programs. Each
of these has their own benefits, but guest spots on hit shows are far easier to pull off. There are age-old examples of politicians stopping by hit
shows; then-House Speaker Tip O'Neill appeared on *Cheers* in 1983,
and that same year Nancy Reagan had a guest spot on *Diff'rent Strokes*.
Massachusetts Governor (and presidential candidate) Michael Dukakis
was on *St. Elsewhere* in 1984 and former House Speaker Newt Gingrich
on *Murphy Brown* in 1996. One can only assume that Amy Poehler has
a serious political interest, because her show *Parks and Recreation* featured appearances from Gingrich (2013), the late Senator John McCain
(2012) former First Lady Michelle Obama (2014), and Former Vice
President Joe Biden was on twice, once in 2012 and a second time in
2015 (D'Abruzzo 2015). These appearances served two purposes. They
allowed politicians to look relatable and fun, and they boosted the ratings of the show they appeared on. These kinds of appearances were so
successful that they inspired innovation. When cable introduced narrowcasting to the public, politicians shifted their attention to more targeted
audiences. Barack Obama did the open for *Monday Night Football* in
2006, John McCain did *WWE Monday Night* RAW in 2008, and all the
presidential candidates hit late night in the 2016 election. This was just
good politicking because it connected voters to their elected officials in
a fun way. These appearances were notable because elected officials went
off-book to do something different. It is incongruous—like watching
animals dressed as humans, or small children cursing.

Interviews on late-night entertainment programs are more difficult to
pull off than a simple guest spot. These kinds of shows are different from
the serious interview shows because their dominant content is light and
generally unpolitical. During the daytime, talk shows such as *Ellen*, *The
View*, and *The Talk* are shows that have included political guests. The late-
night terrain is more populated with a wide range of shows across broadcast and cable, which feature comedy, and politics interspersed with more
cultural fare. These shows include *The Late Show with Stephen Colbert*
(CBS), *The Tonight Show with Jimmy Fallon* (NBC), *Jimmy Kimmel Live!*
(ABC), *Conan* (TBS), *The Late, Late Show with James Corden* (CBS), *Late
Night with Seth Meyers* (NBC), *Saturday Night Live* (NBC), *Last Week*

*Tonight with John Oliver* (HBO), *Full Frontal with Samantha Bee* (TBS), *The Daily Show with Trevor Noah* (Comedy Central), and *Real Time with Bill Maher* (HBO). It is a crowded landscape.

Although there are benefits for politicians to appear on entertainment media, there are risks as well. Some shows are especially uncertain for any politician, since most public figures want to control the story and come out of a media appearance looking good. There are a number of factors that make an entertainment show either dicey or safe include:

- The ways that people watch: Streaming, viral video clips, live programming.
- Audience numbers & demographics of viewership.
- Interview/Appearance type.
- Predictability (You will dance with Ellen) vs. Unpredictability (Colbert is whip smart and will ask tough questions).
- Script control: Predetermined skits.
- Time of show (audience, style).
- Cable vs. Broadcast.

Put together, these risk determinants help guide politicians toward specific programs while they warn against others. *Conan*, *The Late Show with Stephen Colbert*, and *Bill Maher* are dangerous because of the factors above, and because of the live studio audiences who will boo and heckle unreservedly.

There is currently more political humor on late-night television than ever before, and most of it is seethingly anti-Trump. The expanded field allowed late-night comedians to find their niche, and because of their varying perspectives, many found politics to be an area ripe for exploration. What Jon Stewart started on *The Daily Show* became popular and lucrative and, thus, spawned imitators. Some worked (*The Colbert Report*) some did not (*The Nightly Show*) but as different cable networks threw spaghetti at the walls to see what would stick, new faces and voices were added to the lineup. For example, Samantha Bee brought a feminist perspective, Conan O'Brien brought an unpredictability, and South African Trevor Noah, who added an international viewpoint to the airwaves, replaced New Yorker Jon Stewart. Among the most popular and successful is John Oliver who created what I call "advocacy comedy." This is when a comedian crafts his material around a political viewpoint; normally, even political comedians try for the joke first and the lesson second because otherwise the material is not terribly funny. Oliver has turned this on its head. On his show *Last Week Tonight*, he dedicates significant time to one important issue using humor in both discursive and releasing ways. There are new voices and new methods in popular political comedy and they have helped to grow a more diverse landscape. They have also contributed to an increase in the left-wing dominance of political satire.

But it is on broadcast television where the shift from more universal fare into fierce partisan commentary has been more perceptible and sharp. One primary reason for this is that politics has itself become a broader topic of conversation. Five years ago, political humor was a fairly specific area of comedy because most Americans were not as invested in electoral politics or the system writ large. I interviewed comedian and podcaster Marc Maron in 2011 for a different book and asked him about using political material in his stand-up. This was his response:

> The one thing I do know is that 90% of the time if you're going to talk about politics the audience's eyes [are] going to glaze over and not know how to take it in because they don't fucking think about it. (Dagnes 2012)

It was a simpler time. Today, the minute Trump's name is spoken everyone knows *exactly* how to take it in, although the perspectives could be wildly different.

Late-night talk shows, those once hosted by Johnny Carson and Jay Leno and David Letterman, had been places where Americans could go to end the day with a laugh. Today, the hosts have found great success in their aggressive politics, especially those who are vehemently anti-Trump. The shows that have found the most ratings success in the Trump era include *Late Night w/Seth Meyers*, *The Late Show with Stephen Colbert*, and *Jimmy Kimmel Live*. Each of these shows has gained prominence and acclaim as they have all become politically supercharged. For Meyers, Colbert, and Kimmel, President Trump is as much a despised enemy as Hillary Clinton and Barack Obama are to the right-wing media. Similar to the popularity of the right-wing antagonism against the left, the anti-Trump animosity on late night has been a bonanza for ratings. Prior to his return to politics, Stephen Colbert was struggling as the host of *Late Night*, coming in third behind Jimmy Fallon and Jimmy Kimmel, but now he is the dominant force ahead of the others (Obeidallah 2017). Kimmel himself has done extremely well, thanks to the very vocal political stands he has taken on health care and gun control. Kimmel's jump into politics has been indicative of our larger national attention shift in that direction, and he has garnered notice because of this. Kimmel was the host of *The Man Show* and had been seen as a kind of snarky frat boy. *Slate's* Willa Paskin referred to his "merry meanness" which adequately sums up the pre-Trump Kimmel persona (Paskin 2017). This translates well to cruel taunting, as does the second key to his success, which is his self-identified ignorance about politics. Because he had not been especially political before (at least not publically), his new attention to big issues feels authentic. As Mark Harris wrote about Kimmel in *Vulture*:

> He is not the comedian I would have guessed would have become the avatar for a fed-up reaction to our political era — and I recoil from the word 'authentic,' which has too many different meanings to too many different users to be of much value as a discussion point. But these days, Kimmel feels like the real thing — shaky, flummoxed at the way things are going, and increasingly insistent that our elected officials be better people. (Harris 2017)

It is that authenticity that appears to work well for Kimmel, and when he becomes visibly distraught over the health of his newborn son or a mass shooting in his hometown, it feels real. His anger sits comfortably within our political polarization, and audiences have rewarded Kimmel's commentary with good ratings.

There is one exception to the newly charged late-night landscape, and that is *Tonight Show* host Jimmy Fallon. Before the 2016 election, Fallon's silliness and easily shared viral videos made him number one among viewers, a floppy-haired goofball who was having a good time. Once Donald Trump announced his candidacy and the political climate became more passionate, Fallon's shtick was seen as weak and ineffective, and his ratings dropped like a stone. This was especially pronounced when Trump appeared on *The Tonight Show* and Fallon tousled the candidate's hair instead of challenging him on his divisive or incendiary remarks. Excoriated for such jocularity, Fallon found himself on the defensive, literally for years after Trump's appearance. Fallon is the exception that makes the other shows' political bends seem much more pronounced. These late-night talk shows have become so politically charged, and so angry at President Trump, that while they are still funny for some, they are turning off others. CNN media critic Brian Stelter wrote about the newly hostile comedy of late night in the age of Trump:

Trump supporters and conservative media critics have been sharply critical
of the anti-Trump bent of Colbert's "Late Show" and other talk shows.
They argue that it's a turn-off to potential viewers. That may be true,
but the existing audiences for these shows adore comedians like Meyers,
Samantha Bee and John Oliver. The comics are saying out loud what the
viewers at home are feeling. (Stelter 2017)

Entertainment, a term once reserved for things meant to be fun and
diverting, now has become yet another shortcut in our polarization.
Which brings us back to *Roseanne*. In a stroke of convenient timing,
almost immediately following the cancellation of *Roseanne* 2.0, comedian Samantha Bee stepped up to the plate and, on her late-night comedy show on TBS "Full Frontal," called First Daughter Ivanka Trump
the "C-word" which hijacked coverage of Barr's racism and instead
shifted to a loud and angry fight about liberals, conservatives, and
hypocrisy.

Shifting the conversation from Roseanne Barr was no small feat because
it was dominating the news cycles: The left-leaning watchdog group
Media Matters for America did a study of cable news coverage at the time
of the Roseanne Barr explosion to track how much time was devoted
to the sitcom uproar. On the same day that *Roseanne* was canceled, the
*Washington Post* published a Harvard report showing the death toll in
Puerto Rico following Hurricane Maria was 70 times higher than the official count. Media Matters added up the amount of time the cable news
networks devoted to the Puerto Rico story versus the sitcom story, and
researchers found that Barr's tweet and show cancellation was covered 16
times more than the tragedy in Puerto Rico (Vernon 2018). The story
included a chart illustrating the difference in coverage:

| Network | Puerto Rico coverage | Roseanne Barr coverage |
| --- | --- | --- |
| Fox News | 0h0m48s | 1h56m54s |
| CNN | 0h12m3s | 4h48m46s |
| MSNBC | 0h21m18s | 3h38m45s |

Vernon 2018
Total: Puerto Rico story 34 minutes, 9 seconds. *Roseanne*: 10 hours, 24 minutes, 25 seconds

One reason for the disparity in coverage is obvious: One story is simple and easy, the other demanding and upsetting. Another reason concerns the way *Roseanne* fed into our political divisions. The reboot began

as a targeted appeal to a specific group of people, devolved into cultural arguments about groups of American voters, and then sank even lower into a clash about "PC lynch mobs."

The thunderous arguments about liberal hypocrisy and false equivalencies made for good ratings as it easily fed our political polarization. Playing on our emotions and a simple conversation built on a solid foundation of existing and sweeping generalizations, the Barr-Bee conundrum was emblematic of a story that could have been an important conversation starter but instead became a cultural shortcut. Both Barr and Bee apologized to the targets of their offense (Barr to Jarrett, Bee to Ivanka) but the opposing sides of the battle dug in, led by the loudest and most obvious voices in modern American politics. The near-universal condemnation of the racist tweet from Barr was quickly replaced with condemnation of Bee's language. Sarah Huckabee Sanders, White House press secretary, released a statement:

> The language used by Samantha Bee last night is vile and vicious. The collective silence by the left and its media allies is appalling. Her disgusting comments and show are not fit for broadcast, and executives at Time Warner and *TBS* must demonstrate that such explicit profanity about female members of this administration will not be condoned on its network. (Morin 2018)

What had once been the place for all Americans to end a difficult day with mindless humor and a variety of distraction has shifted gears become partisan and very angry.

Since liberals dominate late night, these shows are becoming part and parcel of a new left-wing media bubble. Our polarization is driving our entertainment decisions more than ever, and the left have specific outlets and shows that they consume, while the right has a different set of programming. It is difficult to feel two emotions at once, and so trying to be funny while being angry or scared is a difficult trick, which means that sometimes the joking is shelved in favor of outrage. Perhaps these shows can return to humorous simplicity when the temperature is not so high, but until then the audiences are becoming more ideologically distinct. Late night used to be a place for politicians appear and campaign because they could get in front of a joke, show they are funny and self-deprecating, and also that they could connect with a younger audience. The new sharp anti-Trump tone of late night means right-leaning politicians who used to go on these programs will likely eschew them, which continues the cycle of our isolation: Liberal audiences will not hear from the conservatives policymakers who avoid appearing on them.

This is worsening the divide between us, intensifying the justification for a right-wing media circle that protects conservatives from the snark against them. Caitlin Flanagan wrote about this during the Barr-Bee tumult:

> Though aimed at blue-state sophisticates, these shows are an unintended but powerful form of propaganda for conservatives. When Republicans see these harsh jokes—which echo down through the morning news shows and the chattering day's worth of viral clips, along with those of Jimmy Kimmel, Stephen Colbert, and Seth Meyers—they don't just see a handful of comics mocking them. They see *HBO, Comedy Central, TBS, ABC, CBS,* and *NBC.* In other words, they see exactly what Donald Trump has taught them: that the entire media landscape loathes them, their values, their family, and their religion. It is hardly a reach for them to further imagine that the legitimate news shows on these channels are run by similarly partisan players—nor is it at all illogical. No wonder so many of Trump's followers are inclined to believe only the things that he or his spokespeople tell them directly—everyone else on the tube thinks they're a bunch of trailer-park, Oxy-snorting half-wits who divide their time between retweeting Alex Jones fantasies and ironing their Klan hoods. (Flanagan 2017)

This kind of division within our entertainment choices is both reason for and cause of our larger political rift. It is intensified by the anger that the left feels, which in turn antagonizes those on the right and our divisions deepen.

For his part, President Trump (never one to let an insult go without response) is making things worse. The president tweeted twice in 2017 about late-night hosts. The first: "Late night host are dealing with the Democrats for their very "unfunny" and repetitive material, always anti-Trump! Should we get Equal Time?" and then "More and more people are suggesting that Republicans (and me) should be given Equal Time on T.V. when you look at the one-sided coverage?" Syntax problems aside, Trump was referencing the Equal Time provision mandated by the Federal Communications Commission, which says that if a non-news outlet gives coverage of one candidate, they must provide equal time to opposing candidates. That is a real administrative rule, and it applied during the 2016 presidential campaign. Trump himself triggered a question about the rule when he appeared on *Saturday Night Live* in 2015, which led to the question of whether NBC had to give equal time to the other GOP presidential primary candidates. According to Georgetown University Law Professor Andrew Schwartzman, the airtime given did not have to be on *SNL*, but rather that all candidates "are entitled to the same quantity, day part and price as their opponents" (Pallotta 2015). In response to his tweets against the late-night hosts, *Tonight Show* writer and producer Mike DiCenzo responded on Twitter: "That's not how it works. You're not campaigning. You're the president. Now kindly stop tweeting nonsense and go do your job for once" (Ritzen 2017).

The back-and-forth between Trump and late-night comedians continued in 2018, when in an interview with *The Hollywood Reporter*, Jimmy Fallon expressed his regret for the 2016 hair tousling. The right-wing media circle picked it up, Trump heard about it on *Fox*, and went after Fallon again on Twitter and riffed angrily and personally against the late-night hosts Conan O'Brien, Stephen Colbert, and Jimmy Kimmel during a rally in South Carolina. Calling the three names, he ended his bombast by saying "I mean, honestly, are these people funny?" and the crowd shouted "NO!" In response, Colbert, Fallon, and Conan O'Brien worked together and taped a sketch where they called each other to compare notes: "Hey, low life," Fallon said, to which Colbert responded jovially, "Hey, lost soul. What are you up to?" (Chiu 2018).

Late-night comedians are innovative in ways to troll the president, and with their own entertainment expertise and staffs of comedy writers at their disposal there is no end to the slings and arrows. In 2018, both Stephen Colbert and John Oliver had children's books on the best seller lists; Colbert's was comprised of comments made by Trump after Hurricane Florence. Oliver's book was about Vice President Mike Pence's rabbit. If the old expression is "never pick a fight with anyone who buys ink by the barrel and paper by the ton," the new motto should be something along the lines of "never pick a fight with someone who is a professional entertainer on TV every night in a hyper-mediated age of celebrity."

Back in the 1990s, then-Vice President Dan Quayle weighed in on a plotline from the TV show *Murphy Brown* where the title character (played by Candice Bergen) found herself pregnant and unmarried. The general thought at the time was twofold: First, did Vice President Quayle know that Murphy Brown was a fictional character? And second, why is a sitting Vice President talking about a TV show? The culture has shifted. Amidst the *Roseanne* kerfuffle, there were few outcries asking, "Why does the president care about a sitcom?" because it was so glaringly obvious that the sitcom cared about the president. The country took the bait, first by buying into a show re-launched on the premise that even in the age of "Peak TV," a specific group of voters needed something to watch, then by playing into the simple argument about entirely separate red and blue Americas. Entertainment is now polarization and anger. Everything is personal, the volume turned up.

Which brings us to the topic of sports, an area of entertainment that is *supposed* to involve screaming, cheering, booing, and face painting. What was once an innocent endeavor marked by irrational fealty toward a team representing a city, state, or university (that a fan may or may not have ever been to) has now turned into a national fight about politics. As with entertainment, American sports is not new to political controversy.[12] Athletes have used their fame and platforms to advocate and protest. Examples include Jesse Owens at the 1936 Olympics in Munich, Muhammad Ali refusing to serve in Vietnam in 1967, John Carols and Tommy Smith holding up their firsts in black power solidarity in 1968. Sports and protest are not new, but in recent years, athletes have grown increasingly angry, vocal, and inspired to protest the systemic violence against African-Americans. As athletes have drawn attention to the issues of racism, identity, and police brutality, the national conversation has escalated. This intensification is positive in that it keeps a vital topic in the national consciousness, but it is negative in the way it has become a shortcut in our national polarized anger. Despite the complexity and seriousness of the issues at stake, athletic protests have been reduced to a simplified two-sided debate. The quiet and powerful protests began with specific occurrences but then grew to something larger. The St. Louis Rams walked onto the field with their hands up to protest the events in Ferguson, Missouri. The Miami Heat wore their hoods over their heads in deference to the murder of Trayvon Martin. And most notably, in 2016 Colin Kaepernick took a knee during the national anthem which inspired more football players to do the same. As the number of protests increased at football games across the country, conservatives loudly denounced the actions as un-American, unpatriotic, and abhorrent.

The loudest voice in this dispute, again, was President Trump's. During the campaign, Trump gave an interview about the football protests on KIRO radio in Seattle with Dori Monson and said that perhaps

Colin Kaepernick should expatriate: "I think it's personally not a good thing, I think it's a terrible thing. And, you know, maybe [Kaepernick] should find a country that works better for him. Let him try, it won't happen" (Wilder 2016). After the campaign, Trump continued to weigh in on the NFL protests, tweeting out against the NFL's commissioner Roger Goodell: "Can you believe that the disrespect for our Country, our Flag, our Anthem continues without penalty to the players. The Commissioner has lost control of the hemorrhaging league. Players are the boss!" And at a rally in Alabama where Trump campaigned for Senate candidate Roy Moore, he returned once again to the subject and said: "Wouldn't you love to see one of these NFL owners, when somebody disrespects our flag, to say 'get that son of a b---- off the field right now, out, he's fired!" President Trump continued to rail against the players who took a knee during the National Anthem, likely because it played to his base who fervently roared their approval whenever he broached the subject. At the same time, it kept the protests in the news, which proved effective for the protestors as well. But it deepened the us-them polarity, and when the Philadelphia Eagles won the Super Bowl, most members of the team refused to visit the White House in protest against President Trump.

White House visits from sports teams, a previously apolitical tradition, were a predominantly baseball-focused endeavor for almost a century. President Andrew Johnson hosted two amateur baseball teams in 1865 and President Ulysses Grant hosted baseball's first professional team, the Cincinnati Red Stockings, in 1869. The first championship team to visit was, perhaps appropriately, the 1924 Washington Senators, and so the traditional White House visit began with baseball. In 1963, the Boston Celtics became the first championship basketball team to visit the White House, and in 1980 the Pittsburgh Steelers became the first Super Bowl winners. It was always a win-win for presidents, many of whom were genuine sports fans, all of whom enjoyed the photo opportunity. It was cool for athletes to meet the president and it was a way for the most powerful man in the world to appear accessible. But what once had been a non-political way to celebrate America and sports and athleticism has been caught up in the national anger (Allen 2018). The Golden State Warriors had won the 2017 championship, and two of the team's stars, Steph Curry and Kevin Durant, announced publically that they would not visit the White House in protest of President Trump's actions toward Kaepernick and others:

That we don't stand for basically what our president ... the things that he
said and the things that he hasn't said in the right terms that we won't
stand for it. And by acting and not going, hopefully that will inspire
some change when it comes to what we tolerate in this country and what
is accepted and what we turn a blind eye to. It's not just the act of not
going. There are things you have to do on the back end to actually push
that message into motion. You can talk about all the different personalities
that have said things and done things, from [Colin] Kaepernick to what
happened to [Michael] Bennett to all sorts of examples of what has gone
on in our country that we need to kind of change. And we all are trying to
do what we can, using our platforms, using our opportunities to shed light
on that. ... I don't think us not going to White House is going to miracu-
lously make everything better ... [but] this is my opportunity to voice that.
(Bonesteel 2017)

President Trump responded to Curry and Durant that they and the
team had not been invited in the first place, and the fight endured.
The championship-winning Golden State Warriors visited Washington,
DC anyway, and toured the National Museum of African-American
History with a group of children. Since the President of the USA continued to use the protests to goad his supporters at rallies and followers
on Twitter, it is small wonder that the protests not only continued, but
spread.

ESPN, the cable network that covers sports, had experience dealing
with important subjects such as racism and misogyny, but the heightened
attention to political polarization through a lens of sports came at a bad
time for the network. ESPN was one of the earliest channels on cable
and over the decades became a behemoth, spawning multiple channels
and myriad TV stars. In recent years, however, ESPN was facing serious
financial trouble. It was the most expensive channel on cable TV and so
in order to cut costs and offer so-called skinny bundles to their customers, cable providers began to drop the sports channel. According to the
*Wall Street Journal*, ESPN lost 16 million subscribers in the course of
seven years (Ramachandran 2018). This happened at exactly the same
time when broadcast rights for live sporting events was rising, and as a
result the network was in trouble and executives were feeling tetchy. In
September 2017 amidst the national fight about the kneeling protests,
one of ESPN's star anchors, Jemele Hill, called President Trump a white
supremacist on Twitter.

The president responded in a tweet: "ESPN is paying a really big price for its politics (and bad programming). People are dumping it in RECORD numbers." While the subscription loss was not because of the politicization of sports, the financial problems for the network were there already. John Skipper was then the president of the network and was "furious" with Hill: "If I punish you, he told her, I'd open us up to protests and come off as racist. If I do nothing, that will fuel a narrative among conservatives – and a faction within ESPN – that the network had become too liberal" (Ramachandran 2018). And thus, the sports network became caught in the nation's political polarization. Hill was not suspended then, but she was several weeks later after she encouraged the boycott of the Dallas Cowboys' sponsors when the team's owner threatened to punish a player who took a knee. It was, again, the confluence of corporate boycotts, celebrity, and political protest. Fast forward six months and ESPN remained caught in our national anger because as it happens, ESPN is owned by ABC, the network that aired *Roseanne*. When ABC canceled the sitcom, according to the *New York Post*, network executives at ESPN specifically warned "the most outspoken of its broadcasters" to "be careful of social media" (Marchand 2018).

Controversies involving celebrities are more exciting to cover and discuss than the sausage making on Capitol Hill. The simplistic condensing of difficult topics to easy and angry two-sided fights is not only denigrating to the issues at stake, but harmful for democratic deliberation. Battling over issues and position stands that have moved beyond our news consumption adds up to increased cynicism and institutional distrust, and it deepens our already polarized political climate. Writer Sonny Bunch had a piece in the *Washington Free Beacon* several years ago and wrote that there is a difference between being a political animal and living a politicized life:

> There's nothing wrong with living a *political* life. That is, a life in which politics is one of your interests or your job, something you follow and keep track of and educate yourself on and argue about. The arena of politics is important; political decisions have consequences; and passionately arguing for your preferred political outcomes is nothing to be ashamed of. A politicized life is a different beast, however. It treats politics as a zero sum game or a form of total warfare in which the other side must be obliterated. It alters every aspect of your being: where you shop; what you watch on TV; what sort of music you listen to; who you associate with. If you're

not with the politicized being, you're against him—and if you're against
him, he is well within his rights to ruin you personally and economically.
You, the political other, are a leper to be shunned, lest your thought
crimes infect the rest of society. As I wrote, I find this to be more than a
little disturbing. I don't worry too much about growing partisan gridlock,
but I *do* worry somewhat about an America in which each half the country
hates the other so viscerally that they won't even interact. That's a truly
dangerous state of affairs. (Bunch 2013)

Ideological polarization is exacerbated by this extension of politics into
our larger culture. Bunch is right to worry. The ease with which our
national outrage spreads is both a cause and symptom of grievance politics. Always looking for insult and always finding it is both enraging and
exhausting. The fact that hostile politics runs into our consumer choices
and our entertainment takes away from the joy that these things might
bring to us, replacing it instead with a fury that is difficult to stem.

## Conclusions

Returning to Madison, it is natural for citizens to form groups based on
opinions and beliefs, and if sociologists are to be believed, it is natural for
people to cast aspersions on people outside of their groups. The difference today is that our anger is generalized and unfocused, and we spread
it around with the precision of a shotgun. Political issues have become
divisive components of our politics since we use them as social cues, their
names as shortcuts about ideology and beliefs. Not only does this fire
us up, it also encourages us to find like-minded compatriots for comfort. Americans stay within their bubbles because the alternative poses an
existential threat. Polarization is felt everywhere, citizens are constantly
reminded that there is a war going on within our own house, among our
own citizens, and the only solution is to stay engaged and fight like hell.

One significant problem with our current state of polarization is
that the louder the anger, the more prominence it is given. For example, musician Ted Nugent[13] was in a discussion about gun control with
*InfoWars* host Alex Jones and said about Democrats:

Don't ask why. Just know that evil, dishonesty, and scam artists have always
been around and that right now they're liberal, they're Democrat, they're
[Republicans in name only], they're Hollywood, they're fake news, they're

media, they're academia, and they're half of our government, at least. There are rabid coyotes running around, you don't wait till you see one to go get your gun, keep your gun handy. And every time you see one, you shoot one. (Delk 2018)

When people on the left hear this story, they (understandably) become enraged, which is the reason Nugent went on *InfoWars* to begin with. This raises the volume even more, leading to conservatives wondering why all liberals think they are violent and hateful.

Additionally, the polarized rhetoric is awful at all levels, from the very top of the power structure down. A study conducted by Nithyanand, Schaffner, and Gill showed that when citizens are exposed to discourtesy and vulgarity from political elites, they respond with similar rhetoric. They found a "strong correlation between Trump's rise in popularity and the increasing incivility observed in Republican forums on Reddit" (Nithyanand et al. 2017). The discourse that starts at the top and trickles down makes it contagious. At the Tony Awards (the awards for theater!) actor Robert De Niro took to the stage and said "I'm gonna say one thing: Fuck Trump!" he pumped both fists in the air and got a standing ovation from the audience. This inspired President Trump to respond to De Niro in a tweet the next day: "Robert De Niro, a very Low IQ individual, has received too many shots to the head by real boxers in movies. I watched him last night and truly believe he may be 'punch-drunk'" (Jacobs 2018). The spread of this acrimony is not going to bring the nation together; it will only further the political schism between parties.

Trump is both well known for his insulting language and proud of it, and his divisive language has not been tempered during his term in office. George H. W. Bush called Bill Clinton a "bozo" during the 1992 presidential campaign, which was regarded as "unpresidential" (Baker and Rogers 2018). Things have changed. As Peter Baker and Katie Rogers write in the *New York Times*:

[T]he lesson that Mr. Trump took from his nastier-than-thou campaign was that the more outrageous he was, the more incendiary his rhetoric, the more attention he drew and the more votes he received. Any expectation that he would put the harsh language aside to become more of a moral leader as president has proved illusory. (Baker and Rogers 2018)

Going back to the aforementioned research on incivility, Nithyanand, Schaffner, and Gill also found that such language increased negative partisanship, further driving polarization. The incivility that is so rampant now in our political media has a harmful effect on our political behavior.

A challenge is that many Americans not only mimic the spiteful language but also enjoy it. Even more than being entertaining, the kind of "plain spoken" nature of coarse communication is appealing to some because it appears to be more honest than the diplomatic talk used by most politicians. *Politico* reporter Eliana Johnson told me about a play produced at New York University where actors delivered direct quotes from the three presidential debates; the only hitch was that the producers switched the genders of the candidates. The NYU professors who put on the play expected the audience to denounce a woman using language as harsh as Trump, but were shocked to find that the audience instead found that they appreciated the female Trump's brash style, while they saw the male version of Clinton as dry and "mansplaining" (Jamieson 2017). And these were liberal audiences. At the same time, conservatives think that his combative and offensive style is a thumb in the nose of "political correctness," and that Trump says what they want to say but cannot. "He says, you're right about everything, those other people are idiots and jerks, and all those things you feel but think you shouldn't say in polite company? I'll say them for you!" (Waldman 2016). That the public is untethered from the binds of social acceptability is not a good thing, nor is it a sign of greater honesty in politics. Rather, this kind of free-wheeling offense is contributing to our polarization, further dividing the nation as gains momentum.

There are possible ways to break us out of this polarization, most of which mandate that we forget politics all together. For instance, Matthew Levendusky, an associate professor at the University of Pennsylvania, found that one way to decrease affective polarization was to increase American nationalism, the results of which he found during experiments surrounding the Olympic Games and the July 4th holiday (Levendusky 2018). It would seem that by shifting our focus away from the issues and policies that divide us, and doubling-down on the patriotism that unites us, we can possibly break out of our ideological provinces. This has clearly been accomplished before; America has not always been so divided.

In 2012, the National Republican Campaign Committee created an ad for an incumbent House member from Virginia named Scott Rigell where the congressman said: "Most politicians think Washington is all a game. You put on a jersey and attack the other team. The two parties score points on each other, and our nation's problems get ignored. When my own party's in the wrong, I'm not afraid to say it." It's a positive sentiment, but this was in 2012 and things have changed. I found out about this ad from my former student, Tom Dunn, who works for OnMessage, the Republican ad firm outside of DC. Tom told me about this ad because the idea of "putting on your jersey" has become shorthand for the partisanship of today. The polarization that afflicts us continues because politicos are rewarded for enhancing disunion; there is too much to be gained by disharmony. The ironic thing about this ad was that Rigell was touting his ability to compromise, to be bipartisan and defy the prevalent inclination to attack. He won his reelection campaign in 2012 but in 2016, Scott Rigell announced that he would not support Donald Trump for president, expressing his "dismay at the intensity and toxic nature of partisanship in Congress" (Portnoy 2016). He retired from Congress that year.

## NOTES

1. On one side Fiorina et al. (2008); on the other side, Abramowitz (2010).
2. Haidt is the author of *The Righteous Mind: Why Good People Are Divided by Politics and Religion* (2013) and *The Coddling of the American Mind* (2018) with the Greg Lukianoff, among others.
3. Hetherington is the author of several terrific books on polarization including *Authoritarianism and Polarization* (2009), *Why Washington Won't Work* (2015) and *Prius or Pick Up* (2018).
4. Mason, Liliana, *Uncivil Agreement: How Politics Became Our Identity* (University of Chicago Press, 2018).
5. Berry and Sobieraj, *The Outrage Industry: Political Opinion Media and the New Incivility* (Oxford: 2016).
6. Mutz, *In Your Face Politics: The Consequences of Uncivil Media* (Princeton: 2015).
7. For more on homophily I point readers to sociologists McPherson, Smith-Lovin, and Cook's 2001 paper, "Birds of a Feather: Homophily in Social Networks".

8. Bishop's book, *The Big Sort* (Houghton Mifflin, 2008), was the focus of many academic and popular responses.
9. This led to the incredibly hilarious tweet, because Dick's Sporting Goods was also a Hannity sponsor, that read: "Does the latest brand-name removal from Hannity's show mean that once you are all done smashing your #Keurig machines with hammers and whatever, you have to smash your #Dicks as well?".
10. #GrabYourWallet.
11. Keurig, Starbucks, Proctor, and Gamble, respectively.
12. A very thorough examination of this topic can be found in the 2018 book *The Heritage: Black Athletes, a Divided America, and the Politics of Patriotism* by Howard Bryant.
13. Nugent's discography includes albums such as "Cat Scratch Fever," "Love Grenade," "Full Bluntal Nugity," and "If You Can't Lick 'Em, Lick 'Em," among others.

## Works Cited

Abramowitz, Alan. 2010. *The Disappearing Center: Engaged Citizens, Polarization, and American Democracy*. New Haven: Yale University Press.

Abramowitz, Alan, and Stephen Webster. 2018. Negative Partisanship: Why Americans Dislike Parties but Behave Like Rabid Partisans. *Political Psychology* 39: 119–135.

Abrams, Samuel, and Morris Fiorina. 2012. *The Myth of the "Big Sort"*. Stanford, CA: The Hoover Institution.

Allen, Scott. 2018. *The Traditional White House Visit Began with the 1924 Washington Senators*, February 28. Accessed June 12, 2018. https://www.washingtonpost.com/news/dc-sports-bog/wp/2018/02/28/the-traditional-white-house-visit-began-with-the-washington-senators/?utm_term=.d9bff1556047.

Baker, Peter, and Katie Rogers. 2018. *In Trump's America, the Conversation Turns Ugly and Angry, Starting at the Top*, June 20. Accessed October 6, 2018. https://www.nytimes.com/2018/06/20/us/politics/trump-language-immigration.html.

Berry, Jeffrey, and Sarah Sobieraj. 2014. *The Outrage Industry: Political Opinion Media and the New Incivility*. Oxford: Oxford University Press.

Billig, Michael, and Henri Tajfel. 1973. Social Categorization and Similarity in Intergroup Behaviour. *European Journal of Social Psychology* 3: 27–52.

Bishop, Bill, and Robert Cushing. 2008. The Big Sort: Migration, Community, and Politics in the United States of "Those People". In *Red, Blue, and Purple America: The Future of Election Demographics*, ed. Ruy Teixeira, 50–75. Washington, DC: Brooking Institution Press.

Bitecofer, Rachel. 2018. The Party Decides? In *The Unprecedented 2016 Presidential Election*, ed. Rachel Bitecofer. New York, NY: Palgrave Macmillan.

Bonesteel, Matt. 2017. *President Trump Says Stephen Curry's White House Invitation Has Been 'Withdrawn'*, September 23. Accessed June 18, 2018. https://www.washingtonpost.com/news/early-lead/wp/2017/09/23/president-trump-says-stephen-currys-white-house-invitation-has-been-with-drawn/?utm_term=.46aa9d680875.

Bonfiglio, Joe, interview by Alison Dagnes. 2017. *President, Environmental Defense Action Fund*, February 23.

Brookes, Khristine, interview by Alison Dagnes. 2017. *Communications Director, The Cato Institute*, January 6.

Bump, Philip. 2015. *Obama Is the Most Polarizing President on Record, but It's Not Entirely His Fault*, February 6. Accessed March 12, 2018. https://www.washingtonpost.com/news/the-fix/wp/2015/02/06/obama-is-the-most-polarizing-president-on-record-but-its-not-entirely-his-fault/?utm_term=.a0babfc59f78.

Bunch, Sonny. 2013. *A Political Life vs. A Politicized Life*, March 25. Accessed March 6, 2018. http://freebeacon.com/blog/a-political-life-vs-a-politicized-life/.

Chatterji, Aaron, and Michael Toffel. 2018. The New CEO Activists. *Harvard Business Review* 96: 78–89.

Chiu, Allyson. 2018. *Colbert, Fallon and Conan O'Brien Team Up on Trump*, June 28. Accessed September 11, 2018. https://www.washingtonpost.com/news/morning-mix/wp/2018/06/27/colbert-fallon-and-conan-obrien-team-up-on-trump/?utm_term=.fd0a16b33124.

Chumley, Cheryl. 2018. *Oprah Speech Powerful, but Not Presidential*, January 8. Accessed April 1, 2018. https://www.washingtontimes.com/news/2018/jan/8/oprah-speech-powerful-not-presidential/.

CNN. 1997. *Southern Baptists Vote for Disney Boycott*, June 18. Accessed June 12, 2018. http://www.cnn.com/US/9706/18/baptists.disney/.

Cohen, Marty, David Karol, Hans Noel, and John Zaller. 2008. *The Party Decides: Presidential Nominations Before and After Reform*. Chicago: University of Chicago Press.

Committee on Political Parties. 1950. *Toward a More Responsible Two-Party System*. Washington, DC: American Political Science Review.

D'Abruzzo, Diana. 2015. *Politicians on TV: The Best Cameos from Washington*, June 30. Accessed June 13, 2018. https://www.politico.com/gallery/2015/06/politicians-on-tv-the-best-cameos-from-washington-002037?slide=10.

Dagnes, Alison. 2012. *A Conservative Walks into a Bar*. New York City: Palgrave.

Delk, Josh. 2018. *Ted Nugent Likens Democrats to 'Rabid Coyotes' That Should Be Shot on Sight*, April 7. Accessed October 8, 2018. https://thehill.com/blogs/ballot-box/382117-ted-nugent-likens-democrats-to-rabid-coyotes-says-to-shoot-on-sight.

DellaPosta, Daniel, Yongren Shi, and Michael Macy. 2015. Why Do Liberals Drink Lattes? *American Journal of Sociology* 120: 1473–1511.

Desilver, Drew. 2016. *Turnout Was High in the 2016 Primary Season, but Just Short of 2008 Record*, June 10. Accessed June 11, 2018. http://www.pewresearch.org/fact-tank/2016/06/10/turnout-was-high-in-the-2016-primary-season-but-just-short-of-2008-record/.

Editors. 2008. *Americans Are Increasingly Choosing to Live Among Like-Minded Neighbours: This Makes the Culture War More Bitter and Politics Harder*, June 19. Accessed June 11, 2018. https://www.economist.com/node/11581447.

Ehrenreich, Barbara. 1990. The Wretched of the Hearth: The Undainty Feminism of Roseanne Barr. *The New Republic*, April 2: 28–32.

Filippino, Marc. 2018. *Why CEOs Are Becoming Activists*, February 5. Accessed March 19, 2018. https://www.pri.org/stories/2018-02-05/why-ceos-are-becoming-activists.

Fiorina, Morris P. and Samuel J. Abrams. 2008. Political Polarization in the American Public. *Annual Review of Political Science* 11(1): 563–588.

Fischer, Sara. 2018. *Radioactive Presidency: Trump Is Poison for Brands*, August 8. Accessed September 10, 2018. https://www.axios.com/trump-poison-for-brands-3d9e3ca4-035a-4bbb-b792-8c34e10145c1.html.

Flanagan, Caitline. 2017. *How Late-Night Comedy Fueled the Rise of Trump*, May. Accessed September 11, 2018. https://www.theatlantic.com/magazine/archive/2017/05/how-late-night-comedy-alienated-conservatives-made-liberals-smug-and-fueled-the-rise-of-trump/521472/.

Gaines-Ross, Leslie. 2017. *What CEO Activism Looks Like in the Trump Era*, October 2. Accessed June 13, 2018. https://hbr.org/2017/10/what-ceo-activism-looks-like-in-the-trump-era.

Gallup. 2018. *Donald Trump Job Approval by Party Identification*, September 2. Accessed September 6, 2018. https://news.gallup.com/poll/203198/presidential-approval-ratings-donald-trump.aspx.

Greene, Steven. 1999. Understanding Party Identification. *Political Psychology* 20: 393–403.

Haidt, Jonathan, and Marc Hetherington. 2012. *Look How Far We've Come Apart*, September 17. Accessed March 28, 2018. https://campaignstops.blogs.nytimes.com/2012/09/17/look-how-far-weve-come-apart/.

Hamby, Peter. 2018. *"That Is What Power Looks Like": As Trump Prepares for 2020, Democrats Are Losing the Only Fight That Matters*, May 26. Accessed June 13, 2018. https://www.vanityfair.com/news/2018/05/democrats-are-losing-the-only-fight-that-matters.

Hanson-Long, Kaylie, interview by Alison Dagnes. 2017. *National Communications Director, NARAL Pro Choice America*, February 20.

Harris, Mark. 2017. Jimmy Kimmel Didn't Ask for This—Which Is Why He's the Most Important Host in Late-Night TV. *Vulture*, October 3. https://

www.vulture.com/2017/10/why-jimmy-kimmel-is-the-most-important-host-in-late-night.html.

Harrison, Guy, interview by Alison Dagnes. 2017. *Partner, OnMessage*, May 31.

Herrnson, Paul, interview by Alison Dagnes. 2018. *Professor, University of Connecticut*, April 6.

Hetherington, Marc, and Thomas Rudolph. 2015. *Why Washington Won't Work: Polarization, Political Trust, and the Governing Crisis*. Chicago, IL: University of Chicago Press.

Iyengar, Shanto, and Masha Krupenkin. 2018. The Strengthening of Partisan Affect. *Political Psychology* 39: 201–218.

Iyengar, Shanto, Yphtach Lelkes, Matthew Levendusky, Neil Malhotra, and Sean J. Westwood. 2018. The Origins and Consequences of Affective Polarization in the United States. *American Journal of Political Science*. Washington, DC: Wiley, April 23.

Jacobs, Ben. 2018. *Trump Suggests Robert De Niro Is Brain Damaged Following Actor's Tonys Speech*, June 12. Accessed October 8, 2018. https://www.theguardian.com/us-news/2018/jun/12/trump-robert-de-niro-response-tonys-fuck-speech-twitter-latest.

Jamieson, Amber. 2017. *If Trump Were a Woman: Play Swaps Presidential Candidates' Genders*, January 29. Accessed October 8, 2018. https://www.theguardian.com/us-news/2017/jan/29/clinton-trump-gender-swap-play-her-opponent.

Kolbin, John. 2018. *After Racist Tweet, Roseanne Barr's Show Is Canceled by ABC*, May 29. Accessed September 5, 2018. https://www.nytimes.com/2018/05/29/business/media/roseanne-barr-offensive-tweets.html.

Kweiku, Ezekiel. 2016. *The Real Winners and Losers of Nevada and South Carolina*, February 24. Accessed February 28, 2018. http://www.mtv.com/news/2744685/winners-and-losers-nevada-and-south-carolina/.

LaRaja, Ray, and Brian Schaffner. 2014. *Want to Reduce Polarization? Give Parties More Money*, July 21. Accessed June 11, 2018. https://www.washingtonpost.com/news/monkey-cage/wp/2014/07/21/want-to-reduce-polarization-give-parties-more-money/?utm_term=.acec61f3d172.

Levendusky, Matthew. 2018. Americans, Not Partisans: Can Priming American National Identity Reduce Affective Polarization? *Journal of Politics* 80: 59–70.

Livingston, Michael. 2018. *Here's When Boycotts Have Worked—And When They Haven't*, March 1. Accessed March 7, 2018. http://www.latimes.com/nation/la-na-boycotts-history-20180228-htmlstory.html.

Lowell, Bridget, interview by Alison Dagnes. 2017. *Chief Communications Officer, The Urban Institute*, January 6.

Madison, James. 1787. *The Federalist Papers: No. 10*, November 23. Accessed March 12, 2018. http://avalon.law.yale.edu/18th_century/fed10.asp.

Marchand, Andrew. 2018. *ESPN Warns Outspoken Talent in Wake of 'Roseanne' Controversy*, May 31. Accessed June 12, 2018. https://nypost.

com/2018/05/31/espn-warns-outspoken-talent-in-wake-of-roseanne-controversy/.

Martinez, Gina. 2018. *Despite Outrage, Nike Sales Increased 31% After Kaepernick Ad*, September 8. Accessed September 10, 2018. http://time.com/5390884/nike-sales-go-up-kaepernick-ad/.

Mason, Lilliana. 2018. *Uncivil Agreement: How Politics Became Our Identity*. Chicago, IL: University of Chicago Press.

McLeod, Saul. 2008. *Social Identity Theory*. Accessed February 15, 2018. https://www.simplypsychology.org/social-identity-theory.html.

Morin, Rebecca. 2018. *Comedian Samantha Bee Apologizes to Ivanka Trump*, May 31. Accessed June 1, 2018. https://www.politico.com/story/2018/05/31/samantha-bee-ivanka-trump-apology-615588.

Morning Consult. 2018. *CSR and Political Activism in the Trump Era*. Public, Washington, DC: Morning Consult.

Mutz, Diana. 2015. *In-Your-Face Politics: The Consequences of Uncivl Media*. Princeton: Princeton University Press.

Nithyanand, Rishab, Brian Schaffner, and Phillipa Gill. 2017. *Online Political Discourse in the Trump Era*. arXiv:1711.05303 1-16.

Obeidallah, Dean. 2017. This Thanksgiving, Comedians Should Give Thanks for Trump. *CNN*, November 20. https://www.cnn.com/2017/11/20/opinions/trump-thanksgiving-late-night-comedy-obeidallah-opinion/index.html.

Ohlheiser, Abby. 2018. *TV Roseanne Is a Trump Supporter: Real-Life Roseanne Barr Is Already a Pro-Trump Internet Mainstay*, March 29. Accessed June 11, 2018. https://www.washingtonpost.com/news/the-intersect/wp/2018/01/11/tv-roseanne-will-be-a-trump-supporter-real-life-roseanne-barr-is-already-a-pro-trump-internet-mainstay/?utm_term=.69a02f42399a.

Pallotta, Frank. 2015. *Donald Trump's 'SNL' Stint Could Put FCC's 'Equal-Time' Rule in Play*, October 14. Accessed June 13, 2018. http://money.cnn.com/2015/10/14/media/donald-trump-hillary-clinton-saturday-night-live-equal-time/index.html.

Paskin, Willa. 2017. The New Man Show. *Slate*, October 17. https://slate.com/arts/2017/10/jimmy-kimmels-merry-meanness-makes-him-the-perfect-foil-for-donald-trump.html.

Portnoy, Jenna. 2016. *Rep. Scott Rigell Leaves Virginia Beach GOP After Backing Libertarian for President*, August 6. Accessed October 8, 2018. https://www.washingtonpost.com/local/virginia-politics/rep-scott-rigell-leaves-virginia-beach-gop-after-backing-libertarian-for-president/2016/08/08/55908490-5da6-11e6-9d2f-b1a3564181a1_story.html?noredirect=on&utm_term=.246b50092886.

Ramachandran, Shalini. 2018. How a Weakened ESPN Became Consumed by Politics. *The Wall Street Journal*, May 24.

Ritzen, Tracey. 2017. *Trump Kicked off His Weekend by Angrily Tweeting at 'Unfunny' Late Night Hosts, Demanding 'Equal Time'*, October 7. Accessed June 13, 2018. https://uproxx.com/news/trump-tweet-late-night-equal-time/.

Rubin, Jennifer. 2013. *Why Popular Culture Matters in Politics*, October 28. Accessed June 13, 2018. https://www.washingtonpost.com/blogs/right-turn/wp/2013/10/28/why-popular-culture-matters-in-politics/?utm_term=.7ffdecc5508a.

Schneider, Christian. 2017. *In the Age of Donald Trump, the Crassest Pop Culture Is the Key to Understanding Politics*, November 3. Accessed June 13, 2018. https://www.usatoday.com/story/opinion/2017/11/03/trump-understanding-politics-and-culture-must-come-simultaneously-christian-schneider-column/825728001/.

Severson, Kim. 2012. *Chick-fil-A Thrust Back Into Spotlight on Gay Rights*, July 25. Accessed June 12, 2018. https://www.nytimes.com/2012/07/26/us/gay-rights-uproar-over-chick-fil-a-widens.html.

Stelter, Brian. 2017. Has President Trump Changed Late Night TV Permanently? *CNN*, November 20. https://money.cnn.com/2017/11/20/media/late-night-tv-president-trump/index.html.

Taylor, Kate. 2018. *Companies Are Being Bombarded with Boycott Threats from the Right and Left Over Their NRA Ties—And It Reveals a Dark Truth About America*, February 28. Accessed March 7, 2018. http://www.businessinsider.com/companies-boycott-nra-show-political-polarization-2018-2.

Todd, Brad, interview by Alison Dagnes. 2018. *Partner, OnMessage*, July 16.

Vernon, Pete. 2018. *Puerto Rico's Devastation Takes a Backseat to Roseanne Coverage*, May 31. Accessed June 1, 2018. https://www.cjr.org/the_media_today/puerto-rico-death-coverage.php.

Waldman, Paul. 2016. *Perpetually Outraged, Perpetually Outrageous*, January 16. Accessed October 2, 2018. http://prospect.org/article/perpetually-outraged-perpetually-outrageous-0.

Warzel, Charlie. 2018. *Yelp, the Red Hen, and How All Tech Platforms Are Now Pawns in the Culture War*, June 25. Accessed September 10, 2018. https://www.buzzfeednews.com/article/charliewarzel/yelp-the-red-hen-and-how-all-tech-platforms-are-now-pawns.

Webster, Steven, and Alan Abramoqitz. 2017. The Ideological Foundations of Affective Polarization in the U.S. Electorate. *American Politics Research* 45: 621–647.

Weill, Kelly. 2018. *Roseanne Keeps Promoting QAnon, the Pro-Trump Conspiracy Theory That Makes Pizzagate Look Tame*, March 30. Accessed June 13, 2018. https://www.thedailybeast.com/roseanne-keeps-promoting-qanon-the-pro-trump-conspiracy-theory-that-makes-pizzagate-look-tame.

Wilder, Charlotte. 2016. *Donald Trump Says Colin Kaepernick Should Find a New Country*, August 30. Accessed June 15, 2018. https://ftw.usatoday.com/2016/08/donald-trump-colin-kaepernick-new-country-national-anthem-protest-response.

# CHAPTER 5

# Negative Objectives: The Right-Wing Media Circle and Everyone Else

Everything that has happened in the last fifty years opened the door for something else, something new to fill the media space available and provide a counter to the perceived liberal bias besetting conservatives. What materialized was incredibly profitable, notably successful, and it had culture-changing effects on American politics.

The argument that the media are liberally biased inspired conservatives to work hard in order to get their point of view into the public space. Despite the fact that there are now conservative voices dominating politics, the perception that the conservative media are victims of persecuting unfairness persists, allowing for a persecuted tone on the right. The argument that conservatives remain oppressed has encouraged an enduring defensiveness that belies the success of the right-wing media. Conservatives dominate talk radio, outnumbering their liberal counterparts by a wide margin with far bigger audiences. *Fox News* has been the number one rated cable news program (by a wide margin) every single month for over 16 years. *Breitbart* was so successful that its boss became a senior advisor to a president. The network of distinctly right-wing media outlets might be small in number compared to the mainstream media, but their power and influence are formidable, thanks to a very devoted and substantial audience. Until relatively recently, the mainstream media had been the principal force in the American news system; they started big, stayed vast, and they did not change. Their audiences remain considerable, but so too are their competition, which means that the audience of the mainstream news media is far more fragmented

© The Author(s) 2019
A. Dagnes, *Super Mad at Everything All the Time*,
https://doi.org/10.1007/978-3-030-06131-9_5

than that of the right-wing media circle. The right-wing media grew in strength, audience, and political power, but despite their ascendancy, they continue to rail against the mainstream media, to the point that they have spun off into a wholly separate ideological communication system.

We are polarized and we are angry, but our media split is not one of equal division. On one side is the large expanse of the mainstream media, which includes news outlets that maintain journalistic ethics plus those that are purposely leftist, and on the other side is a small circle, tightly closed, self-reinforcing, furious, oppositional, and very different from their opposition. While conservative news sources have existed for decades as direct responses to the perceived liberal mainstream media, today a very selective right-wing media sphere views *everything* outside of their circle as not only insufficiently conservative, but antagonistically liberal. Will Sommer is a writer for *The Daily Beast* and an expert in right-wing media. He publishes a tipsheet called "Right Richter," and I asked him about the major players in the right-wing media circle. Together we identified the following:

| Internet | Television | Talk Radio |
| --- | --- | --- |
| Drudge | Fox News | Rush Limbaugh |
| Breitbart | Sinclair Broadcasting | Sean Hannity |
| Daily Caller | One America News | Mark Levin |
| Red State | | Dennis Praeger |
| Daily Wire | | Laura Ingraham |
| Newsmax | | Salem Broadcasting |
| InfoWars | | |
| Town Hall | | |
| Gateway Pundit | | |
| Western Journal | | |

CRTV (Sommer, Editor, Right Richter 2018a)

These outlets are united in their political positions, although they tend to focus on specific issues and give short shrift to others. I spoke with Howard Polskin who publishes a tipsheet called "TheRighting," and he told me that several common subjects appear within this circle: "Anti-immigration, the boarders, anti-intellectualism... they don't like professors. Anti-Hollywood, anti-elitism, anything transgendered – that's such a hot button – anti-Hillary and Bill. You can see the big themes emerging" (Polskin 2018).

This influence sphere shares not only an ideological viewpoint, but their frequently stated purpose is predicated on exposing, antagonizing, or fighting everyone else. Outlets are clear in their stated missions of providing purposely conservative content while poking the liberal mainstream media in the eye. For example, *Breitbart* states that their content is "curated and written specifically for the new generation of independent and conservative thinkers." The head of *One American News Network* (OANN) states that their goal is to "provide a platform where more voices can be heard, voices that are ignored, libertarian and conservative voices." And from the *Western Journal*: "Every day, WesternJournal.com publishes conservative, libertarian, free market and pro-family writers and broadcasters." This is markedly different from a legacy outlet that purports to be an actual news organization. Being purposely conservative means that these outlets come to the news of the day with a preexisting angle they want to emphasize, and they frequently reaffirm an argument or line of thinking from another conservative organization within the circle. They do so while taking glee in opposing their perceived antagonists. Examples of the liberal eye poking: *Daily Wire* posts: "Our goal is simple: unmask leftists in the media for who they are, destroy their credibility with the American public, and devastate their funding bases." From *Gateway Pundit*: "We report the truth - And leave the Russia-Collusion fairy tale to the Conspiracy media."

Players in this circle are argumentative and unrepentant, and their audience is adamant of their virtues, faithful adherents to their messaging. When the right-wing media circle posits a narrative which is repeated on multiple platforms, their audience believes it and adheres to it faithfully, regardless of accuracy. Even with the abundance of news and political content available, right-wing media consumers tend to read, watch, and listen within this bubble, dividing the public between the faithful and the non-believers.

The upshot of this entirely separate system is that the American public now have two wholly detached versions of the truth and are completely untrusting of the other side, consistently asking how someone reading, listening, or watching the opposing media could possibly believe what it reports. Those on the right are aghast at the dominance of *The New York Times* and declare its liberal bias without having to produce one single example as evidence, calling the mainstream media "fake news" without data to back this up. Those outside the right-wing media circle are gobsmacked by the opinions shared within the circle and have no clue as to how they came up with these perspectives to begin with, casting everything within the circle as fraudulent, without making important distinctions or understanding why they believe as they do. This ideological divorce came about for all of the reasons already articulated in this book: the 50-year rage against the liberal media, the technology that expanded options, the money that could be made from this technological boom, and the polarization that is currently chocking our political system. The outcome of these factors colliding is an information system with two truths, forcing two sides, increasing our national anger. The disconnect between the media spheres has led to several interrelated dilemmas.

One important problem is that most people are sick to death of the news. A study from the Pew Center reports that 7 in 10 Americans have news fatigue, the sensation of being so overwhelmed by information that people check out (Gottfried and Barthel 2018). Those who stay engaged are the people who are the angriest, which means that they are fed a consistent diet of rage to keep them going. This happens across all political media platforms, regardless of ideology, and it further increases the vitriol. Because many Americans are worn out by the volume and tone of the news, the outrage machine has to work extra hard to attract new, less engaged people as an audience. The combination of these two factors is that just when people think the conversation has turned nastier than ever before, it gets worse. Not only that, the nastiness becomes normalized and the ever-increasing wrathful rhetoric bleeds down to everyday vernacular and keeps the volume raised nonstop because the uncivil ferocity and rage spewed in the media are contagious. Examples abound. On the left, Rep. Maxine Waters (D-CA) called on the public to publically shame members of the Trump administration. After receiving death threats in response to this call for uncivil behavior, Waters said: "If you shoot me, you'd better shoot straight. Because there's nothing like a wounded animal" (King 2018). President Trump responded on Twitter that Waters was "an extraordinarily low IQ person" in one tweet, and in another: "Crazy Maxine Waters, said by some to be one of the most corrupt people in politics, is rapidly becoming, together with Nancy Pelosi, the FACE of the Democrat Party. Her ranting and raving, even referring to herself as a wounded animal, will make people flee the Democrats!" This prompted continued and increased personal vitriol against Rep. Waters on one side, on the other myriad cases of Americans approaching administration officials in public places just to yell at them. Elsewhere, former Trump campaign staffer Cory Lewandowski appeared on *Fox News* and said "Womp womp" in response to the story of an immigrant child with Down Syndrome separated from his mother (Haag 2018). Ten days later in Huntsville, Alabama, a man was arrested for yelling "WOMP WOMP!" and brandishing a gun during immigration rally (Selk 2018a).[1] The tone in this country is contagious, encouraged by our leaders, and the spread of hostility is seemingly infinite. So that's one problem.

Another problem is that the missions of the mainstream and right-wing media circles are dissimilar, and thus, the news and opinions coming from either are disconnected. The mainstream news media is generally comprised of the so-called legacy outlets, news organizations that have produced journalism for decades. Their goal is to remain solvent amidst massive competition while holding on to the norms of a profession that seems to be shifting under their feet. New, digitally native outlets have to elbow their way onto a crowded field of traditional and established outlets, all of whom compete against one another. Conversely, the mission of the right-wing media circle is to oppose those outside of it at all costs, which means the first thing to come from inside the circle is an accusation against their opponent. Seeing themselves in a foxhole, they do not compete against one another as much as they fight for attention and audience support. They are accommodating of their ideological position above all, returning to their stands, sometimes regardless of fact. This creates an entirely separate set of "truths," facts, and realities that are detached from one another. Some argue that the partisan news of today is reminiscent of the past and that the objective journalistic standards of the twentieth century were the anomaly. While elements of this might be true, what we have now is way more than a partisan news system; we have two entirely separate spheres of information dissemination and two distinctly singular interpretations of the news.

A compounding issue is that the President of the United States not only endorses this separate media system, but also encourages the opposition. Consistently calling the mainstream media "fake," the president casts doubt on any news outlet that does not wholly support him and views the right-wing media ecosystem as the sole source of legitimate information. This has a similar trickle-down effect to the spread of vitriolic language. Trump has called the press the "enemy of the people," and in doing so encouraged others to treat the press similarly. At rallies, Trump fires up his supporters with chants of "CNN sucks!" He consistently encourages his base to spew venom at the White House press corps traveling him on trips. But even more than this trickle-down vilification to the public, the President of the USA sets an example for other politicians to follow. A spokesman for the Environmental Protection Agency called a reporter a "piece of trash" (Greenwood 2018). Officials at the department of Health and Human Services tweeted out personal insults to sitting senators who were critical of the president, and one of these staffers has a license plate that reads: "FAKENWS" (Diamond 2018). This kind of anti-press rhetoric is as communicable as the uncivil discourse already discussed, both of which are unhelpful in a deliberative democracy where the First Amendment guarantees press freedom.

The anti-press bombast also profoundly affects trust in the news media, and not surprisingly the distrust is more prominent on the right. A 2018 poll showed that 92% of Republicans think that traditional news outlets knowingly report false or misleading stories (Fischer, 92% of Republicans Think Media Intentionally Reports Fake News 2018b). Democrats, on the other hand, trust the news far more, which leads to an uncomfortable divergence of information. When the stories and news accounts inside the right-wing media circle differ from those in the mainstream media circle, the audience not only believes that the right-wing media circle is right, but right 100% of the time *and* they believe the mainstream media is purposely deceiving them.

The final and, perhaps, most complicating problem is that as wide as the mainstream circle is, the right-wing media circle is limited. Outlets within the circle are conservative, and some do exemplary political reporting and analysis, but the most striking quality of the right-wing media circle is that such a small group of outlets vary dramatically in their validity. The right-wing media circle includes major, dominant outlets like *Fox News* and conspiracy-laden, fact-deficient outlets like *InfoWars*. Additionally, major players within the circle play footsie with extremists, as members of the alt-right are one part of the devoted audience base. These fringe elements are given legitimacy by high-ranking journalists and politicos who link, share, and approve of their messages. This muddies the waters inside the circle, blending fact, fiction, conspiracy, and racism together. President Trump's son, Donald Trump Jr., is one mainstream figure who has helped mix up the sources. Trump Jr. has spread conspiracy theories about the so-called deep state, likes and shares material from fringe figures, and keeps the alt-right engaged with the Trump presidency. This kind of mainstreaming means that extremists are mixed in with the rest of the right-wing media circle, and is one big reason that those outside the circle say that Trump supporters are racist.

All put together, there are reasons that the right-wing media circle evolved, grew, and now dominate, but there are serious problems that emerge from these entirely unconnected media circles. The media polarization separates us both expressively and practically; the divergent information orbits in which we communicate lead to the kind of exaggerated enmity that now mark our political discourse. It is dangerous for a democratic system, built on compromise, to operate in such a toxic climate. Examined in this chapter are the different media spheres that exist, and the ways that polarization is found in, and fed by, the news media we have today.

## Ideological Media: Development and Types

People frequently use the term "news," sometimes without specification or accuracy. There are two different realms of "news," one having to do with actual news and the other not so much. The primary function of the actual news media is to inform through journalism, where reporters and investigators go out to find the facts of an event, and then describe these facts in enough detail to explain a situation clearly. This definition of news also includes analysis, which is where opinion works its way into the factual description of events. In real journalism, opinion is important because the truth can be complicated and analysis offers ways of making sense of the world. In most newspapers, analysis is labeled clearly so as not to confuse the readers. These journalistic outlets specifically delineate news from analysis with an emphasis on the first, rather than the second. More common today are "news" organizations that provide abundant commentary on the work supplied by actual journalists without doing much reporting of their own.

This is the other kind of news outlet, one where opinion reigns and facts are fungible, and this is where the modern partisan press is situated. Unlike a journalist who deals in facts, a pundit is someone who opines. Punditry itself is not a bad thing; analysis is important and different perspectives can be enlightening, but opinion without a basis in fact is not analysis. Modern punditry is less informed and far more strident than it has been in the past and it is more prevalent. Talk radio was an early pioneer in opinion delivery as hosts have to fill hours of airtime with enough entertainment to maintain their listening audience. This evolved to television where cable news channels have stocked their morning and prime-time lineups with pundits who are similarly entertaining in their rage.

Building on cable news punditry, the idea of ideological news spin grew even more dramatically with the Internet, and as a result, today there is *much* more opinion to be found than there is straight-up journalism.

In 2008, scholars Kathleen Hall Jamieson and Joseph Cappella published a seminal book about the conservative media of this time called *Echo Chamber* (Jamieson and Cappella 2008). The echo chamber in question consisted of talk radio and *Fox News*, and the system that Jamieson and Cappella examined was the forerunner to the right-wing media circle we have today. They traced the rise of talk radio from the expansion of FM in the 1960s and 1970s, which opened up radio space significantly. Into the void came the radio hosts who may have inspired the expression: "talk is cheap." The end of the Fairness Doctrine in 1985, paved the way for an all-opinion, all the time radio broadcast and thus began the talk radio revolution of the 1980s and 1990s. Jamieson and Cappella identified the most important players in this echo chamber, and these players remain essential today. Leading the pack was Rush Limbaugh, the king of talk radio. Prominent conservative politicians went on his show because his listening audience was devoted and active, which granted "El Rushbo" greater strength. Limbaugh's dominance made him the unofficial head of the Republican Party at times. Other talk radio hosts followed his example to become important conservative media figures themselves. Limbaugh remained the undisputed champ of talk radio until 2018 when *Talkers* magazine ranked Sean Hannity #1 above Limbaugh for the first time (ever) in their annual "Heavy Hundred" list of powerful hosts (Ho 2018). Other talk radio hosts followed Rush's model, and Glenn Beck, Laura Ingraham, Mark Levin, and Dennis Prager became popular and powerful within conservative circles. The success of talk radio naturally opened the door to television punditry, which was helped greatly by cable technology.

If broadcast news is called this because it transmits news broadly, ideologically opinionated news can be considered narrowcasting. There are reasons for media organizations to narrowcast their news, most of which (not surprisingly) have to do with money. According to Hunter College economist Lisa George, cutting price only works so much, because news organizations have to have edge in a highly competitive media climate. This is how partisanship intensified during the cable expansion of the 1990s. With so many new cable TV channel options available, targeting a loyal audience and meeting their needs was an ideal solution to market fragmentation. While fact-based journalism and nuanced analysis have their places, they run in short supply on the airwaves. If 24-hour cable news channels have taught us nothing, they have been instructive as to the abundance of time and space to fill. With a glut of airtime and infinite possibilities, news producers worked hard to attract an audience. Early in the cable revolution, television executives figured out that the news alone was not interesting or abundant enough to hold an audience for 24 hours.[2] Hence, there was an explosion of the kind of chat-show, news-adjacent programming once reserved for Sunday mornings on broadcast networks. This was lucrative for the cable networks because punditry is less expensive than journalism, and it proved to be immensely entertaining for the public because it inspired an audience to put on their jerseys and root for a team. This bred audience loyalty as it increased the partisan divide and raked in ad revenue for the cable news networks. It appeared to be a win-win-win.

It was a successful formula because so-called news junkies tend toward the partisan anyway, that so-called base of political enthusiasts. This created a built-in audience, and it worked because partisanship blossoms in passionate disagreement. While the yelling on cable news is abundant today, it was not always so heated. Televised political wrangling first appeared several decades ago when two intellectuals debated the politics of the day from opposing ideological sides. *Firing Line* was hosted by William F. Buckley from 1966 to 1999, and was the longest running show of its kind. Buckley allowed his guests to articulate their arguments against his arguments, an idea that today seems extraordinary. Buckley made the show unique, an intellectual discussion between equals who could disagree agreeably. Norman Mailer once described Buckley as a combination of "commodore of the yacht club, Joseph Goebbels, Robert Mitchum, Maverick, Savonarola, the nice prep school kid next door, and the snows of yesteryear." Quoted in a *Salon* piece about the ending of the show in 1999, Bill Kristol said: "Buckley really believes that in order to convince, you have to debate and not just preach, which of course means risking the possibility that someone will beat you in debate" (Lehman 1999). Buckley rarely lost a debate, but he was willing to take that risk in order to articulate a conservative point of view on television to a larger audience. *Firing Line* was a different way for Buckley to bring conservatism onto the liberal media, and according to the 1999 piece in *Salon*, Buckley "went out of his way to include other points of view." Victor Navasky, who was the editor of *The Nation* at the time, was quoted in that 1999 article that he would miss the program when it went off the air. When asked what he would miss about it, Navasky responded that he would miss "Buckley's raised eyebrow, his sneering tone and his predictable, and sometimes eloquent, statements of his Neanderthal perspective" (Lehman 1999). A cutting observation, perhaps, but a thoroughly civil one.

This civility began to slip as the TV medium expanded and *Firing Line* inspired imitators. Tossing aside the lengthy responses and courteous debate, these shows emphasized a more dramatic kind of fight. Shows like *Agronsky and Company*, *The McLaughlin Group*, and the original *Crossfire* featured ideologically opposed DC insiders yelling about policies and elections and politicians. In 1996, Howard Kurtz, now on *Fox News*, was a *Washington Post* media reporter and he wrote a book called *Hot Air* about the new media culture of partisan bickering. Comparing *The McLaughlin Group* (which featured journalists yelling at each other), to *The PBS News Hour with Jim Lehrer* (which did not), Kurtz described the impetus for all the shouting and drama; the public did not want to think. They wanted to be amused:

> If people wanted high-minded journalism, more of them would watch Jim Lehrer. In a talk show nation, as John McLaughlin understands all too well, viewers want to be entertained. On that score, he has delivered in a way that has changed the very nature of talking-head television. The cardinal sin in the Age of McLaughlin is to be boring. (Kurtz 1996)

The yelling grew even louder when 24-hour news outlets had to keep things interesting, avoid the boring, and make their audiences devoted followers. That is when the networks began to take sides. Starting with *Fox News Channel* in the late 1990s and continuing into the twenty-first century, the American news media moved in a kind of Big Sort of their own.

*Fox News* was the first of its kind, forging a new path to political niche programming by claiming it was the antidote to the liberal media. During the Bush (43) administration, *Fox News* received talking points from the White House and the right side of the ideological spectrum stayed on message. Jamieson and Capella's echo chamber illustrated how Republican leaders and conservative media figures created a feedback loop that both enhanced the goals of the GOP while marginalizing the mainstream news media, and it was the successful beginning of the system to come. Lest we believe that the demonization of the mainstream media is something new and original, one needs only to look back to this echo chamber of ideological press during the Bush years. In a 2005 piece for *The Nation*, noted media scholar Eric Alterman wrote that two Bush officials spoke about the way that administration was able to use the media to speak directly to their supporters. These officials sound as if they work for Trump today:

> We're an empire now, and when we act, we create our own reality. And while you're studying that reality–judiciously, as you will–we'll act again, creating other new realities, which you can study too, and that's how things will sort out. We're history's actors...and you, all of you, will be left to just study what we do.' For those who didn't like it, another Bush adviser explained, 'Let me clue you in. We don't care. You see, you're out-numbered two to one by folks in the big, wide middle of America, busy working people who don't read the *New York Times* or *Washington Post* or the *LA Times*. (Alterman 2005)

This sounds so familiar to what is currently the state of the polarized media, with a heavy emphasis on the standard anti-coastal elite argument that pits "real Americans" against the effete and out of touch media snobs. This was even before the right-wing media circle included ideological Web sites, which expanded reach and intensified the opposition. These ideological sites link to other right-wing sources, which helps to provide a carefully culled set of resources. They connect personally with their audience, and they provide online conduits for radio and television content providers. They also encourage and engross the most engaged activists in politics today, because people are able to bond immediately online from far-away places. Together, these Web sites helped foment the right-wing media ecosystem that we have today.

Initially, Internet activism came from the left. While the conservative echo chamber was gaining influence in the Bush (43) administration, Democrats became early web innovators. In 2004, presidential candidate Howard Dean was one of the first politicians to go online to organize meetups and coordinate support. During the Bush years, as the Republicans were coordinating their messaging efforts on talk radio and cable, the left began to organize their opposition online. *Axios* mapped the launch of 89 political Web sites in the past 20 years and, not surprisingly, found that there was a rise in left-leaning sites during the Bush years (Fischer, The Recent Explosion of Right-Wing News Sites 2017).

Fighting against something is easy and entertaining; indignation and wrath are communicable emotions. During the early years of the twenty-first century, the Democrats had both advantages of out-party indignation and online savvy, and they used these to push against a president with whom they clamorously disagreed. When Obama came to town, the right-wing sites grew in number and strength. Thus, beginning with the conservative echo chamber and the new online activism of the left, two distinctly ideological media systems began to take shape. The left-wing media differs from the mainstream media, but both are outside of the right-wing media ecosystem, and this is why we have different truths today.

## LEFT-WING MEDIA

Despite the cries of conservative hostility to this idea, there is a difference between the left-wing ideological media and the mainstream press. The left-wing ideological media began in print with *The Nation* and *Mother Jones* and expanded its offerings from there. When the purposely left-wing media is called "liberal," they respond with something akin to "heck YEAH we're liberal." It is a collection of outlets operating on different platforms and includes not only political blogs and magazines and cable news pundits, but also entertainment personalities and celebrities. All of whom are resolutely and proudly progressive. *MSNBC's* evening pundit lineup is comprised entirely of leftist thinkers and talking heads, and their *Morning Joe* program is ostensibly hosted by a conservative, former Republican congressman Joe Scarboro. But this is the show that was described to me in an interview (off the record) as the show that liberals watch to prove to their friends that they can stomach conservatives... which makes the show not very conservative at all. *MSNBC* does not have the ratings or influence that *Fox News* does, and thus seeing it as the cable response to *Fox News* is erroneous, but it is staunchly leftist. Liberal Web sites now have Donald Trump, a singular figure at whom they may bark, and consequently, sites like *Talking Points Memo, Daily Kos, Think Progress, Crooks and Liars*, and *Alternet* have audiences as dedicated as those who adhere to the right-wing blogs. Also in the "firmly liberal" column are now the late-night talk shows on broadcast, marrying into the comedic family of liberal satirists on cable. My past research investigated why political satire leans left[3] which is how I can say with some authority that there was an existing liberal bias in political comedy. What is different today, as discussed in the previous chapter, is that a sharp left turn has taken place on the formerly apolitical late-night talk shows on broadcast television. These are the purposely left-wing media structures, but they do not form the kind of sphere of the right-wing media circle.

This is where false equivalencies and what-about-isms are most frequently flung. When confronted with the idea of a right-wing media circle with *Fox News* as its epicenter, many consumers of the circle's content will say "what about *MSNBC?*" In truth, most of the media organizations within the right-wing ecosystem garner more attention (quantified with ratings and web traffic) and have more influence on their audience than the outlets on the left have with theirs. This is why comparing the two is in intellectually dishonest.

The liberal media line up does not conjoin the way that the right-wing media outlets do for several reasons. Conservatives argue that left-wing coordination is unnecessary because the larger mainstream media are already so liberal, but journalists push back against this characterization. The mainstream media will rarely collaborate with ideological outlets for fear of being branded as biased themselves. Additionally, unlike the right-wing media, the left lacks a singular narrative under which they can unite. To quote Will Rogers: "Democrats never agree on anything, that's why they're Democrats. If they agreed with each other, they'd be Republicans" (Rogers n.d.). Finally, many of the efforts designed specifically to produce a purely liberal media outlet have historically fallen flat. For example, *Air America* was launched in 2004 to serve as a counter-balance to the dominance of right-wing talk radio. The network had a purposely leftist slant and was not short on talent: prominent personalities included Al Franken, Janeane Garofalo, Rachel Maddow, Lizz Winstead, Sam Seder, Cenk Uygur, and Marc Maron. It did not last. It floundered financially several years into its existence and then folded for good in 2010, not for lack of trying. More recently, a new progressive OTT video service called the *Political Voices Network* was launched to try to respond to the right-wing OTT sites such as CRTV, *The Blaze*, and *One American News Network*. This video service aims to tap into the streaming trend while it provides an alternative to the conservative options already running (Fischer, New Streaming Network Launching for Liberals 2018a). Too new to gauge its success, it joins an already crowded OTT landscape. None of these streaming services has the audience or strength of an actual television network, but instead adds to a larger ideological network. That the left is trying to do this illustrates the power of the right-wing media ecosystem, and at the same time, it helps to show that these streaming networks, at least for now, are not the natural competition to legacy broadcasting.

It is likely that because much of the public regards the mainstream media as liberal, having an *actual* liberal media is either redundant or simply too niche to be a formidable entity of its own. As a result, the left-wing media circle is simply not as strong or influential as their counterpart on the right. Even with out-party anger, the left-wing media does not compete with the right-wing ideological media. It also does not garner the attention of the mass public (or of political elites) the way the mainstream media does.

## THE MAINSTREAM MEDIA

There is an important difference between journalism and political puffery: journalists find the news stories sometimes referred to as "original fact reporting" and political puffery provides spin about the findings. In between is punditry, which runs along a continuum from thoughtful exploration to partisan howling. These three forms of content blend into a mishmash, which can be confusing for the news audience who are inundated with information and have way too many options to peruse. As former CNN reporter Frank Sesno said: "One of the dangers is thinking that people know the difference between the editorial page and the front page, between a commentator or pundit commenting on something alongside a reporter who's supposed to be providing facts. In this environment, when you have news, talking points and opinions all colliding, it can be really disorienting to the audience" (Farhi, Sean Hannity Thinks Viewers Can Tell the Difference Between News and Opinion. Hold on a Moment 2017a). News organizations and pundits assist in this confusion. Calling something "news" does not necessarily make it so; viewers frequently turn on the *Cable News Network (CNN)* to see three or more guests yelling at one another. That is not exactly "news." Similarly, calling oneself a "journalist" does not a reporter make. *Fox News* pundit Sean Hannity has called himself an "opinion journalist" or an "advocacy journalist," which is a confluence of meanings and essentially nonsensical. When organizations with "news" in their name provide commentary and information in a seamless blend, the confusion is understandable. Along these lines *CBS* White House correspondent Major Garrett made an emphatic point to me about the difference, because news organizations provide so much material which should not be weighted evenly: "Journalism isn't content" (Garrett 2017). In a time when the politics is so prevalent in the minds of the American public, it is easy to lose sight of the differentiation. This is why it is similarly essential to make distinctions between the mainstream news media and the left-wing political media.

In 2017, the *Washington Post's* Erik Wemple crafted a working definition of "mainstream news media," a term used rather disparagingly in the past decade.[4] Wemple uses the first two rows of the White House briefing room seating chart to determine the most important "mainstream news" outlets (see chart below) and notes that *Fox News* is in the front row. He also makes an important distinction between the news and opinions sides of *Fox*, quoting *Fox's* White House correspondent John Roberts (who used to work at *CNN* and *CBS* as well) to say he is as scrappy and challenging a reporter as the other White House reporters in the room (Wemple 2017).

The ideal of the "news media" is to be original and provide factual reporting. The models taught in journalism schools uphold an unbiased standard rooted within a storytelling structure that emphasizes detail and fact, in order to inform rather than to persuade. For these purposes, the mainstream news media are defined as outlets who gather facts and are regarded as important enough to have permanent seats in the front two rows of the White House briefing room. Arguably, the White House beat is for reporters whose job it is to break important news about the most important politician in the world.

### The White House Briefing Room Permanent Seats

| Broadcast | Cable news | Wire services | Radio | Print |
| --- | --- | --- | --- | --- |
| ABC | CNN | Associated Press | CBS Radio | New York Times |
| CBS | Fox News | Reuters | NPR | Washington Post |
| NBC | | Bloomberg | AP Radio | Wall Street Journal |
| | | McClatchy | ABC Radio | National Journal |

The most prominent outlets within the mainstream media are considered "legacy" outlets because they have been in the news business for a very long time. This is a chronology of news sources with White House Briefing Room seats:

| News organization | Year founded |
| --- | --- |
| Associated Press | 1849 |
| The New York Times | 1851 |
| Reuters News Service | 1851 |
| McClatchy News Service | 1857 |
| The Washington Post | 1877 |
| The Wall Street Journal | 1889 |
| CBS | 1927 |
| NBC | 1940 |
| ABC | 1951 |
| National Journal | 1969 |
| National Public Radio | 1970 |
| CNN | 1980 |
| Fox News | 1996 |

Almost all of these news companies have been in journalism long enough to have a traditional view of their roles and duties. Reporters from these news outlets see themselves as fact-finders, informing the public of the events of the day from an objective perch. Yet this definition is imperfect because there are so many interpretations of the mainstream media. Former Alaska Governor Sarah Palin famously referred to it as the "lamestream media" and the right generally agrees with this characterization. The left has a problem with the mainstream media as well, as articulated by Noam Chomsky who defines it as a series of corporate-owned and controlled outlets bent on brainwashing the viewing public. As with most things, where you stand depends on where you sit.

The most important quality of the mainstream news media is that their profitability rests entirely on their reputations as neutral fact-finders, and to bring in revenue these outlets compete against one another to break news and report stories first. For example, the way the *New York Times*, *Washington Post*, and *Wall Street Journal* make money is through their investigative journalism, which is why they still fight so hard against one another to break major stories. Media critic James Warren wrote a piece for *Vanity Fair's Hive* that was called "Is *The New York Times* vs *The Washington Post* vs Trump The Last Great Newspaper War?" Warren chronicled these two newspaper giants as they expand staff and tech in order to stay powerful and ferociously compete against one another. An important point is that the competition between the two is keeping both legacy newspapers afloat. Writes Warren: "Breaking story after story, two great American newspapers, *The New York Times* and *The Washington Post*, are resurgent, with record readerships" (Warren 2017).

The competition between major mainstream media outlets has been so profitable; the resulting economic growth actually has a name: The Trump Bump. This refers to the financial gains of certain news outlets thanks to the chaos of the Trump White House, led by a showman with roots in the entertainment business. There is subsequent growth in many national news organizations that cover politics and the White House, and with their eyes on 2020 some of the biggest names n journalism are staffing up. *The New York Times, Washington Post, The Atlantic, the Los Angeles Times,* and *Politico* are all adding reporters (Allen, Trump Media Frenzy Grows: Politics on Steroids, 24/7 2018).

Digitally native news sites such as *Vox, Politico, Buzzfeed,* and the sky-rocketing *Axios,* join them within the mainstream media. Additionally, there are also news-adjacent outlets, like the morning shows on broadcast television, which produce political content among other fare. *ABC's* "Good Morning America," *CBS's* "This Morning," and *NBC's* "Today Show" uphold the "broad" aspect of broadcasting and aim right down the middle through story selection, content production, and guest selection. As politics continues to spread into our other cultural areas, some previously nonpolitical and centrist productions have become more politicized, which makes them difficult to categorize.

This is one of the most significant challenges for the mainstream media; because the news has morphed into different forms thanks to constantly evolving technology, identifying a straight mainstream news outlet beyond the well-established and prominent legacy media organizations can be tricky. A complicating factor is that the definition of "news" is increasingly fuzzy. When push alerts breathlessly notify citizens about policy debates and vote totals, presidential tweets, and celebrity scandals equally, it is challenging to identify the "mainstream news." At its essence, the mainstream news media has minimal partisan bias and does original reporting of the facts. But because conservatives have so effectively railed against the mainstream media, convincing people that a mainstream outlet has minimal partisan bias presents a substantial challenge. This is why so many conservatives stick within the right-wing media circle; they are increasingly untrusting of the mainstream media. This distrust, however, is universal and the left cocoons themselves within their own media filter bubble, although this bubble is more expansive. In 2017, four researchers from Harvard analyzed "hyperlinking patterns, social media sharing patterns on Facebook and Twitter, and topic and language patterns" to help explain how news consumers on the left and right shared stories and linked to other sites. They had a very large sample (1.25 million stories, published by 25,000 sources) to determine the news media diet of different Americans (Benkler et al. 2017). They found sorting on both the right and the left, but by plotting their data points about who links and shares to which media source, the researchers found that the left-wing media circle was not nearly as tight as the right-wing circle. By focusing on pro-Clinton and pro-Trump audiences, researchers found that the pro-Clinton audience engaged with legacy media outlets, while the pro-Trump audiences stayed within their circle:

> The size of the nodes marking traditional professional media like *The New York Times, The Washington Post*, and *CNN*, surrounded by *the Hill, ABC, and NBC*, tell us that these media drew particularly large audiences. Their color tells us that Clinton followers attended to them more than Trump followers, and their proximity on the map to more quintessentially partisan sites—like *Huffington Post, MSNBC*, or *the Daily Beast*—suggests that attention to these more partisan outlets on the left was more tightly interwoven with attention to traditional media. The *Breitbart*-centered wing, by contrast, is farther from the mainstream set and lacks bridging nodes that draw attention and connect it to that mainstream. (Benkler et al. 2017)

The left-wing cocoon includes both purposely liberal outlets and news organizations within the mainstream news media. It is larger, fragmented, and more widespread: less a circle than a splotch. In other words, there are two media spheres but they are not equal in size, scope, or concentration. The right-wing media circle is vastly different from the rest of the media, both left and mainstream, in its mission and its audience.

## THE RIGHT-WING MEDIA CIRCLE

The modern right-wing media circle has a distinctive character from the left-wing and mainstream media, and utilizes very specific tactics. Taking the existing conservative narrative of liberal media bias and amplifying it dramatically, the warrior journalists in the right-wing media bubble believe they are the sole providers of the truth. Matt Boyle, the Washington editor of *Breitbart*, gave a speech in DC in the summer of 2017, which McKay Coppins detailed in the *Columbia Journalism Review*:

'Journalistic integrity is dead,' [Boyle] declared. 'There is no such thing anymore. So everything is about weaponization of information.' Standing behind a mahogany podium in a baggy dark suit, Boyle preached with the confidence of a true believer. In a stuttering staccato, he condemned the nation's preeminent news outlets as 'corrupted institutions,' 'built on a lie,' and a criminal 'syndicate that needs to be dismantled.' Boyle and his compatriots were laboring to usher in an imminent—and glorious—journalistic apocalypse. 'We envision a day when CNN is no longer in business. We envision a day when *The New York Times* closes its doors. I think that day is possible.' (Coppins 2017)

This is the essence of the right-wing media circle's vision: It is them against the world. This circle is isolated, reinforcing, and unchallenging of those whom they support. Separate from the rest of political media, those within this circle maintain that all others beyond their own sphere of influence are defective. Beyond merely taking a conservative stand in their reporting and punditry, as had been done in the past, this new system takes a far more aggressive position, predicated on the idea that everyone is liberal. Lloyd Grove of *The Daily Beast* said it well: "To the right-wing media, every other form of media is left leaning and the legacy media, *CNN, The New York Times*, etc., they will insist that from now until doomsday that their journalism is unbiased.... And those of us in the mainstream media vehement resist the notion that we are left-wing, but that's the organizing principal [of the those on the right]" (Grove 2017). The end-state is winning the war against the left.

To the right-wing media, there is little to no distinction between the journalism found in major legacy newspapers and *MSNBC* pundit Rachel Maddow; the "fake news" mainstream media is an entity without demarcations or differentiation. This puts the right-wing media into an unusual stance that is both defensive and offensive concomitantly; defensive because they claim to be victims of anti-conservative discrimination and offensive because, as *Breitbart's* Boyle stated in the summer of 2017, their goal is the "full destruction and elimination of the entire mainstream media" (Coppins 2017). This has staggering effects on what is called gatekeeping, which is the ability of a news organization to shape the public's political awareness through story selection. What the right-wing media covers, and the stories that they refuse to report, are important indicators of their own biases. They cover the stories that fit into their narratives, reaffirming other organizations within their sphere while they buttress a narrative. When a major story breaks that is damning to the right-wing media's narrative or to their heroes, they frequently and willfully ignore the story or give it short shrift. The only competition within the right-wing media circle is for clicks and traffic, and this is accomplished not by breaking news but by being first with the narrative that the circle has already established. *Daily Beast* reporter Will Sommer noted that this collection runs as a well-oiled machine. Within the right-wing media ecosystem, there is an established messaging pattern where information goes from Internet to talk radio to *Fox News* and then around again. As these narratives circulate within the right-wing media circle, they strengthen and spread since the outlets confirm what their mates are reporting. The audience of the right-wing media circle will hear the same storylines on a multitude of platforms, which buoys the stories and adds support of their veracity.

The undisputed center of this circle is *Fox* because it extends from mainstream audiences into the circle. It is popular, employs credentialed journalists, and is easily accessed by its older audience. *Fox News* is also the originator of the kind of ideological information system we have today; they have the experience and a record of success. It was the first of its kind to show that "news need not be *about* politics but can *be* politics":

> Using the genre of news as a cover, *Fox* confidently creates and dramatizes all sorts of contestable and debatable ideas about public life using the codes and conventions of established journalistic practice. And through this confluence of niche audiences, feelings of community, ideological performance, and news genre, *Fox* has established itself as the most successful cable news operation in the United States. (Jones 2012)

Accordingly, *Fox News* is the center of the circle, and the other outlets help feed the cable channel with guests and they reaffirm *Fox's* narratives. The right-wing Web sites posture aggressively are enormously popular, vital in their ability to attract and maintain and engaged (and enraged) audience. One young conservative activist told me that "the left innovates and the right perfects." Just as left-wing ideological sites originated in opposition to the Bush (43) administration, some of the most influential right-wing sites launched in furious conflict against Barack Obama. They have grown influential, in no small part thanks to the support of other outlets within the sphere. When these right-wing sites joined the existing echo chamber of *Fox News* and talk radio, the influence circle began to solidify. The difference between these sites and those on the left is that the right-wing sites grew stronger and connected to other conservative platforms more directly. There is some overlap between outlets, and perhaps the greatest strength of the news organizations within the ecosystem is the way they consistently reaffirm the narratives set to oppose their antagonists.

*Buzzfeed* reporter Charlie Warzel writes about the right-wing media and has his own tipsheet called *InfoWarzel*, the title being a mashup of the conspiracy Web site *InfoWars* and his last name. Warzel crafted a theory called the "Upside Down Media" to help explain how this reinforcing circle of messaging and misinformation works. Similar to Sommer, Warzel sees an informal connection between media outlets that is reinforcing and supportive:

> Each new bit from every new actor plays off the last and each outlet lends its own brand of spin (from *Gateway Pundit's* total skewing of the truth to Drudge's incendiary headlines to *Infowars'* focus on set-ups and conspiracy). They're a well-oiled machine at this point. And by the time a good debunk of all of this pops up, they'll simply ignore it and then say, 'meh, we don't care about that anymore' and manufacture the next false outrage. (Kafka 2017)

Since many of these right-wing media figures featured on these different mediums appear across varying platforms, they can provide the kind of continuous reiteration and confirmation of stories and slants. As the authors of the Harvard report write about the 2016 election, this meant that the audience of the right-wing media circle were frequently insulated from fact:

> Over the course of the election, this turned the right-wing media system into an internally coherent, relatively insulated knowledge community, reinforcing the shared worldview of readers and shielding them from journalism that challenged it. The prevalence of such material has created an environment in which the President can tell supporters about events in Sweden that never happened, or a presidential advisor can reference a non-existent 'Bowling Green massacre.' (Benkler et al. 2017)

Will Sommer also examined this insulation, which has afforded right-wing media figures an immense amount of power to help shape the conversation. Unlike the Bush (43) years when the administration would disseminate talking points to media outlets, according to Sommer, now it is the right-wing media that leads with a narrative when one is required (Sommer, Reporter, Daily Beast 2018b). When news breaks that is bad for the right, someone within the media circle will come forward to try to define the response. Floating a possible set of talking points ends up setting the agenda since once a talking point resonates, the rest of the media sphere will reaffirm this reaction.

Warzel's "upside down media" not only encourages this insulation, but is specifically designed to perpetuate it. He has identified four recurring reaction stages when bad news hits the sphere, and describes a system that both buttresses and expands upon corresponding sources:

Phase 1: Quiet Period

Phase 2: Blaming The Usual Suspects/Dismissal
        Mainstream Media Malpractice Defense
        Fake News Defense
        Hit Piece/Distraction Defense
        Anonymous Sourcing Defense
        The Deep State Leaks Defense

Phase 3: Changing The News Cycle

Phase 4: Close The Loop/Merge The Dueling News Cycles (Warzel, How
        the Pro-Trump Media Responds to a Crisis in Just 4 Steps 2017b).

The varying elements of Phases 2 and 3 are especially visible when the right-wing media circle struggles to change the subject or find an alternative for blame. There have been many examples of this, stretching back from the 2016 presidential campaign.

The "Access Hollywood" tapes dropped one month before the 2016 election which revealed, among other things, that then-candidate Trump said about women: "You know, I'm automatically attracted to beautiful — I just start kissing them. It's like a magnet. Just kiss. I don't even wait. And when you're a star, they let you do it. You can do anything.... Grab'em by the pussy. You can do anything" (Transcript 2016).

The three broadcast networks covered the tape and the ensuing political fallout. *ABC* noted prominent Republicans denouncing the candidate. *CBS* covered the politicians withdrawing support, noting Mike Pence was "beside himself." *NBC* addressed the chaos within the Trump campaign and the damage done to the Republican Party. On *Fox News*, however, reporting focused on the mainstream media's coverage of the "Access Hollywood" tape, and since *NBC* released the tape headlined their coverage with a "BIAS ALERT" banner. Tucker Carlson argued that the withdrawal of GOP support for Trump was actually due to policy differences. The network moved effortlessly into a retrospective examination of Bill and Hillary Clinton (McGarrell 2018).

Similarly, when Special Counsel Robert Mueller indicted former Trump campaign Chief Paul Manafort, *Fox News* shifted attention to a story about Uranium One (Peter 2017). Uranium One was a Canadian company with ties to both Russia and the Clinton Foundation, and it garnered much attention on the right but little attention elsewhere. *Fox* also led several segments questioning the validity of the Mueller investigation, the legitimacy of the FBI, and reiterated the obvious guilt of Hillary Clinton. Once *Fox News* aired these alternative stories or questions, other right-wing media outlets repeated them and in this regard, the ecosystem is able to magnify their position and their audience hears the same line of argument on multiple platforms, which gives it even more credibility.

The audience is the most important part of the puzzle, since they are the viewers, listeners, and readers to watch listen, and click enough to make the news outlets profitable. An audience comes to any media outlet in obvious ways, but the advent and politicization of social media has increased the volume of traffic and disagreement fomented and shared. Social media began as an innocent place to share vacation photos (Facebook), videos (YouTube), and naked selfies (SnapChat), but soon became politically weaponized. Since social developed during the Obama administration when Republicans were the aggrieved out-party, social grew up to be a protest player especially on the right. The real fire and fury of the right-wing media comes from the reinforcements by fellow travelers, and this is where social media is so powerful. The social media algorithms (examined in Chapter 3) support the idea that the public was feeling more strongly about politics than it was thinking about them, and social enhanced these feeling exponentially. To recap: the *Fox News*, talk radio echo chamber was already employed when right-wing Web sites grew in opposition to the Obama administration, and social media connected everyone together, amplifying their reach. All of these platforms feed base and primal ideological worries and thus encourage a partisan media system built to emphasize division.

The right-wing media circle, which had heretofore been a collection of fringe outlets, is now a set of news organizations that are legitimized, prominent, and powerful. Returning to that research which examined how news consumers linked to and shared stories, it is clear that this right-wing media circle has a dedicated and devoted following. The study showed that those who read, shared, and linked to stories within the right-wing media circle generally remained within these confines. The authors went on to describe this as "asymmetric polarization," and found that there was a tight circle of sharing among right-wing sites that was not found on the left. Those within the circle work together, connect to one another, reinforce the opinions and narratives within the sphere, and (as identified by *Axios'* Sara Fischer) do not compete against each other, at least not in the way that the mainstream media does (Fischer, Axios, 2017). As the report notes, this circle has formidable power.

> What we find in our data is a network of mutually-reinforcing hyperpartisan sites that revive what Richard Hofstadter called 'the paranoid style in American politics,' combining decontextualized truths, repeated falsehoods, and leaps of logic to create a fundamentally misleading view of the world. 'Fake news,' which implies made of whole cloth by politically disinterested parties out to make a buck of Facebook advertising dollars, rather than propaganda and disinformation, is not an adequate term. By repetition, variation, and circulation through many associated sites, the network of sites make their claims familiar to readers, and this fluency with the core narrative gives credence to the incredible. (Benkler et al. 2017)

Their negative objective drives the right-wing media messaging, their reinforced support provides an intellectual buttress, and their audience feeds their popularity and funds their continued endeavors. Much of this has to do with President Trump.

## 24 HOUR TRUMP

It is difficult to understand how the right-wing media still rails against their "elite" media opponents when they themselves are elites now; many of these outlets have seats in the White House briefing room[5] or have

White House Press credentials,[6] their former employees work in the West Wing,[7] or their current employees date a member of the First Family.[8] Yet they continue to claim victimhood as they protest against those outside of their circle of influence. They are influential now because of the divisions within the Republican Party today, because of the new nationalism that is widespread on the right, and because the most powerful person in America is a devoted fan of their work. The popularity of the right-wing media has grown, in part, because of their loyalty toward one man; this has changed the right-wing media from partisans taking pro-GOP stands to a singular devotion to Donald Trump. Early in the campaign, Trump pulled ahead of a large pack of very conservative competitors, thanks (in part) to the support from the most prominent actors inside the right-wing media circle. Matt Drudge, *Fox's* Sean Hannity, Ann Coulter and Steve Bannon from *Breitbart* went all-in for Trump. The rest of the right-wing media circle followed suit as the audience went all-in as well. When asked in interviews, supporters at Trump rallies said that they liked his bravado, his "authenticity" and his seething disdain for politics. Leon Wolf is managing editor at *Red State*, a conservative Web site, and said of Trump's support that some people are "naturally attracted to obnoxious people who are largely ignorant of actual policy" (Darcy 2016).

What was once a concentrated support of an established ideology has turned into sharp, focused adoration for Donald Trump and hatred for his political opponents. In this manner, it is less pro-conservative than it is anti-liberal. The question of whether his supporters love him because he is a disruptor, or whether he disrupts to gain support is a chicken and egg question that is almost beside the point. Trump's faithful and committed base has not only coopted the GOP; they have given structure to the right-wing media circle as well. This has resulted in a media circle that is more oppositional than productive. According to *Breitbart's* Boyle, the goal of this circle is to "hold the global permanent political class in contempt" (Darcy 2016). As a result, these outlets are also doing less original reporting than they once were, publishing more commentary than journalism, providing a full-throated defense of the president in the process. It had not been this way prior to Donald Trump's election. Commentator Ben Howe wrote that many conservative news outlets used to provide real journalism that extended beyond the ecosystem, but "something happened on the way to Donald Trump," and there was less original reporting from these outlets as a result (Howe 2018). This is likely for several reasons. Given legitimacy by Trump's election and because of their fealty for him, the oppositional aspect of journalism, the investigative impulse that leads to digging and fact-finding, has been largely negated by those who support him. Additionally, all the Trump's attacks on the "fake media" differentiated the right-wing media outlets from everyone else. This probably had a secondary effect where the mainstream media closed its ranks to the right-wing media outlets, and the conservative media closed ranks as well. The president now makes regular distinctions between "fake news" outlets (*CNN*) and "real news" (*Fox News*), rejecting the first to call on the latter. In 2018, *Politico's* magazine featured a story highlighting the new conservative media establishment, listing its most prominent figures. The article gave the credit (or the blame) of the new right-wing media circle to President Trump:

> Donald Trump has transformed conservative media as much as he has Republican politics. An establishment once the province of tweedy editorialists and the mannered heirs of William F. Buckley has been overthrown by a new set of brash characters, from name-brand provocateurs like Sean Hannity and Laura Ingraham to a younger generation making their mark in social media.... It's a boisterous and unapologetic bunch, mostly but not all pro-Trump. If they share one unifying trait, it's their appetite for courting controversy and baiting liberals—one that connects viscerally to a wide swath of conservative Americans eager to see political correctness and the "mainstream media" taken down a peg or two. (Mahaskey 2018)

Another reason for the closed ranks of the right-wing media circle can be directly connected to the affective polarization addressed in Chapter 4. When the mood of the electorate is rooted in antipathy toward the opposition, not only will the right-wing media support Trump, they will see the mainstream media as opposing him. This is not a baseless contention, since much of the original reporting from the legacy news has uncovered stories damning to Trump, his campaign, his businesses, his family, and his administration. Journalists argue that they are reporting the truth; Trump supporters reject this notion and frequently argue that all the stories about the president paint him in a negative light. This divide does nothing to bring the two sides together, but it does help maintain the profit margins in a political climate where polarization is lucrative.

President Trump's attacks against the press are fully supported by the right-wing media circle because they share his view that the rest of the press are illegitimate and part of a leftist cabal out to get them. In this way, Trump and those inside the circle reinforce one another, and numerous media critics point to the "feedback loop" between Trump and the right-wing media circle. Isaac Stanley-Becker in *The Washington Post* imagined President Trump's own social media as an echo of our filter bubbles: "Trump's carefully curated feed is a reflection of the ideological chasm that's dividing the media and splintering society.... right-wing media insulates Trump, and his most devoted supporters, from blunt assessments of his administration" (Stanley-Becker 2018). This feedback loop, where Trump provides forage to right-wing outlets who fawningly cover him and reaffirm his decision-making, is especially pronounced between the president and *Fox News*. Specific programs and personalities on the network are particularly popular with the president, inspiring *The New York Times* to call the network's morning show "Fox and Friends" the "most powerful TV show in America." The relationship between Trump and "Fox and Friends" began well before his presidential run, and then citizen-Trump called into the show weekly. Now that he is president, the relationship has solidified to the point that one former White House staffer reported that the president schedules his meetings around the program (Choi 2018). According to *CNN*, the president's Instagram account reposted 85 photos or videos from either *Fox News, Fox Business* or "Fox & Friends" from May 22 to August 22, 2018, which worked out to be 24% of the 358 posts (Schwartz 2018c). *Vox* found that the president's Twitter feed showed a call and response between the president and "Fox and Friends," and that the show's hosts began to incorporate more language including the president in their remarks as a result (Maza 2018). And Adam Gabbatt wrote in *The Guardian* that "Fox and Friends" plays an outsize role in American politics today, while also gaining a tremendous amount from the relationship:

> The show manages to serve as a court sycophant, whispering in the ear of the king, criticizing his perceived enemies and fluffing his feathers. But the relationship between Trump and his favorite show isn't one-sided. "Fox & Friends" gets plenty out of it, too. Free publicity through the president's regular tweets and endorsements, and free influence through being able to influence his agenda. (Gabbatt 2017)

The close relationship between "Fox and Friends" and the president is not seamless. In 2018, President Trump watched "Fox and Friends" and apparently misunderstood a joke told by the hosts. Building on the false accusation that billionaire George Soros was paying protestors against Brett Kavanaugh's confirmation to the Supreme Court, the morning show hosts joked that those protestors would be even madder when they did not get paid. Trump did not get the joke, and in his call-and-response fashion tweeted during the show: "The paid D.C. protesters are now ready to REALLY protest because they haven't gotten their checks - in other words, they weren't paid! Screamers in Congress, and outside, were far too obvious - less professional than anticipated by those paying (or not paying) the bills!" (Selk, Trump Apparently Misunderstands 'Fox & Friends' Joke, Makes Baffling Tweet 2018b).

Americans who watch *Fox News* see a tremendous amount of Trump because the president is omnipresent on the network. Media Matters, a left-leaning media think tank, reported that from April until November of 2018, in the run-up to the midterm elections, *Fox News* gave almost 21 hours of coverage to Trump political rallies which is equivalent to more than $34 million in free advertising. At the same time, *MSNBC* and *CNN* gave the same rallies less than 40 minutes combined (Power 2018).

The blurring lines between Trump and *Fox News* personalities grow blurrier. *Fox News* host Sean Hannity let Trump lawyers Rudolph Giuliani and Jay Sekulow guest host his radio program in August of 2018 (Feldman 2018). Trump refers to the network as an extension of himself, using words like "we" and "us" about the network's hosts. At a rally in Ohio, Trump told the crowd about the *Fox News* audience: "So we're blowing them away. And that's good, because those are the people that love us" (Thomsen 2018). Thus, this feedback loop helps the president advertise himself and his positions as it lends legitimacy to the antagonistic mission of *Fox News* and others within the right-wing media circle. The President of the USA is anti-left, and has a cadre of news outlets to support him.

The result of this hostile feedback loop is the conflation of President Trump and the larger American political system. By inserting himself as the larger focal point of American politics, Trump demands a relentless fealty among his supporters that seeps its way into unrelated areas. It has created an "us versus them" division in America where compromise is not feasible, because the only stated goal of any debate is total victory. Trump's supporters may have come to his side already angry, but he has fueled and intensified this rage by cocooning himself and his supporters in an alternate media universe. As a result, American politics today is tribal, divided, and furious.

## THE IMPORTANCE OF BEING BREITBART

There is much to be learned about the pro-Trump aspect of the right-wing media circle by further examining the trajectory of *Breitbart*. In 2007, the late Andrew Breitbart started a pro-Israel, ideologically conservative Web site dedicated to the "destruction of the old media guard" and named it after himself. The site eventually broke into three different components assailing the liberalism of "Big Government, Big Hollywood, and Big Journalism" and it generally took the well-honed line that the media were too liberal and that conservatives were getting shafted. Andrew Breitbart died in 2012 at the age of 43, and subsequently the Web site moved even more rightward and dramatically more antagonistic. Steve Bannon took the helm and under his direction, *Breitbart* became more politically aggressive, disparaging both the left and establishment Republicans as well. Bannon hosted a radio show on the site and featured guests from the fringes of conservatism, many from the alt-right movement, who shared his worldview; "Bannon's political philosophy boils down to three things that a Western country, and America in particular, needs to be successful: Capitalism, nationalism, and 'Judeo-Christian values'" (Guilford and Sonnad 2017).

On his show, Bannon featured Trump prominently and the *Breitbart* Web site became the go-to place for the nationalism that was growing on the right. According to a 2016 Southern Poverty Law Center article, the Web site, which had been consistently nationalist in tone, became even more so during the run-up to Donald Trump's presidential campaign:

Over the past year the media outlet has been openly promoting the core issues of the Alt-Right, introducing these racist ideas to its readership – much to the delight of many in the white nationalist world who could never dream of reaching such a vast number of people. Breitbart has always given a platform to parts of the radical right, most notably elements of the organized anti-Muslim and anti-immigrant movements. Breitbart has also organized conferences featuring nativist speakers and published op-eds and interviews with movement leaders. But since 2015, *Breitbart* began publishing more overtly racist diatribes about Muslims and immigrants. (Piggott 2016)

Bannon was so successful in leading *Breitbart* that the site became the hub of the right-wing circle, so much so that it temporarily moved *Fox News* out of its central position during the campaign. Bannon himself was so triumphant that upon Trump's election, he was tapped to be a senior advisor to president, serving as a kind of co-Chief of Staff. And because of both of these success stories, *Breitbart* not only thrived, but also spawned imitators as others began to copy their formula and mimic their confrontational style. *Fox News*, which remained incredibly powerful on cable even as *Breitbart* ascended online, turned their attention to their Web site in late 2017, "beefing it up" to become "a little Breitbart" (Schwartz, Fox News Website Beefs Up and 'Goes a Little Breitbart' 2017). Yochai Benkler is a Harvard professor who was one author of the study already referenced, and *Politico* interviewed him about the changes on the *Fox News* Web site:

> During the primary, when *Fox News* was more critical of Trump — and *Breitbart* turned against *Fox*, attacking it in several headlines — Benkler said the site's influence decreased. '*Fox News* became less prominent, fewer Twitter shares, fewer Facebook shares,' he said. But that changed during the general election. 'It's only when they line up, after Trump essentially wins out, that they return to their position of prominence,' he said. 'In many senses, it was a capitulation of *Fox News* to the *Breitbart* line....If you're seeing major changes now, it makes sense as a competitive strategy.' (Schwartz, Fox News Website Beefs Up and 'Goes a Little Breitbart' 2017)

The imitation of *Breitbart* extends beyond *Fox News*. In 2018, media watchers noted the growth of "Baby *Breitbarts*," smaller Web sites operating the same way *Breitbart* does but at a local level. There are Baby *Breitbarts* in Maine, Arizona, and Tennessee, and they have filled a gap left by the decline of actual local news coverage. Unlike real news outlets, these Web sites follow the *Breitbart* model by covering local races and legislation with an "anti-establishment, right-wing perspective." With names that sound like legitimate journalistic enterprises, these small, ideological outlets are appealing to conservative politicians in statewide races, but are concerning for those who watch political journalism. The issue is that readers may come to the Web site without knowing that is it not a real news site, but is instead a partisan outlet. Kathleen Culver, director of the Center for Journalism Ethics at the University of Wisconsin, was quoted in *Politico*: "In general, when people try to adopt the forms of journalism without the norms of journalism, we really do have to be concerned that they're trying to put one over on people. It makes it very hard for citizens. It makes it very hard to navigate this information environment and find credible sources that you can rely on" (Schwartz, Baby Breitbarts to Pop Up Across the Country? 2018b). The economics of these small, ideological outlets make them powerfully attractive for conservatives who want more *Breitbarts* around. Their costs are low since their staffs are small, they do not print their materials, and they do not need significant infrastructure to broadcast. Accordingly, two editors of *The Tennessee Star*, one of these Baby *Breitbarts*, estimates that it would only cost around $300,000 to launch more of these sites in battleground states (Schwartz, Baby Breitbarts to Pop Up Across the Country? 2018b).

This shift toward a more *Breitbart*-y approach has had several important consequences. Imitating *Breitbart* means amplifying the rhetoric. When partisan news sites copy the *Breitbart* formula, in order to do so successfully they have to become louder and more punitive. For *Fox News*, which shifted toward the *Brietbart*-style, the tone has become both sharper and determinedly Pro-Trump. According to *Vanity Fair's* Gabriel Sherman, an expert on all-things *Fox News*, the network has taken on the role of championing the president; this is very much on purpose:

> *Fox* producers saw ratings drop whenever something negative about Trump was said on air. Since then, *Fox* has shed prominent Trump critics like Megyn Kelly, George Will, and Rich Lowry, while bulking up on pro-Trump voices such as Seb Gorka, Laura Ingraham, and Mark Levin. 'The network has become a safe space for Trump fans,' said an executive. Those who didn't get on board felt the pressure. Last spring, Bob Beckel, a former co-host of *The Five* and vocal Trump detractor, found an unsigned note in his office telling him to back off Trump.... (Sherman 2018)

In terms of pitch, the combination of a unified message and a pro-Trump stand has meant an entirely different approach to some of the biggest stories in the news. An example can be found in the aforementioned coverage of Special Counsel Robert Mueller's investigation into connections between the Trump campaign and the Russian government. The audience of the right-wing media circle are hearing a more deliberately anti-government tone with special attention to the so-called deep state.

The term "deep state" has become code for supposedly bad government actors who are out to get President Trump because they ostensibly support Hillary Clinton, Barack Obama, and other left-leaning politicians. This term had been used in other countries but was first brought to the USA in 2014 by former Republican congressman Mike Lofgren who used the expression to explain the unknown actors in our current military industrial complex. In an essay on *Bill Moyers'* Web site, Lofgren defines the "deep state" as "…a hybrid association of elements of government and parts of top-level finance and industry that is effectively able to govern the USA without reference to the consent of the governed as expressed through the formal political process" (Lofgren 2014). While Lofgren makes a compelling case for how these unelected actors influence foreign policymaking, it is doubtful that he intended for this to become code for a massive conspiracy theory about Donald Trump and FBI agents, but that is exactly what has happened. Lofgren's definition lends itself pliably to such a contortion, and thus the term has gained prominence, especially on *Fox News*.

*The Daily Beast's* Will Sommer addressed the newly antagonistic temperament of *Fox News*: "*Fox* has always pushed a political message. But this angry, anxious tone is a new thing" (Sommer, Fox Gets Mad 2018a). He theorized that the reasons for this new deep state pitch and *Fox's* increasingly bellicose posture are two-fold. First, *Fox News* is opposing the Mueller investigation to deliver a pro-Trump message to their Trump-loyal audience: "*Fox* was walloped during the presidential campaign for not going far enough right and getting accused of 'cucking out' on Trump. This time around, *Fox* is happy to deliver what the audience wants" (Sommer, Fox Gets Mad 2018a). This leads to the second reason that *Fox News* has amplified their anti-government offensive: They have to keep up with the competition, since the other right-wing news organizations are echoing this narrative.

This is why as right-wing news outlets successfully emulate *Breitbart*, they end up seizing *Breitbart's* audience in the process. *Breitbart* grew its audience during the 2016 presidential campaign and maintained readership when their candidate won the election and their editor in chief was tapped to be White House senior advisor. But one year into the Trump presidency, amidst a very *Breitbart*-y cohort now occupying the right-wing media sphere, the Web site has seen a massive drop in unique visitors: from 15 million in October 2017 to 7.8 million in February 2018 (Schwartz, Breitbart's Readership Plunges 2018a). In a *Politico* article, former *Breitbart* editor Ben Shapiro attributed this fall to Steve Bannon's dismissal from the site earlier in the year. I asked Will Sommer what he thought, and he wrote me this response:

... *Breitbart* is doing less original reporting (admittedly it's harder for them to get WH exclusives now), so that's part of the drop. They're also experiencing the same FB issues all the right-wing sites are, and it's natural for traffic to drop when the administration they're supporting is in power. Plus: general organizational chaos there with Bannon gone.... They still have a lot more traffic than their rivals. Maybe the most interesting part is that it suggests the rest of the right-wing media (particularly *Fox*) has been Breitbartified, so they're no longer the only ones offering that product. (Sommer, Editor, Right Richter 2018a)

As this circle has been established and is increasingly effective, it has changed the way politics is discussed, because as it shifts the conversation on the right, it then influences the broader political conversation as well. Those within the circle are supportive of one another, which allows for a limited narrative as well as a simple and adherent resonance. There is cooperation among these outlets because they have a common purpose, which is to defend their position as they oppose those regarded as enemies. Their audience is dependable but limited; those who are steadfast consumers of right-wing media are self-selected, constant, and limited in number. They are also dedicated supporters of Donald Trump.

## ALT-RIGHT, ALT-LIGHT, THESE KIDS ARE *NOT* ALRIGHT AND MANY ARE CONSPIRACY THEORISTS

An important segment of Trump's supporters includes those on the fringes and this brings up the new positioning of the alt-right in American politics. The "Alternative Right" (alt-right) is the name for the far right edge of the conservative wing on the American political spectrum. The alt-right organizes around the white nationalist ideas about preserving white culture and the victimization of white men by minorities and women. Members of the alt-right initially organized online, in Reddit sub-forums and on 4Chan and 8Chan where they posted outrage anonymously. Fueled by anger and resentment, the alt-right began to take shape in 2010 when white supremacist Richard Spencer founded the Alternative Right blog. The movement grew under the cultivation of Steve Bannon who saw that a large swath of disaffected guys had time and energy to spare. Before working at *Breitbart*, Bannon invested in a company called Internet Gaming Enterprise (IGE) where he was introduced to an online community of very angry, jingoistic young white male videogamers. The story of IGE is long and somewhat complicated, but the condensed version is that IGE hired low-wage Chinese video gamers to play online, amassed rewards for winning games, and then sold these rewards to players, which allowed people to buy their victory instead of slogging through a long video game. American gamers found out about this, howled in xenophobic protest, and the company ultimately failed. But the episode was illustrative because it was how Bannon first tapped into this population segment. The event became known as "Gamergate."

In interviews with Joshua Green who (literally) wrote the book about him, Steve Bannon said, "These guys, these rootless white males, had monster power" (Snider 2017). He saw the political potential of a throng of angry young men and worked on bringing them over to *Breitbart* when he took the helm there. Bannon was able to accomplish this task by hiring Milo Yiannopoulos to write about technology for *Breitbart*, specifically "Gamergate," which attracted those rootless white males with monster power. "I realized Milo could connect with these kids right away," Bannon told Green. "You can activate that army. They come in through Gamergate or whatever and then get turned onto politics and Trump" (Snider 2017). The alt-right then had a place at the *Breitbart* table, which was the greased chute to other outlets within the right-wing media circle. Yiannopoulos wrote a lengthy piece for *Breitbart* in 2016 explaining the alt-right in supportive terms. He distinguished members of the alt-right from skinheads (skinheads are dumb, the alt-right is "dangerously bright"), stating the alt-right is a form of natural conservatism, and describing its members as young, fun, and full of vitality: "Previously an obscure subculture, the alt-right burst onto the national political scene in 2015. Although initially small in number, the alt-right has a youthful energy and jarring, taboo-defying rhetoric that have boosted its membership and made it impossible to ignore" (Bokhari and Yiannopoulos 2016).

Not surprisingly, since members of the alt-right are consistently advocating and instigating violence, the Southern Poverty Law Center (SPLC) has a different take on them. Because the alt-right is a collection of unalike groups (do not call them diverse!), rather than a unified organization, it can be difficult to categorize, but the SPLC identifies that groups within this collection include neo-Nazis, Skinheads, and representatives from white supremacist hate groups. The extreme right has been a mainstay of American politics for the entirety of our national history, but not since Reconstruction has it been so politically legitimized. The reason for this validity is Donald Trump. When Steve Bannon brought the alt-right movement to *Breitbart* and politicized the angry young men while championing Trump as a presidential candidate, he supplied a base of supporters who were devoted to Trump and became reliably active. Unlike the politicians before him, Trump refused to renounce the fringe of the GOP. Past candidates and elected officials took pains to distance themselves from the extreme right, but not Trump. Instead, by using divisive issues and racist rhetoric to energize his supporters, members of the alt-right felt they had found a kindred spirit. During the 2016 presidential campaign, when then-candidate Trump was endorsed by a total of twelve newspapers, and one of them was *The Crusader*, the official newspaper of the Ku Klux Klan. In 2018, according to Howard Polskin who tracks these things for *TheRighting*, the extremist site *The Daily Stormer* had as much web traffic as a regional newspaper (Polskin 2018). These sites are popular among a segment of the president's base, but slightly more subtly, those espousing racist and xenophobic tendencies avoid the KKK and read *Breitbart* instead.

When Bannon moved to the White House as senior advisor to the president, this gave Bannon and *Breitbart* even more power and acceptability. It mainstreamed the alt-right because their anti-establishmentarianism blended in with that narrative about Trump supporters being ignored by the coastal elites. This quote comes from AlternativeRight. com: "After finding a patron in Donald Trump, the Alt-Right acquired the ability to go on the offensive. Properly understood, the election of Trump was the first step towards reopening a long-closed road to patronage and power for radical Rightists, by overthrowing the right-liberal professional losers and restoring a true conservative elite in their place" (Lawrence 2018). The movement of the alt-right into the more mainstream media culture is one important indication of how much the right-wing media circle has grown and developed in recent years. What before was unacceptable is now part and parcel of a system of reinforcing narratives for an audience that is not only devoted, but also willing to fight for the Republican Party in order to achieve their goals.

This is where having a well-known foil comes in handy.

## SWORN ENEMIES AND CONSPIRACY THEORIES

For any ideological media outlet, fighting an adversary gins up the kind of anger that is the fuel of polarization. This is more easily accomplished when out of power because when your team runs the table, there is less to fight against. When your team is in charge, well-known adversaries and conspiracy theories provide the kind of useful antagonists to rail against. Alex Jones heads up *InfoWars*, the conspiracy theory media platform launched in 1999. *InfoWars* rose to popularity in the Trump campaign and now boasts traffic of more than 50 million total visits per month. In 2018, *Facebook, Apple, YouTube* and eventually *Twitter* removed *InfoWars* content from their platforms because the site violated hate speech rules. This was expected to hurt *InfoWars* traffic, but it had the opposite effect: both the Web site and the *InfoWars* stores saw a more than 30% increase in web traffic (Timberg 2018). The key to Jones' popularity is his ability to spot danger in the opposition, and frequently that opposition is the US government. Jones' tirades vary in topic, from the moon landing to September 11th to the massacre at Sandy Hook Elementary in Newtown, Connecticut. They rarely vary in culprit. When Jones turns his attention to more specific enemies, he habitually returns to familiar storylines about well-known foes. Jones was a strong supporter of "Birtherism," the false theory that Barack Obama was not born in the USA. Donald Trump also perpetuated this conspiracy. The two share a penchant for the conspiratorial that may be one reason Trump is a strong supporter of *InfoWars*. After the 2016 election, according to Alex Jones, Trump called him personally to thank him for his assistance: "He said, 'Listen, Alex, I just talked to kings and queens of the world, world leaders, you name it, but he said it doesn't matter, I wanted to talk to you, to thank your audience'" (Killelea 2017). The two also share a serious dislike for former president Barack Obama. Describing the potency of Alex Jones' enmity toward Barack Obama, an article from *Buzzfeed* argued that having such an antagonist was the key to Jones' success:

> Former *Infowars* employees suggested that Jones' secret fear was that his opposition would someday run out — especially if Obama lost re-election. One recalled Jones pacing back and forth on Election Day in 2012, nervous over the prospect of losing the polarizing president that had helped usher in ratings gold. "He just kept saying, 'Oh my God, if Obama loses,

we're out of business,'" the employee said. "One of the guys in there asked, 'You didn't vote for Obama, did you?' And Alex said nothing. Just a grimace. I don't know what it meant." (Warzel, Alex Jones Will Never Stop Being Alex Jones 2017a)

Having a foil to blame and incriminate makes for excellent media content, and at the same time it allows for a distraction when the news is going against a preferred narrative. Returning to those well-worn and easily understood foils is fairly common, which is why Hillary Clinton remains a popular topic of conversation on the right, regardless of her political irrelevance. Because these recognizable enemies are in relatively short supply, and because the party that controls most of the branches of government in Washington is not, technically, the right-wing's opposing party, conspiracy theories within this circle have flourished. Hence, another consequence of this closed media circle is that it allows its audience to believe accusations and ideas unchecked, regardless of their veracity or believability. InfoWars is still regarded as fairly fringe, which is why some of the ideas on that site are pretty wild, but conspiracies still proliferate on the right. A 2016 study from Uscinski, Klostad, and Atkinson in *Political Research Quarterly* found that:

>...partisanship strongly affects the propensity to see a conspiracy when the conspiracy theory has a partisan element. In this experiment, Republicans were more likely to see a conspiracy behind media coverage than either Independents or democrats. This is because suspicion of liberal media bias has been mainstream belief of Republican elites for decades; such suspicion has not generally been a part of Democratic rhetoric. (Uscinski et al. 2016)

In other words, the antagonism against the mainstream media by the right-wing media bubble feeds the conspiracy theories. Today, these theories come in the form of poorly sourced conjectures that bounce around the circle like a pinball in a machine without an egress and are not limited to the fringe outlets. For example, as recently as 2017, polling showed that the majority of Republicans still believe former President Barack Obama was born in Kenya, despite the fact that the allegation was definitively proven to be incorrect by none other than the Republican governor of Hawaii (Glum 2017). Nastier conspiracies continue to proliferate between the right-wing media sources, such as the 2016 murder of Democratic National Committee employee Seth

Rich, which the right-wing media alleged to be the work of the Clinton machine. Rich was shot very late at night near his Capitol Hill home, and because of his DNC employment, *Fox News* began an investigation into unsubstantiated rumors about his death. Subsequently, rumors about this investigation quickly spread to the other right-wing media sources and the conspiracy theory took off from there. From *Breitbart* to *InfoWars* to *Gateway Pundit* to *Zero Hedge* to the most popular hosts on *Fox News*, right-wing media figures promoted the theory that the Seth Rich murder was somehow orchestrated by Hillary Clinton's presidential campaign and Wikileaks. Rich's parents are now suing *Fox News* for promulgating the conspiracy theory and causing personal harm to the family (Coaston 2018).

For the more fringe right-wing outlets, conspiracy theories are fed and extended on web forums like 4Chan where anonymous posters spread wild stories that are eagerly consumed by a believing audience. 4Chan is an imageboard that allows online communities of people to gather and share rumors. The 4Chan board called "/p/" is designated as the "politically incorrect" political forum and it gained traction during the 2016 presidential campaign. *Vox* described it as: "the sort of place where neo-Nazis and people who believe women shouldn't have basic human rights used to meet before we started verifying them on Twitter and electing them to public office" (Martineau 2017). The Q Anon conspiracy began here in 2017 after Trump said that a military dinner was "the calm before the storm." In October 2017, someone calling himself "Q" created a message thread titled "The Calm Before the Storm," and began posting messages about President Trump's master plan to "stage a countercoup against the deep state." The plot that Q proffered was that all of the presidents before Trump were in on a vast deep state conspiracy, past presidents going back to Reagan were part of a criminal conspiracy to make their empire stronger. This was a complicated web of bad actors, according to the Q Anon adherents, which included not just politicians but also bankers, financiers, and entrenched bureaucrats. The good news, according to Q and those who followed his postings with laser-sharp intensity, was that President Trump had been convinced to run for president in order to end the cabal. In this world, Donald Trump is the only guy in a white hat who will save America. Claiming he was a high-level government official with Q-level security clearances, Q alleged big things were happening:

According to Q, Trump was never really involved with Russia, and isn't actually under investigation by Mueller & Co. On the contrary, Q insists that it's actually Clinton and Obama who were corrupted by Putin (and are now actually under investigation by Mueller) because they're obviously just evil, money-hungry globalists who'll do anything for the highest bidder. (Oh, yeah, and they're also apparently into raping and killing children, though the crowd is split over whether this is because they're satanists or just part of some weird blackmail scheme involving the CIA.) (Martineau 2017)

This is an attractive conspiracy theory because it involves all of the boogiemen for the right (Clinton, Obama, Mueller) and makes President Trump a hero while absolving him of any culpability. Now known as "The Storm," this thread has become madly popular with users layering on theory after theory: Barack Obama will be sent to Guantanamo Bay, MS-13 really murdered Seth Rich. All of these could be chalked up as nonsense, but *Fox News* pundit Sean Hannity has retweeted a "Q Annon" posting from 4Chan, giving the forum the kind of legitimacy that moves it toward the more normalized right-wing media bubble. Other celebrities[9] have joined in the Q chorus, and at a Republican campaign rally attended by President Trump in 2018, the "Q" signs in the audience made it to prime time coverage. This kind of mainstreaming gives Q a kind of acceptability that past conspiracy theories have been denied, and at the same time, the pro-Trump tone of Q makes it attractive to maintain. Will Sommer summed it up: "The Storm's success as a conspiracy theory lies in how it wraps up every murky narrative on the right into a kind of mega-narrative where Trump and his voters are always, always winning" (Sommer, Meet "The Storm," The Conspiracy Theory Taking Over the Pro-Trump Internet 2018b).

Q Anon followers maintain that Trump himself is in on the conspiracy since he has used the number "seventeen" in public remarks with seeming off-handedness. Q is, of course, the 17th letter of the alphabet. So when President Trump said at a rally that he had only been to Washington DC "seventeen times," or when he tweeted that the Russia investigation was a witch hunt, where Robert Mueller is "totally conflicted, and his 17 Angry Democrats that are doing his dirty work are a disgrace to USA!" Q Anon supporters get excited, thinking that the President of the USA is secretly communicating with them. Trump is conspiracy friendly himself, since he was one of the most prominent of the "Birthers," has alleged that vaccines directly cause autism, and that the late Supreme Court Justice Antonin Scalia was murdered because he was supposedly found with a pillow over his face. That President Trump would not stop the Q Anon conspiracies from proliferating is hardly a surprise. He fed this idea further in 2018 when radio host and prominent QAnon promoted Michael Lebron posed for a picture with President Trump in the White House. In a social media post, Lebron assured his followers that the President "knows about" the theory (Weigle 2018).

Many of the conspiracy theories involve buzzwords and codes, using a kind of language to communicate in what Sommer refers to as "high context culture" (Sommer, Reporter, *Daily Beast* 2018b). This term refers to the coded language of the right-wing media circle where allusions to past conspiracy theories remain active and ready to launch. In an interview, Sommer said about this high context culture:

> Once you get into *Breitbart, Gateway Pundit, InfoWars,* even Sean Hannity, it becomes so self-referential that it's like you're tuning into a soap opera on episode 500… conspiracy theories get mentioned and dropped…. These things build up into these really obscure references that you only get if you've been following along for a while. (Sommer, Reporter, *Daily Beast* 2018b)

In this manner, conspiracy theories in the right-wing media ecosystem unite their devotees while they encourage the kind of grouping that social identity scholars were talking about. These conspiracy theories are destructive, because their creators have devoted followings whom they are able to lure into a make believe land, an alternate reality that does not connect to real-world circumstances.

While having conspiracies can unify the ideologically adherent, believing them full-bore is hazardous. So too is simply staying within a single filter bubble without venturing out. This has become a concern for some on the right who see a danger in the current two-truth media system. Having such a closed set of media figures and ideological supporters can lead to "epistemic closure," a phenomenon that occurs when our filter bubbles and tightly exclusive discussion circles encourage closed-minded discourse and discouraging opposing thought, leading to a tendency to engage in fantasy. Patricia Cohen wrote about this in the *New York Times* in 2010 after the term began to gain prominence in conservative circles.

A scholar named Julian Sanchez from the Cato Institute had written an article about the conservative echo chamber of that time. Remember: this is the echo chamber of Jamieson and Cappella, which was limited to *Fox News* and talk radio. Sanchez argued then that the conservative media "become worryingly untethered from reality as the impetus to satisfy the demand for red meat overtakes any motivation to report accurately" (Cohen 2010). The article referenced a debate about discourse and intellectualism within the conservative movement that foreshadowed the current divide within the Republican Party, and in doing so presaged the right-wing media bubble, which currently eschews any opposing thought.

The *Daily Beast's* Will Sommer noted that this epistemic closure has shifted considerably in the past several years. While conservatives have consistently disregarded *The New York Times* out of hand, the rise of Trump has made the closure even more narrow: "The rise of Trump cleaved it off even further when you start getting conservative outlets that don't support Trump relegated to [being called] "mainstream media," or "cuck," whatever you want to call them. Then it pushes people even further toward the fringes" (Sommer, Editor, Right Richter 2018a). This is where the conspiracy theories can gain more prominence, says Sommer, because the epistemic closure allows unsubstantiated stories to bounce around the right-wing media circle freely.

It was not always like this. In fact, because the news media now includes forms and functions so wildly advanced, it was *never* like this, even when the political parties ran the newspapers. What is different now is the power this right-wing media has not only to disseminate the messages, but also to craft the messages themselves and spurn all others. Conservative blogger Noah Millman was quoted in the 2010 *Times* piece, arguing that this may be a function of a generational divide: "Young conservatives in the late 1980s and early 1990s saw their movement go from strength to strength — and learned that conservatism was always right and that people who didn't see that were fools" (Cohen 2010).

The right-wing media bubble does indeed see those outside of their circle as fools (and worse), which has led to two totally distinct information systems. Charlie Warzel wrote a piece that was titled "2017 Was the Year That the Internet Destroyed Our Shared Reality" about today's media which consists of unconnected spheres of truth:

They are operating in wholly separate universes, each armed with its own sets of facts, fomented by a White House–led war on the media and amplified by easily weaponized social platforms. 2017 was the year we lost our shared reality: a year where a pro-Trump media pushed conspiracy-theorizing and hyperpartisanship further toward the center of popular culture, revealing not just parallel media institutions, but parallel universes of information. (Warzel, The Year That the Internet Destroyed Our Shared Reality 2017c)

The dangers of operating in two separate universes are obvious: it is impossible for a political system predicated on compromise to function properly if there is no common language or no set of agreed-upon beliefs on which politicians can deliberate. When there are financial rewards for alternative truths and replacement realities, problem-solving seems unlikely.

## Conclusions

Politics has always been vital to our broader culture, but we did not hear about it as frequently or as fervidly as we do today. Certainly, in the 1960s the temperature was similarly high, but we were spared the constant flood of information and commentary that our currently expansive and ubiquitous media presently permits. Additionally, there is so much money to be earned because of this attention to politics, it is impossible to imagine a situation where news organizations hold back for the greater good. As media expert Ken Doctor wrote: "publishers are witnessing a baby digital boom, and its parents are that odd couple of our times, Donald J. Trump and John Oliver" (Doctor 2017). As long as outlets like *The New York Times, The Washington Post, Pro-Publica, The Atlantic,* and *The New Yorker* see massive increases in their subscriptions, they will continue to tend to the journalism that is both incredibly important for the survival of the nation and utterly overwhelming for the public. Additionally, the profitability of political fighting means that we will continue to hear what University of Wisconsin political scientist Michael Wagner calls "extreme quotes from partisans." These extreme quotes are newsworthy—and also lucrative (Wagner 2017). This keeps the pressure on politicians to continue to amplify their rhetoric in order to gain attention, as it also entices the news media to cover these verbal bombings.

The political climate and the news media that cover it are suffering from a similar constituent malady. Without a very large center to demand composed compromise and serious deliberation, most of the political discourse today is frenzied and intemperate, taking place out on the wings away from common ground. Discussions today end up loudly broadcast on the media by actors who serve to antagonize or resolutely reaffirm without much moderation. There is a resulting lack of trust from the American public who watches and listens and reads about all of this, and it is dangerous. Because there is so much news breaking out of Washington today, Americans turn to a polarized media system as a balm to soothe the chaos. The problem is that the partisan news media are intensifying the turmoil, which does nothing to calm our temper. Conspiracies and comedy may be forms of entertainment for two different population segments, but even this entertainment is increasing the stress.

In *Echo Chamber,* Kathleen Hall Jamieson and Joseph Cappella looked for the positive attributes of the conservative media bubble. They wrote that such attention to information with a consistently conservative perspective would help to encourage a sense of community among those on the right, and also inform the audience enough to argue effectively. The authors were certainly correct about this, as the community has grown tighter and more argumentative. Jamieson and Cappella also warned all of the dangers of this system: the ideological insulation, the cocooning of opposing thought, the enmity toward opposing views, the outrage, and the personal attacks (Jamieson and Cappella 2008). The left, for their part, amplifies the division by tending to their own adherents, casting aspersions on those who oppose them with equal animosity and force. This is where we have landed.

No one could not have predicted the separate media universes we have today, the total lack of a "shared reality" (Warzel, The Year That the Internet Destroyed Our Shared Reality 2017c). The technological advancements and the ways that politicians have adapted to this new messaging were impossible to foresee. But Hannah Arendt foretold this exact state in 1951 when writing about totalitarianism. Arendt, worried about the citizenry in the face of dishonest power, knew that the media were the key to mass manipulation.

> In an ever-changing, incomprehensible world the masses had reached the point where they would, at the same time, believe everything and nothing, think that everything was possible and that nothing was true. ... Mass propaganda discovered that its audience was ready at all times to believe

the worst, no matter how absurd, and did not particularly object to being deceived because it held every statement to be a lie anyhow. The totalitarian mass leaders based their propaganda on the correct psychological assumption that, under such conditions, one could make people believe the most fantastic statements one day, and trust that if the next day they were given irrefutable proof of their falsehood, they would take refuge in cynicism; instead of deserting the leaders who had lied to them, they would protest that they had known all along that the statement was a lie and would admire the leaders for their superior tactical cleverness. (Arendt 1951)

This is where we are, and so this is what needs to be changed if we are to stop sorting and start acting as if we are all citizens of the same collective democracy. The reinforcing polarizations of our news media and our politics fortify our divisions, and that is problematic for the public, for those who see value in our nation and the conversations of our democracy.

## Notes

1. During the opening prayer.
2. This was, obviously, pre-2016.
3. See Dagnes, *A Conservative Walks into a Bar* (2012).
4. Wemple, Erik, "Is Fox News part of the mainstream media? It depends." *The Washington Post* (March 14, 2017).
5. *Newsmax, One America News.*
6. *Gateway Pundit, The Daily Caller, Breitbart.*
7. *Breitbart's* Steve Bannon, *Fox News'* Bill Shine.
8. *Fox News* personality Kimberly Guilfoyle and Donald Trump Jr.
9. Curt Schilling, Roseann Barr.

## Works Cited

Allen, Mike. 2018. *Trump Media Frenzy Grows: Politics on Steroids, 24/7*, October 9. Accessed October 9, 2018. https://www.axios.com/newsletters/axios-am-7c89485a-3bfc-40b1-87cc-f594d0436d7d.html?utm_source=newsletter&utm_medium=email&utm_campaign=newsletter_axiosam&stream=top.

Alterman, Eric. 2005. *Bush's War on the Press*, April 21. Accessed July 2, 2018. https://www.thenation.com/article/bushs-war-press/.

Arendt, Hannah. 1951. *The Origins of Totalitarianism*. New York, NY: Schocken Books.

Benkler, Yochai, Robert Faris, Hal Roberts, and Ethan Zuckerman. 2017. *Study: Breitbart-Led Right-Wing Media Ecosystem Altered Broader Media Agenda*, March 3. Accessed November 12, 2017. https://www.cjr.org/analysis/breitbart-media-trump-harvard-study.php.

Bokhari, Allum, and Milo Yiannopoulos. 2016. *An Establishment Conservative's Guide to the Alt-Right*, March 29. Accessed June 21, 2018. http://www.breitbart.com/tech/2016/03/29/an-establishment-conservatives-guide-to-the-alt-right/.

Carter, Brandon. 2017. *Conservative Media Outlets Gain Seats in White House Briefing Room*, June 6. Accessed March 24, 2018. http://thehill.com/homenews/media/340323-conservative-media-outlets-gain-seats-in-white-house-briefing-room.

Choi, David. 2018. Trump Schedules His Meetings Around 'Fox and Friends' Segments, According to Former White House Official. *Business Insider*, July 31. https://www.businessinsider.com/trump-fox-new-and-friends-schedules-meetings-2018-7.

Coaston, Jane. 2018. *Seth Rich's Parents Are Taking Their Fight Against Fox News to Court*, March 23. Accessed March 26, 2018. https://www.vox.com/2018/3/23/17129414/seth-rich-fox-news-lawsuit-conspiracy-theories.

Cohen, Patricia. 2010. *'Epistemic Closure'? Those Are Fighting Words*, April 27. Accessed March 29, 2018. https://www.nytimes.com/2010/04/28/books/28conserv.html.

Coppins, McKay. 2017. *What If the Right-Wing Media Wins?* Fall. Accessed March 20, 2018. https://www.cjr.org/special_report/right-wing-media-breitbart-fox-bannon-carlson-hannity-coulter-trump.php.

Darcy, Oliver. 2016. *Donald Trump Broke the Conservative Media*, August 26. Accessed June 21, 2018. http://www.businessinsider.com/conservative-media-trump-drudge-coulter-2016-8.

Dellinger, A.J. 2018. *FCC Reportedly Planning to Change Rules to Save Sinclair's Takeover of Local News Before Court Can Kill It*, June 6. Accessed July 9, 2018. https://gizmodo.com/fcc-reportedly-planning-to-change-rules-to-save-sinclai-1826818478.

Diamond, Dan. 2018. *Meet the HHS Officials Who Tweet Like Trump*, June 29. Accessed July 3, 2018. https://www.politico.com/story/2018/06/29/health-officials-tweet-like-donald-trump-663026.

Doctor, Ken. 2017. *Trump Bump Grows into Subscription Surge—And Not Just for the New York Times*, March 3. Accessed April 1, 2018. https://www.thestreet.com/story/14024114/1/trump-bump-grows-into-subscription-surge.html.

Eakin, Marah. 2016. *The Telecommunications Act of 1996 Gave Us Shitty Cell Service, Expensive Cable*, August 11. Accessed July 2, 2018. https://tv.avclub.com/the-telecommunications-act-of-1996-gave-us-shitty-cell-1798250823.

Farhi, Paul. 2017a. *Sean Hannity Thinks Viewers Can Tell the Difference Between News and Opinion. Hold on a Moment,* March 28. Accessed July 11, 2018. https://www.washingtonpost.com/lifestyle/style/sean-hannity-thinks-viewers-can-tell-the-difference-between-news-and-opinion-hold-on-a-moment/2017/03/27/eb0c5870-1307-11e7-9e4f-09aa75d3ec57_story.html?utm_term=.6ecf861c9b91.

———. 2017b. *What the Latest James O'Keefe Video Leaves Out,* June 28. Accessed July 10, 2018. https://www.washingtonpost.com/lifestyle/style/what-you-dont-see-in-okeefe-video-may-be-as-important-as-what-you-do/2017/06/28/dcb67446-5b7c-11e7-a9f6-7c3296387341_story.html?utm_term=.d14f498c85b5.

Farhi, Paul, Jack Gillum, and Chris Alcantara. 2018. *In This Town, You Can Flip the Channel All You Want—The News Is Often the Same,* June 14. Accessed July 10, 2018. https://www.washingtonpost.com/graphics/2018/lifestyle/sinclair-broadcasting/?utm_term=.bbbfee977e9d.

Farhi, Paul, interview by Alison Dagnes. 2017. *Reporter, Washington Post,* July 19.

Feldman, Josh. 2018. Fox News Contributor Says Giuliani, Sekulow Guest-Hosting for Hannity Is a 'New Level of Coziness'. *Mediate,* August 12. https://www.mediaite.com/tv/fox-news-contributor-says-giuliani-sekulow-guest-hosting-for-hannity-is-a-new-levelof-coziness/.

Fischer, Sara. 2017. *The Recent Explosion of Right-Wing News Sites,* February 23. Accessed March 3, 2018. https://www.axios.com/the-recent-explosion-of-right-wing-news-sites-1513300575-1a623983-75d6-41a1-88ee-49e50a461777.html.

———. 2018a. *New Streaming Network Launching for Liberals,* January 2. Accessed July 9, 2018. https://www.axios.com/newsletters/axios-media-trends-59e82c34-adfc-432b-aa98-00f361627740.html.

———. 2018b. *92% of Republicans Think Media Intentionally Reports Fake News,* June 27. Accessed July 3, 2018. https://www.axios.com/trump-effect-92-percent-republicans-media-fake-news-9c1bbf70-0054-41dd-b506-0869bb-10f08c.html.

Fischer, Sara, interview by Alison Dagnes. 2017. *Axios,* July 19.

Gabbatt, Adam. 2017. Trump and The Fox & Friends Show. Think Ego, Not News. *The Guardian,* September 17. https://www.theguardian.com/media/2017/sep/17/fox-and-friends-fox-news-donald-trump.

Garrett, Major, interview by Alison Dagnes. 2017. *CBS News White House Correspondent,* August 14.

Glum, Julia. 2017. *Some Republicans Still Think Obama Was Born in Kenya as Trump Resurrects Birther Conspiracy Theory,* December 11. Accessed March 26, 2018. http://www.newsweek.com/trump-birther-obama-poll-republicans-kenya-744195.

Gold, Hadas, and Oliver Darcy. 2018. *Salem Executives Pressured Radio Hosts to Cover Trump More Positively, Emails Show*, May 9. Accessed July 2, 2018. https://money.cnn.com/2018/05/09/media/salem-radio-executives-trump/index.html.

Gottfried, Jeffrey, and Michael Barthel. 2018. *Almost Seven-in-Ten Americans Have News Fatigue, More Among Republicans*, June 5. Accessed July 3, 2018. http://www.pewresearch.org/fact-tank/2018/06/05/almost-seven-in-ten-americans-have-news-fatigue-more-among-republicans/.

Greenwood, Max. 2018. *EPA Spokesperson Calls Reporter 'A Piece of Trash'*, June 6. Accessed July 3, 2018. http://thehill.com/policy/energy-environment/391045-epa-spokesperson-calls-reporter-a-piece-of-trash.

Grove, Lloyd, interview by Alison Dagnes. 2017. *The Daily Beast, Editor at Large*, July 17.

Grynbaum, Michael. 2017. *White House Grants Press Credentials to a Pro-Trump Blog*, February 13. Accessed March 24, 2018. https://www.nytimes.com/2017/02/13/business/the-gateway-pundit-trump.html.

———. 2018. *Fox News Once Gave Trump a Perch. Now It's His Bullhorn*, July 1. Accessed July 11, 2018. https://www.nytimes.com/2018/07/01/business/media/fox-news-trump-bill-shine.html.

Guilford, Gwynn, and Nikhi Sonnad. 2017. *What Steve Bannon Really Wants*, February 3. Accessed March 25, 2018. https://qz.com/898134/what-steve-bannon-really-wants/.

Haag, Matthew. 2018. *'Womp Womp': Corey Lewandowski Mocks Child with Down Syndrome Separated from Mother*, June 20. Accessed July 2, 2018. https://www.nytimes.com/2018/06/20/business/media/corey-lewandowski-womp-womp-down-syndrome.html.

Hemmer, Nicole. 2018. *How Breitbart Became Just Another Right-Wing Trump Cheerleader*, January 12. Accessed March 25, 2018. https://www.washingtonpost.com/outlook/how-breitbart-became-just-another-right-wing-trump-cheerleader/2018/01/12/fa90bec0-f6f6-11e7-a9e3-ab18ce41436a_story.html?utm_term=.621402a2ad5a.

Ho, Rodney. 2018. *Talkers Magazine Heavy Hundred 2018: Sean Hannity Beats Rush Limbaugh for First Time*, May 21. Accessed July 2, 2018. https://www.ajc.com/blog/radiotvtalk/talkers-magazine-heavy-hundred-2018-sean-hannity-beats-rush-limbaugh-for-first-time/vNBjGaSb8GWnhGHc0AshoL/.

Howe, Ben. 2018. *Dear Conservative Media: Do Some More Damn Reporting*, May 11. Accessed May 12, 2018. https://www.thedailybeast.com/dear-conservative-media-do-some-more-damn-reporting.

Jamieson, Kathleen Hall, and Joseph Cappella. 2008. *Echo Chamber: Rush Limbaugh and the Conservative Media Establishment*. London: Oxford University Press.

Johnson, Charles. 2017. *BUSTED: The @WashingtonPost's Paul Farhi (@ farhip) Lies About @JamesOKeefeIII To Cover For @CNN*, June 30. Accessed July 10, 2018. http://gotnews.com/busted-washingtonposts-paul-farhi-farhip-lies-jamesokeefeiii-cover-cnn/.

Jones, Jeffrey. 2012. "Fox News and the Performance of Ideology." *Cinema Journal* 51 (4):178–185.

Kafka, Peter. 2017. "Full Transcript: BuzzFeed's Charlie Warzel and CNN's Oliver Darcy on Recode Media." *Recode*, August 27. Accessed March 21, 2018. https://www.recode.net/2017/8/27/16211416/transcript-buzz-feed-charlie-warzel-cnn-oliver-darcy-trump-drudge-breitbart-conservative-recode-media?curator=MediaREDEF.

Killelea, Eric. 2017. *Alex Jones' Mis-Infowars: 7 Bat-Sh*t Conspiracy Theories*, February 21. Accessed September 21, 2018. https://www.rollingstone.com/culture/culture-lists/alex-jones-mis-infowars-7-bat-sht-conspiracy-theories-195468/.

King, Ledyard. 2018. *Maxine Waters Confronts Death Threats: 'If You Shoot at Me, You Better Shoot Straight'*, June 30. Accessed July 3, 2018. https://www.usatoday.com/story/news/politics/onpolitics/2018/06/30/maxine-waters-confronts-threats-families-belong-together-rally/748361002/.

Kurtz, Howard. 1996. *Hot Air: All Talk All the Time*. New York, NY: Times Books.

Lawrence, J. 2018. *Thoughts on the State of the Right*, April 12. Accessed June 21, 2018. https://alternativeright.blog/2018/04/12/thoughts-on-the-state-of-the-right/.

Lehman, Susan. 1999. *Media Circus*, January 7. Accessed July 9, 2018. http://www.salon.com/media/lehm/1999/01/07lehm.html.

Lima, Christiano. 2018. *Trump Jr.: Dad's Ambassador to the Fringe*, April 4. Accessed July 9, 2018. https://www.politico.com/story/2018/04/08/trump-jr-conspiracy-theories-far-right-506795.

Lofgren, Mike. 2014. *Essay: Anatomy of the Deep State*, February 21. Accessed March 29, 2018. http://billmoyers.com/2014/02/21/anatomy-of-the-deep-state/.

Mahaskey, M. Scott. 2018. *The New Conservative Media Establishment*, May/June. Accessed May 15, 2018. https://www.politico.com/magazine/story/2018/04/27/the-new-conservative-media-establishment-218107.

Martin, Gregory, and Josh McCrain. 2018. *Yes, Sinclair Broadcast Group Does Cut Local News, Increase National News and Tilt Its Stations Rightward*, April 10. Accessed July 2, 2018. https://www.washingtonpost.com/news/monkey-cage/wp/2018/04/10/yes-sinclair-broadcast-group-does-cut-local-news-increase-national-news-and-tilt-its-stations-rightward/?utm_term=.8c60e2f7f6b4.

Martineau, Paris. 2017. *The Storm Is the New Pizzagate—Only Worse*, December 19. Accessed March 26, 2018. http://nymag.com/selectall/2017/12/qanon-4chan-the-storm-conspiracy-explained.html.

Matsa, Katerina Eva. 2017. *Local TV News Fact Sheet*, July 13. Accessed July 9, 2018. http://www.journalism.org/fact-sheet/local-tv-news/.

Maza, Carlos. 2018. The Trump-Fox & Friends Feedback Loop, Explained. *Vox*, February 9. https://www.vox.com/2018/2/9/16997022/strikethrough-trump-fox-friends-feedback-loop-explained-tweet.

McClennen, Sophia. 2018. *How Sinclair Is Taking Over Local News and Pushing the Country to the Right*, April 14. Accessed July 9, 2018. https://www.salon.com/2018/04/14/how-sinclair-is-taking-over-local-news-and-pushing-the-country-to-the-right/.

McGarrell, Audrey. 2018. *Framing of Access Hollywood Tape by Network*. Academic Research, Shippensburg, PA.

Namako, Tom. 2018. *An "Ashamed" Fox News Commentator Just Quit the "Propaganda Machine"*, March 20. Accessed March 25, 2018. https://www.buzzfeed.com/tomnamako/ralph-peters?utm_term=.uyg9mdPQJk#.afXDlRmg7N.

Peter, Jeremy. 2017. *Alternative Narrative Emerges in Conservative Media as Russia Inquiry Widens*, November 3. Accessed October 8, 2018. https://www.nytimes.com/2017/11/03/us/politics/conservative-media-trump-clintons.html.

Piggott, Stephen. 2016. *Is Breitbart.com Becoming the Media Arm of the 'Alt-Right'?*, April 28. Accessed March 22, 2018. https://www.splcenter.org/hatewatch/2016/04/28/breitbartcom-becoming-media-arm-alt-right.

Polling, Monmoth. 2018. *National: Public Troubled by 'Deep State'*, March 19. Accessed June 21, 2018. https://www.monmouth.edu/polling-institute/documents/monmouthpoll_us_031918.pdf/.

Polskin, Howard, interview by Alison Dagnes. 2018. *TheRighting, Editor*, August 6.

Power, Liz. 2018. How Cable News Covered Trump's Rallies Before the 2018 Midterms. *Media Matters*, October 9. https://www.mediamatters.org/research/2018/10/09/How-cable-news-is-covering-Trumps-rallies/221625.

Rogers, Will. n.d. *Will Rogers Today*. Accessed July 11, 2018. https://www.willrogerstoday.com/will_rogers_quotes/quotes.cfm?qID=4.

Schwartz, Jason. 2017. *Fox News Website Beefs Up and 'Goes A Little Breitbart'*, December 23. Accessed March 25, 2018. https://www.politico.com/story/2017/12/23/fox-news-website-breitbart-312326.

———. 2018a. *Breitbart's Readership Plunges*, March 20. Accessed March 25, 2018. https://www.politico.com/story/2018/03/20/breitbart-readership-plunge-steve-bannon-474801.

———. 2018b. *Baby Breitbarts to Pop Up Across the Country?*, April 30. Accessed May 3, 2018. https://www.politico.com/story/2018/04/30/breitbart-tennessee-fake-news-560670.

———. 2018c. *Sinclair Preps to Challenge Fox News*, May 3. Accessed July 10, 2018. https://www.politico.com/story/2018/05/03/sinclair-broadcast-challenge-to-fox-news-566757.

Selk, Avi. 2018a. *Man Arrested After Shouting 'Womp, Womp' and Pulling a Gun on Immigration Protesters*, July 1. Accessed July 2, 2018. https://www.washingtonpost.com/news/post-nation/wp/2018/07/01/man-arrested-after-shouting-womp-womp-and-pulling-a-gun-on-immigration-protesters/?utm_term=.abfaea3cefe0.

———. 2018b. *Trump Apparently Misunderstands 'Fox & Friends' Joke, Makes Baffling Tweet*, October 10. Accessed October 11, 2018. https://www.washingtonpost.com/politics/2018/10/09/trump-tweeted-again-not-even-his-fans-know-what-hes-talking-about/?noredirect=on&utm_campaign=f33457956f-EMAIL_CAMPAIGN_2018_09_11_04_47_COPY_01&utm_medium=email&utm_source=CNN%20Media%3A%20Reliable%20Sou.

Shalby, Colleen. 2017. *Trump Retweets Alt-Right Media Figure Who Pushed 'PizzaGate' and Seth Rich Conspiracy Theories*, August 14. Accessed July 9, 2018. http://www.latimes.com/politics/la-pol-updates-everything-president-trump-retweets-alt-right-blogger-who-1502769297-htmlstory.html.

Sherman, Gabriel. 2018. *"A Safe Space for Trump": Inside the Feedback Loop Between the President and Fox News*, January 11. Accessed March 15, 2018. https://www.vanityfair.com/news/2018/01/inside-the-feedback-loop-between-the-president-and-fox-news.

Snider, Mike. 2017. *Steve Bannon Learned to Harness Troll Army from 'World of Warcraft'*, July 18. Accessed June 21, 2018. https://www.usatoday.com/story/tech/talkingtech/2017/07/18/steve-bannon-learned-harness-troll-army-world-warcraft/489713001/.

Sommer, Will. 2018a. *Fox Gets Mad*. Right Richter, Washington, DC: Patreon.

———. 2018b. *Meet "The Storm," the Conspiracy Theory Taking Over the Pro-Trump Internet*, January 12. Accessed March 26, 2018. https://medium.com/@willsommer/meet-the-storm-the-conspiracy-theory-taking-over-the-pro-trump-internet-3ec94bf7d8a3.

———. 2018c. *Normalizing InfoWars*. Right Richter, Washington, DC: Patreon.

Sommer, Will, interview by Alison Dagnes. 2018a. *Editor, Right Richter*, March 23.

———. 2018b. *Reporter, The Daily Beast*, January 8.

Stanley-Becker, Isaac. 2018. In Trump's Right-Wing Media Universe, It Was a Day Like Any Other. *The Washington Post*, August 22. https://www.washingtonpost.com/news/morning-mix/wp/2018/08/22/how-right-wing-media-dealt-with-adevastating-day-for-trump/?utm_term=.da3063cffa60.

Stelter, Brian. 2018. *Sinclair's New Media-Bashing Promos Rankle Local Anchors*, March 7. Accessed July 10, 2018. https://money.cnn.com/2018/03/07/media/sinclair-broadcasting-promos-media-bashing/index.html.

Swaine, Jon. 2018. *Sinclair TV Chairman to Trump: 'We Are Here to Deliver Your Message'*, April 10. Accessed July 9, 2018. https://www.

theguardian.com/media/2018/apr/10/donald-trump-sinclair-david-smith-white-house-meeting.

Thomsen, Jacqueline. 2018. *Trump Touts Fox News, Attacks Cable News Competitors at Rally. The Hill*, August 4. https://thehill.com/homenews/administration/400424-trump-touts-fox-news-attacks-cable-news-competitors-atrally.

Timberg, Craig. 2018. *As Alex Jones Rails Against 'Big Tech,' His Infowars Stores Still Thrive Online*, September 10. Accessed September 21, 2018. https://www.washingtonpost.com/technology/2018/09/10/alex-jones-rails-against-big-tech-his-infowars-stores-still-thrive-online/?utm_term=.21beb86e2b8e.

Transcript. 2016. *Transcript: Donald Trump's Taped Comments About Women*, October 7. Accessed October 9, 2018. 9https://www.nytimes.com/2016/10/08/us/donald-trump-tape-transcript.html.

Uscinski, Joseph, Casey Klofstad, and Matthew D. Atkinson. 2016. What Drives Conspiratorial Beliefs? *Political Research Quarterly* 69 (1): 57–71.

Wagner, Michael, interview by Dagnes. 2017. *Associate Professor, University of Wisconsin*, April 6.

Warren, James. 2017. *Is The New York Times vs. The Washington Post vs. Trump the Last Great Newspaper War?*, July 30. Accessed March 14, 2018. https://www.vanityfair.com/news/2017/07/new-york-times-washington-post-donald-trump.

Warzel, Charlie. 2017a. *Alex Jones Will Never Stop Being Alex Jones*, May 3. Accessed March 21, 2018. https://www.buzzfeed.com/charliewarzel/alex-jones-will-never-stop-being-alex-jones?curator=MediaREDEF&utm_term=.em2Kl5dE7k#.bkKGgDo4LP.

———. 2017b. *How the Pro-Trump Media Responds to a Crisis in Just 4 Steps*, May 16. Accessed March 2, 2018. https://www.buzzfeed.com/charliewarzel/how-the-pro-trump-media-responds-to-a-crisis-in-just-4-steps?curator=MediaREDEF&utm_term=.ny88dRJV20#.wuQQgo3ANM.

———. 2017c. *The Year That the Internet Destroyed Our Shared Reality*, December 28. Accessed March 29, 2018. https://www.buzzfeed.com/charliewarzel/2017-year-the-internet-destroyed-shared-reality?utm_term=.gxpwQW5Vn#.nhzjzavM5.

Weigle, Dave. 2018. *Trump Posed with Prominent Conspiracy Theorist in Oval Office Photo*, August 24. Accessed October 9, 2018. http://www.chicagotribune.com/news/nationworld/ct-trump-photo-conspiracy-theorist-20180824-story.html.

Wemple, Erik. 2017. *Is Fox News Part of the Mainstream Media? It Depends*, March 14. Accessed March 25, 2018. https://www.washingtonpost.com/blogs/erik-wemple/wp/2017/03/14/is-fox-news-part-of-the-mainstream-media-it-depends/?utm_term=.5b9a328e9ba9.

CHAPTER 6

# Consequential, Problematic and Perhaps Resolvable

The political temperature is so high right now that people feel constantly burned. A routine polling question asks Americans if the country is going in the right direction or along the wrong track and the vast majority of respondents today say "wrong track," which seems too genteel and underplays the fierce national mood. Fights about people, policy, and politics are commonplace; 2018 Quinnipiac polls showed that 91% of those polled thought the hostility in politics was a "serious problem" (Peters 2018). Carolyn Lukensmeyer is the executive director of the National Institute for Civil Discourse that was founded after the shooting of former-Congresswoman Gabby Giffords with the intent of calming down the rhetoric. The Institute assists in conflict resolution, and Lukensmeyer reports that the requests for assistance are increasing because of our destructive political culture and our resentment toward one another: "This is now deep in our homes, deep in our neighborhoods, deep in our places of worship and deep in our workplaces. It really is a virus" (Peters 2018).

Much of the anger that has spread throughout our culture comes from a sense of frustration on both sides of our divide. Americans feel ignored and left out of the political process and that feeling of being snubbed is enough to enrage anybody. The problem is that anger is profitable for the media; it keeps people engaged and attentive to both the outlets that inform and to the outlets that provoke. The media reflect our wishes, providing us with what we want; the "rule of anticipated importance" states that the media cover what people *will* want. Because the public is so frustrated, the media provide us with support for our

© The Author(s) 2019
A. Dagnes, *Super Mad at Everything All the Time*,
https://doi.org/10.1007/978-3-030-06131-9_6

disappointment, in essence saying: "You are right to be frustrated, and here are more reasons why you should be". While satisfying to hear, this validation only serves to infuriate us further and deepen the divide.

The most successful media outlets have perfected their ability to attract and keep an audience, and in doing so they advance our anger. The blame also falls to the public who foster this system by tuning in and buying into the rage, perpetuating the cycle by feeding the outrage machine with ratings and clicks. Our anger did not suddenly appear. It has been building for a long time, slowly and almost imperceptibly, and not only have we become inured to the ire, we have adjusted our emotional temperatures to meet the fury around us.

The currently polarized political media are either the result of our division or the cause of it, but either way the system we have is the culmination of 50 years of development. A slowly growing distrust of the news media and the political system led to the right's frustration with both, and opened the door for something new to replace a news media stacked against them. Incredible technology that has become commonplace expanded the platforms for this new media system, but while the technology connects us at the exact same time it emboldens our division. Our cultural shortcuts allow us to sort ourselves, and in a confusing world these shortcuts provide comfort and familiarity but they also oversimplify complicated issues and help to demonize a perceived opponent. Creating a separate media that is tailor-made for a specific segment of the American public might have been ideologically satisfying for some voters and lucrative for many media moguls, but in the end it separates us. The right-wing media circle sows doubt, pedals fear, demands unquestioning allegiance, and creates an alternative set of facts that maintain the anger and expands the polarization. Without a specific set of gatekeepers to tamp down on the unacceptable, motivated by a negative objective that aims its wrath against everyone else, the right-wing media circle validates its audience's frustration while it feeds it's anxieties. Fueled by well-worn victimization, moved solely by the desire to win a war against anyone outside their circle, the right-wing media succeeds through its ability to divide.

At the same time, the mainstream media's inability to look at an America beyond their own perspectives led to the palpable frustration of those who felt, understandably, ignored. Additionally, the mainstream press continue to take the bait when President Trump, who grabs every opportunity to rail against them, trolls them. Trump's anti-press narrative succeeds because it extends the existing narrative of media bias, intensifies the outrage, and legitimizes the right-wing media circle's negative objective of being anti-left instead of pro-conservative. Trump's successful campaign against the press had been in the making for decades as conservatives planted seeds of distrust, but those seeds would not have grown so fruitfully were there not real grievances on the right to begin with. Republican advertising consultant Brad Todd told me in an interview that Trump's election cemented the idea that the establishment in Washington was out of touch and under representative of a swath of the public. The anti-DC sentiment among a large portion of the Republican base extended to conservatives who had agreed to the TARP bailout in 2008, and according to Todd this changed the ideological question of "who's left, who's right" to a different question of "who's inside the Beltway, who's outside?" (Todd, Partner, OnMessage 2018). To this end, the entire Washington establishment, including politicians and journalists, were suspect and Trump seized this perspective and made it his own. Former White House advisor Stephen Bannon supported this populist theory of Trump's election: "This is Trump at war — war with the elites; war with the permanent political class; war with the opposition party media, tech oligarchs, the Antifa anarchists. This is the reason Trump is president — to take on the vested interests in this country for hard working Americans" (Parker 2018). *CBN* reporter David Brody was a guest on *Meet the Press* and said: "I'd say on the Republican side they got exactly what they wanted, a guy that was going to shake things up… the truth of the matter is 62% think the media is biased" (Wemple 2018a). Brody is not wrong. Trump lawyer Rudolph Giuliani connected this argument of liberal bias to the successful Trump campaign against the press: "He's trying to point out that there's a very, very heavy political motivation to everything they're doing. This has been the argument since Barry Goldwater and Ronald Reagan, that we're not treated fairly. I think that problems of us are exaggerated into big national scandals, and problems for them are just not looked at" (Parker 2018). Lara Brown from George Washington University and *CBS News* Chief White House Correspondent Major Garrett both agreed with Giuliana's sentiment about the perception of unfair treatment. They each made the point that the conservative enmity toward the press did not begin with Donald Trump, but reached a zenith under President Obama. Brown noted: "A huge portion of the American people thought that [the press] was in the tank for the Obama administration and that they did not cover him aggressively" (Brown 2017). Garrett concurred and said about the perception that the press was anti-conservative was especially pronounced during Obama because: "there was the sense that even when he was being scrutinized, it wasn't at the maximum level. There was always a hand tied behind the media's back. I heard this all the time that: 'yeah, yeah. You ask him questions but you don't really get after him" (Garrett 2017).

It follows that when the mainstream media covers Trump endlessly and with great scrutiny, his supporters think that the press is unfairly out to get him. Yet Trump brought with him a set of qualities that demands the attention. He is a media maven, a television guy who manipulates the press into covering him all the time. He is brash and obnoxious, a showman who craves the spotlight. He is a businessman who (a) is not a politician in that he does not abide by the rules and norms of politics and (b) came to the White House with myriad legal troubles in his wake. His supporters may love him for all of these reasons, but they are also the reasons that the press covers him as they do.

Bret Stephens wrote in *The New York Times*: "For a president who cares more about ratings than he does about polls, this is the ultimate vindication. He minds less if you hate him so long as he knows that you're thinking about him" (Stephens 2017). The world is thinking about Trump and in America, that unrelenting attention amplifies our divide. Personalized discourse and vitriol are becoming normalized, accepted across the ideological spectrum. As a result, there are damaging consequences to all of this anger and harmful outcomes of a society with a polarized news system that delivers different truths to the nation. That said, does not necessarily have to be a permanent state. We can change the culture with work and attention to the factors that maintain the enmity and the effects of our division.

## EFFECTS

1. Without a common set of facts, the political system breaks down.

American democracy is predicated on compromise which is totally impossible when two sides are armed with entirely different sets of realities. Without a shared narrative, lawmakers cannot craft policy because there is no agreement on where problems begin and end. Without a collective truth, citizens cannot properly understand the complexity of the world around them. Without a common conversation, we cannot disagree without any hope of resolution. This leads to a public segmentation where people feel ignored or worse, which then amplifies our divide.

2. Our debased rhetoric decreases our interest in politics and problem-solving.

The near-constant barrage of news that purposely enrages the public dulls our senses. It becomes more difficult to shock and awe, which means that in order to do so there must be a consistent increase in the volume of the alarms. This has a two-pronged effect of its own: On the one hand, we begin to see appalling behavior and astonishing animosity as part and parcel of our democratic process. When this happens, the delegitimization of our government is inevitable. Following that undermining, when the public is overwhelmed and unquestioning, it is easier to give up entirely. As Nausicaa Renner, digital editor of the *Columbia Journalism Review*, writes: "As soon as we accept something as the human condition, we stop talking about it or holding others to account; we simply adapt, admit defeat, lower our expectations" (Renner 2018). When we abandon our democratic principals, it becomes even less likely we can solve the problems that surround us or even work together to benefit the nation.

3. We have run out of mean things to say to one another.

When the public consistently hears invectives hurled by political opponents at one another, that kind of language not only becomes normalized but also boring. Using once-feared words in public becomes ordinary, and politics becomes personal. To keep up the name-calling in an interesting way, the insults have to increase in tone and tenor, and at some point these words lose their power. Case in point, the word "Nazi". At one time, being called a Nazi was the worst thing an American could be called, but the word lost its punch because we became so accustomed to hearing it. Rush Limbaugh called leftist women "Feminazis" and the left responded by calling George W. Bush a Nazi, and as a result when *actual* Nazis marched in a violent "Unite the Right" rally it was not nearly as astonishing as it should have been. By upping the ante with every insult, at some point we simply ran out of words. This is why, in order to paint the left as deplorable, those on the far right frequently resort to using "pedophile" to slander a politician they do not like. There is nothing worse than a pedophile, and all other words feel weak with overuse.

4. Our language is now dehumanizing.

When we "other" our opponents and use descriptive words to lower them to animals, not only do we degrade our discourse, we lack the desire to understand a conflicting viewpoint. Allison Skinner is a psychology researcher at Northwestern University, and she has written about the modern use of dehumanizing language. Warning about the dangers of such rhetorical flourishes, Skinner writes:

> Once someone is dehumanized, we usually deny them the consideration, compassion and empathy that we typically give other people. It can relax our instinctive aversion to aggression and violence. Studies have found that once a person has dehumanized another person or group, they're less likely to consider their thoughts and feelings. (Skinner 2018)

Characterizing our rivals as animals makes it exponentially more challenging to live in common spaces. When President Trump uses such language, he talks in terms of "us" and "them," and in doing so show that he only represents part of the country, worsening our division.

5. The public's attention span has shrunk.

A study done by the Google News Lab in 2018 showed that the public might be paying more attention to the news, but our attention is easily diverted and we focus on one topic for short bursts of time: "The study shows that while Trump's presidency has been action-packed, the public's attention span doesn't seem to last for long. The visible spikes of increased Googling on a topic indicate that Trump-related news captures the public's interest, but that attention quickly fizzles out or is captured by the next bombshell report or firing" (Kight 2017). Our inability to focus on one topic for too long discourages a deeper analysis of problems or any kind of collaborative discussion about solutions.

Additionally, as the public increasingly lives in filter bubbles these shortened attention spans preclude hearing an opposing thought. As the public bounces from topic to topic quickly and without real comprehension, it exacerbates the aversion to more challenging fare. Listening to differing opinions is vital to make sense of the world around us, and this is a skill that is in progressively short supply.

6. Mistakes made, purposely or by accident, are rampant.

An ideologically focused news system that is built for speed can be sloppy because people make mistakes under pressure. The time constraints and push to be first add significant pressure to the news industry. Additionally, sometimes the truth is tossed aside in favor of a pleasing hit of righteous indignation. During the 2018 confirmation hearings of Brett Kavanaugh to be an Associate Justice on the Supreme Court, a professor in California named Christine Ford came forward to accuse Judge Kavanaugh of sexual assault, and in an effort to support the Trump nominee, someone found her "Rate My Professor" Webpage and tried to use her record against her. The right-wing media circle, led by *The Drudge Report*, ran with Ford's student ratings, using their depictions of her as a "mad" and "troubled" professor. The story spread to *Gateway Pundit*, *The Mark Levin* radio show, and was also mentioned on *Fox News*. The problem was that they found the wrong Professor Ford, targeting Christine Adams Ford, a professor of human services at California State University, Fullerton instead of Christine Blasey Ford, who teaches psychology and statistics at Palo Alto University (Collins 2018). As *CNN*'s Alex Koppelman tweeted: "Turns out when you make a movement and a business out of being deliberately ignorant about everything the press does to get stories right, you end up being wrong a lot…" (Reliable Sources Tipsheet 2018).

It was not always this way. Several journalists with whom I spoke told me that early in their careers if they made a mistake it was not only rare but so humiliating as to be seared into their memory. Major Garrett told me that he made three mistakes in his journalistic career and he remembered every single one of them vividly (Garrett 2017). David Zurawik told me that when he was just starting out as a print reporter, he made a minor error on an obituary. When he came into work the next day, his editor screamed at him: "We sell 200,000 papers a day. How are you going to go to those 200,000 homes and correct this mistake that you made because you were careless?" (Zurawik 2017) In this current media climate, mistakes are more easily tolerated and the quality of the news diminishes in the process.

7. The verbal assaults against the press will eventually lead to real violence.

When journalists are called "the enemy of the people," it is small wonder that violence might ensue. The threat of violence against the press, encouraged by the president's language, has prompted several networks to employ security guards to accompany their staff to the president's political rallies. According to *MSNBC* reporter Katy Tur, the public is seemingly unaware of the threats against the press that are now regular occurrences: "What you do not see are the nasty letters or packages or emails. The threats of physical violence. 'I hope you get raped and killed,' one person wrote to me just this week. 'Raped and killed.' Not just me, but a couple of my female colleagues as well" (J. Schwartz 2018). In 2018, the FBI arrested a California man who called the *Boston Globe* and said, in a mimicry of Trump's language: "You're the enemy of the people, and we're going to kill every fucking one of you". The suspect, Robert Chain, also said: "We are going to shoot you motherfuckers in the head," and when authorities investigated, they found 20 firearms in Chain's home (Follman 2018). Sometimes this ramped-up rhetoric is just hyperbole, and sometimes people have a hard time making that distinction.

8. This entire media system has flattened expertise.

With so many voices to be heard from and so many opinions offered on countless platforms, the value of expertise has been poleaxed. Thanks to social media, which allows anyone the ability to post their opinions and receive plaudits for uninformed beliefs, this is a common phenomenon. There are several drawbacks from a glut of information. The first is that the overall lack of media literacy among the public prevents the ability to find solid, fact-based information. When someone looks for information and settles upon the first ten hits of a Google search, they might not be finding the most substantial research on a topic. A compounding problem is that because anyone can opine, many opinions are themselves without substantive research. Without cues as to validity or significance, these baseless opinions can be weighed more than their actual worth. Tara Brabazon is a scholar from the University of Brighton in England and she wrote about what she calls the "Google Effect," where the overabundance of information devalues fact, scholarship, and research (Brabazon 2006). The result is "low grade information" from amateurs, which does little to meaningfully contribute to the national conversation. I spoke with Dr. Darrell West from The Brookings Institution about the abundance of information available to Americans today, and he remarked that although the public might have access, they were not consuming what they actually needed: "There is tremendous information available to people but it doesn't mean what they need is going to rise to the top. What is attracting the most attention at times is the most distracting and the least helpful" (West 2018). The public is less informed as we become more entertained.

Each of these effects is problematic on their own, dangerous when put together. There are, however, potential answers to the crisis we are currently facing.

## POSSIBLE SOLUTIONS

Even as the media expand in size and scope and our attention spans dwindle, all is not lost. There are two primary areas of potential improvement; the first is to change the behavior of the public, the second is to improve the structure of the media.

### Media Literacy

There is a growing body of research on media literacy, which examines the best ways to access and analyze truthful information. This is especially important in an age of "fake news" and two entirely separate systems of news dissemination. In a paper titled "Media Literacy: A Foundational Skill for Democracy in the 21st Century" that was published in the *Hastings Law Journal*, Tessa Jolls and Michelle Johnsen address the challenges of protecting against the threats that come from more access to information. They write: "The most democratic way to address this challenge is teaching society to be wiser information consumers and producers through critical thinking and a pedagogy that empowers them to evaluate, analyze, and choose critically whether to act on information" (Jolls and Johnsen 2018). There are a number of media literacy organizations that educate and provide resources. These include the Center for Media Literacy, Media Literacy Now, and the National Association for Media Literacy. Each of these groups aims to bring a broader discussion of media literacy into the public discourse with an eye toward improved media consumption. I also strongly recommend Bruce Bartlett's book *The Truth Matters* which is a handy and vital source on this topic.[1]

## *Listening*

A healthier media diet is one possible solution, and another is improved communication, which can be accomplished through active listening. Instead of remaining cloistered in our filter bubbles, an antidote to epistemic closure is to actively engage with a variety of voices. Along these lines, a project called "Story Corps" has been launched to try to bring people together because, as they say, it is hard to hate up close. This effort encourages storytelling and active listening as a way to bridge our political divide (StoryCorps 2018). StoryCorps builds on the theory that listening to others can further help us understand the core values of our fellow citizens, which will in turn encourage unity. Robb Willer, a sociology professor at Stanford, studies polarization and has found that when people try to persuade political opponents, they lose ground. Instead, Willis says, people should take the time to form coalitions with one another based on their core values. The only way to do this is to listen:

> Liberals and conservatives must take the time to really listen to one another, to understand one another's values and to think creatively about why someone with very different political and moral commitments from their own should nonetheless come to agree with them. Empathy and respect will be critical if we are going to sew our country back together. (Shashkevich 2017)

Political scientist Michael Wagner has written extensively about communication and democracy, and he agreed that listening to others was vital. Wagner went a bit further to recommend that people seek out those who differ in opinion in order to gain perspective and empathy:

> You need to make an effort to find people who are different then you and sit down with them in an environment where your goal is not to try to persuade them that you are right. Your goal is to just hear what they have to say and maybe share what you have to say.... So many people on both sides feel a deep resentment toward people on the other side... because many people's frustration is that they don't feel heard or respected. (Wagner 2017)

Feeling ignored is powerfully destructive and active listening goes far to ameliorate those negative feelings. Additionally, there is value in crowdsourcing. By listening to the opinions of others, our opinion may or may not change, but our beliefs can strengthen and grow from their exposure to differing perceptions. The only way to sharpen our ideas is by learning more about them, and as we do this, we can gain perspective from the thoughts of other people.

### Voting for Elected Officials Who Are Politicians

This solution has nothing to do with job experience, much more to do with the concept of what it is to be "political". The word has been so thoroughly trashed in modern conversation that it has ceased to have an actual meaning. To be political is to be engaged with the actions of governing, and to govern is to lead a community. There are different ways to think about how to lead, but at the root of being an elected official is representation. When our divisions are so mighty and our political language so intemperate, more than ever citizens need leaders who have faith in the system they work hard to get elected to. With confidence that the government can solve problems, hashing out the solutions becomes more of a collective effort, encouraging citizens to disagree without being disagreeable.

The idea of nonpoliticians leading the citizenry is not in itself a bad thing and is certainly not limited to one side of the political aisle. Increasingly, Americans from both parties are making names for themselves as outsiders who can singlehandedly solve problems without the system at all. There are two problems with this: First, no one has the skill set, but perhaps more to the point American democracy was specifically designed to be a collaborative process with separated powers and checks and balances. The partisan media rewards posturing and braggadocio because it is interesting and exciting, but it is not necessarily useful. Returning politicians to the political realm, asking for some diplomacy and regard for the whole republic, could help.

### Supporting Local News

Another set of solutions lie in the structures of the news media. Most media experts agree that one key to bridging our political divisions is strengthening local news, encouraging their growth in the face of increased national competition. Local news brings citizens the information about issues that are most immediately important, and these outlets keep the citizenry tethered to their decision makers. Local newspapers and their direct connection to the communities they cover serve to unite people with their neighbors, which can help grow ties to end division. As *Washington Post* columnist Margaret Sullivan writes: "In our terribly divided nation, we need the local newspaper to give us common information — an agreed-upon set of facts to argue about" (Sullivan 2018). Additionally, better local news would help to restore faith in the institutions that are currently suffering from a distinct lack of trust. If one problem with trust in government is the idea that Washington is far away and ineffective, seeing the hard work and efficacy of local government would break that narrative. Local news outlets are the only ones covering a city council meeting; their survival is crucial to monitor elected officials and this, in turn, would "help us break out of our national filter bubbles," to bridge the gaps between the citizenry and our elected officials (Hart and Fischer 2018).

### Increasing Diversity in Journalism

Other solutions can be found in making structural changes to the news media. For one, the mainstream press corps is astoundingly homogenous in terms of race, gender, ideology, and geography, and this lack of diversity encourages the kind of filter bubbles that made Americans angry in the first place. In 2018, *The New York Times* and *Politico* each had seven White House correspondents, all of whom were white. The same racial sameness can be said for the White House reporting staff from the *Wall Street Journal*, *USA Today*, and *Reuters* (Farhi 2018). Sarah Glover, president of the National Association of Black Journalists, is quoted in an article about this homogeny: "The lack of diversity in the White House press corps is unsettling. News organizations should have staff that reflect the communities they serve. ... A White House press team without ethnic diversity is a complete missed opportunity" (Farhi 2018). There is also a lack of gender diversity in the press corps as well. In an interview on *CNN*, former *Today Show* anchor Katie Couric remarked that this leads to implicit biases all around: "All three evening news anchors are male. The vast majority of executive producers at every network are male," and that this leads to "cultural conditioning that causes us to look at people a certain way" (Wattles 2018). Ideological and geographic homogeny lead to another kind of conditioning, one loudly noted by conservatives who argue that the news media are predominantly left leaning and concentrated on the coasts. Accordingly, in order to reduce the ideological polarization, it might be wise to include more reporters who are right leaning and live in the center of the country. As GOP strategist Brad Todd wrote in a piece for *The Federalist*:

> It is understood as gospel among Republican strategists that few journalists understand the chemistry or architecture of Republican primaries. Too few reporters personally relate to the motivations of conservative voters, or even have enough acquaintances to have developed an appreciation for the mindset. (Todd 2017)

In an interview, Todd expanded on this idea, noting that the uniformity of the mainstream press corps was why so many journalists missed the cues leading up to the 2016 presidential election (Todd, Partner, OnMessage 2018). Put together, increasing the diversity of newsrooms could go a long way to repair our disunion.

### Technology Solutions to Tech Problems

There is technology on the horizon that has the potential to help. If algorithms are one reason our filter bubbles remain unpopped, changing these structures would help. So too would technology that increases trust in the media by filtering out the garbage. Along these lines, there are sites and programs developed specifically to combat fake news and increase trust in the media. Most of these efforts have been developed by nonprofit media think tanks and groups within the journalism industry, and they include the News Integrity Initiative, The Journalism Trust Initiative, Internews, Accountability Journalism Program, Trusting News, Media Manipulation Initiative, and The Trust Project (Fischer, Look at This List 2018b). All of these have been launched to provide some reality testing to various sources and sites, but as *Axios'* Sara Fischer notes, there are so many of them it is difficult to gauge their success. A promising development comes from NewsGuard Technologies, which uses real journalists to rate news and information sites in order to sort between fake news and legitimate sources. Using a nine-point checklist to determine trustworthiness, NewsGuard rates the sites: "Sites that don't clearly label advertising lose points, for example. Sites that have a coherent correction policy gain points. If you install NewsGuard and browse Google, Bing, Facebook, or Twitter, you'll see either a red or green icon next to every news source, a binary indicator of whether it meets NewsGuard's standards" (Lapowski 2018). These kinds of services, dependent on people instead of algorithms, can add a level of value and trust to our online news consumption, and there is clearly more development in the works.

## The American People

The last answer to our divided political climate can be found within the citizenry and structure of the American democracy. Our system was built for deliberation, and although we are not reaching our full potential at this exact moment, that does not negate the fundamental truth of our system. Roderick Hart, author of *Civil Hope*, made this point clearly when he said that democracy was built for continued conversation:

> The strength of a democracy lies in its weaknesses and in the willingness of its people at the grassroots level to argue about those weaknesses without stopping.... We've always been divided in lots of way. The question is: Are we still arguing? If we're still having that interchange, that's as good as a democracy gets. (Hard 2017)

The challenge will be to continue the discussion and keep moving forward. America has faced tests in the past and this is a significant one. But my hope is that we are up to the task.

## CONCLUSIONS

The polarized political media we have today are the result of different factors and though the resulting problems are substantial, there is hope in the solutions. When citizens work just a bit harder to pierce their filter bubbles, and news organizations try to structure their outlets and content better, the combination of these forces can be powerful. Perhaps these efforts will lead toward greater trust in the electoral system and the news media, which will stem the polarization. The biggest catch, however, is that these solutions take time to implement. Building trust in government cannot be accomplished overnight, nor can we repair the colossal animosity of our partisanship. Compounding this is the fact that we have become more interested in immediate gratification of later, and want change quickly. Cultural changes take time, careful consideration, and work.

I asked the Brookings Institution's Darrell West how we could change our national tone, how we could resume a normalcy that felt more positive. West answered:

> I don't think there's any immediate fix that's going to take care of the problem. We're in a situation where we have to think long term, and it may be years before some things change in a way that's going to improve the system. We need to be laying the foundation now.... It's good to put out the ideas that you think will work and then hope that the political moment arises that leads to implementation. (West 2018)

It took years to get to where we are, and it will take years for us to move to something different and, hopefully, better. Planting the seeds now to bloom later is an optimistic exercise but a useful one because it mandates that we look forward and not just to the immediate.

An important seed to plant is the belief in real journalism. Citizens will never agree on the solutions to our biggest policy questions, which are exactly why we have a democracy to represent our interests, and why we need reporters to inform citizens about the facts of our government. As David Zurawik from *The Baltimore Sun* said about journalists:

> We are the ones that give citizens information that they can use to judge all the lies and spin that's coming at them from people in government, that's coming at them from advertising, that's coming at them most media outlets. This is worthy information, independent source of verified information that should keep you from going mad amid all these lies, all this spin... If you don't have that, you don't have a democracy. If you don't have an independent source of trustworthy information, your votes can be controlled. Your lives can be controlled. (Zurawik 2017)

Agreement is not the end-goal of a deliberate democracy; compromise is. Accordingly, it is vital to have a press to provide us with a factual foundation upon which we can productively disagree. As James Bennet, Editorial Page Editor of *The New York Times* said: "We're really at risk of losing sight of the notion that disagreement can be constructive –that it's pretty rare for any of us to be entirely right or wrong about anything" (Bennet 2018). We also need a free and trusted press to hold our leaders accountable to the voters, and to push back on the current inclination of polarization and division as a political tactic. As men are not angels, some will continue to choose division over harmony, seeing gain from short-term victories that are shallow and insincere. We need the press to hold our lawmakers accountable, and to hold the public responsible too for our decisions. As *CBS News*'s Major Garrett said: "If from the time you wake up to the time you go to bed, all the news you consume makes you happy, you're doing it wrong" (Garrett 2017). And this is why we need faith in journalism.

We can remind ourselves of the importance of the press as we work toward repairing the trust we have lost. *C-SPAN* founder Brian Lamb gave me a copy of "The Journalist's Creed," written by Walter Williams who was the first Dean of the Missouri School of Journalism. A plaque with this statement hangs in the National Press Club in Washington, and it is a useful reminder of what is possible. The "Creed" ends with this statement:

> I believe that the journalism which succeeds best — and best deserves success — fears God and honors Man; is stoutly independent, unmoved by pride of opinion or greed of power, constructive, tolerant but never careless, self-controlled, patient, always respectful of its readers but always unafraid, is quickly indignant at injustice; is unswayed by the appeal of privilege or the clamor of the mob; seeks to give every man a chance and, as far as law and honest wage and recognition of human brotherhood can make it so, an equal chance; is profoundly patriotic while sincerely promoting international good will and cementing world-comradeship; is a journalism of humanity, of and for today's world. (Fancher 2009)

Our national anger shakes our faith in the country and it feels like a permanent condition. In truth, we can stop the fury and antagonism if we choose to. Perhaps by knowing how this rage began, we can end it. Knowledge of the symptoms can produce a cure.

Then, we will not have to be super mad at everything all the time.

# NOTE

1. Bartlett, Bruce, *The Truth Matters: A Citizen's Guide to Separating Facts from Lies and Stopping Fake News in Its Tracks* (New York, 2017).

# WORKS CITED

Bennet, James. 2018. *Introducing "The Argument," A New Podcast from The New York Times Opinion*, October 5. Accessed October 5, 2018. https://www.nytco.com/introducing-the-argument-a-new-podcast-from-the-new-york-times-opinion/.

Brabazon, Tara. 2006. The Google Effect: Googling, Blogging, Wikis, and the Flattening of Expertise. *Libri* 56 (3): 157–167.

Brown, Lara, interview by Alison Dagnes. 2017. *Director, George Washington University Graduate School of Political Management*, August 21.

Bump, Philip. 2018. *Trump Eliminates the Middleman in His War Against Journalists*, October 1. Accessed October 2, 2018. https://www.washingtonpost.com/politics/2018/10/01/trump-eliminates-middle-man-his-war-against-journalists/?utm_term=.fc19da30e362.

Carolan, Liz. 2018. *Trusted News Sources Curbed Social Media Impact on Swedish Vote*, September 12. Accessed September 26, 2018. https://www.irishtimes.com/opinion/trusted-news-sources-curbed-social-media-impact-on-swedish-vote-1.3625682?mode=amp&__vfz=c_pages%3D11000002670848.

Chan, Sewell. 2017. *Number of Jailed Journalists Hits Record High, Advocacy Group Says*, December 17. Accessed September 30, 2018. https://www.nytimes.com/2017/12/13/world/europe/journalists-jailed-committee-to-protect-journalists.html.

Choi, David. 2018. Trump Schedules His Meetings Around 'Fox and Friends' Segments, According to Former White House Official. *Business Insider*, July 31. https://www.businessinsider.com/trump-fox-new-and-friends-schedules-meetings-2018-7.

Collins, Ben. 2018. *Far-Right News Sites Smear California Professor After Misidentifying Kavanaugh Accuser*, September 17. Accessed October 1, 2018. https://www.nbcnews.com/tech/tech-news/far-right-news-sites-smear-california-professor-after-misidentifying-kavanaugh-n910471.

Fancher, Michael. 2009. *The 21st Century Journalist's Creed*, September 16. Accessed October 4, 2018. https://niemanreports.org/articles/the-21st-century-journalists-creed/.

Farhi, Paul. 2018. *The White House Press Room Is Overwhelmingly White. Does That Matter?* September 30. Accessed October 1, 2018. https://www.Washingtonpost.com/lifestyle/style/the-white-house-press-room-is-overwhelmingly-white-does-that-matter/2018/09/30/3b99ca00-bdb3-11e8-8792-78719177250f_story.html?utm_term=.32ae9be83815.

Feldman, Josh. 2018. *Ari Melber Rips Into Giuliani and Sekulow's 'Bizarre' Hannity Guest-Hosting Gig*, August 10. Accessed September 26, 2018. https://www.mediaite.com/tv/ari-melber-rips-into-giuliani-and-sekulows-bizarre-hannity-guest-hosting-gig/.

Fischer, Sara. 2018a. *NewsGuard Launches First Product with Help from Microsoft*, August 23. Accessed September 30, 2018. https://www.axios.com/newsguard-launches-first-product-2143fc9e-470f-44b6-b8f1-6006646d26db.html.

———. 2018b. *Look at This List*, October 9. Accessed October 9, 2018. C:\Users\ADDagn\AppData\Local\Microsoft\Windows\INetCache\Content.Outlook\W1R1E418\email.mht.

Follman, Mark. 2018. *Trump's "Enemy of the People" Rhetoric Is Endangering Journalists' Lives*, September 13. Accessed September 26, 2018. https://www.motherjones.com/politics/2018/09/trump-enemy-of-the-people-media-threats/.

Friedman, Uri. 2017. *The Real-World Consequences of 'Fake News'*, December 23. Accessed September 30, 2018. https://www.theatlantic.com/international/archive/2017/12/trump-world-fake-news/548888/.

Gabbatt, Adam. 2017. Trump and The Fox & Friends Show. Think Ego, Not News. *The Guardian*, September 17. https://www.theguardian.com/media/2017/sep/17/fox-and-friends-fox-news-donald-trump.

Garrett, Major, interview by Alison Dagnes. 2017. *CBS News Chief White House Correspondent*, August 21.

Gold, Hadas. 2016. *Donald Trump Takes Credit for Public Distrust of the Media*, September 15. Accessed September 25, 2018. https://www.politico.com/blogs/on-media/2016/09/donald-trump-takes-credit-for-distrust-of-media-228221.

Grynbaum, Michael. 2018. *'Fake News' Goes Global as Trump, in Britain, Rips the Press*, July 13. Accessed September 30, 2018. https://www.nytimes.com/2018/07/13/business/media/trump-cnn-london.html.

Hard, Roderick, interview by Alison Dagnes. 2017. *Professor, University of Texas at Austin*, April 8.

Hart, Kim, and Sara Fischer. 2018. *Two Possible Solutions as Trust in Media Tanks*, February 8. Accessed September 30, 2018. https://www.axios.com/newsletters/axios-am-fe5cac47-0a13-467f-bf99-2589eeb9c2ee.html.

Horton, Alex. 2018. *Fox News Host Lobs 'Fake News' Tweet At … Another Fox News host*, August 5. Accessed September 26, 2018. https://www.washingtonpost.com/news/arts-and-entertainment/wp/2018/08/05/fox-news-host-lobs-fake-news-tweet-at-another-fox-news-host/?utm_term=.3fb6da097f23.

Jolls, Tessa, and Michelle Johnsen. 2018. Media Literacy: A Foundational Skill for Democracy in the 21st Century. *Hastings Law Journal* 69 (5): 1379–1408.

Keith, Tamara. 2018. *President Trump's Description of What's 'Fake' Is Expanding*, September 2. Accessed September 25, 2018. https://www.npr.org/2018/09/02/643761979/president-trumps-description-of-whats-fake-is-expanding.

Kight, Stef. 2017. *The Insane News Cycle of Trump's Presidency in 1 Chart*, September 17. Accessed September 26, 2018. https://www.axios.com/the-insane-news-cycle-of-trumps-presidency-in-1-chart-1513305658-b2393db8-4d82-41fc-92c6-acda4f3dd8db.html.

Lapowski, Issie. 2018. *NewsGuard Wants to Fight Fake News with Humans, Not Algorithms*, August 23. Accessed September 30, 2018. https://www.wired.com/story/newsguard-extension-fake-news-trust-score/.

Matthews, Dylan. 2018. *No, a Former Kavanaugh Clerk Didn't Flash a "White Power Sign." Here's What Really Happened*, September 5. Accessed October 1, 2018. https://www.vox.com/2018/9/5/17821946/white-power-hand-signal-brett-kavanaugh-confirmation-hearing-zina-bash-4chan.

Maza, Carlos. 2018. The Trump-Fox & Friends Feedback Loop, Explained. *Vox*, February 9. https://www.vox.com/2018/2/9/16997022/strikethrough-trump-fox-friends-feedback-loop-explained-tweet.

Parker, Ashley. 2018. *'Totally Dishonest': Trump Asserts Only He Can Be Trusted Over Opponents and 'Fake News'*, August 30. Accessed September 25, 2018. https://www.washingtonpost.com/politics/trump-pushes-a-reality-where-opponents-are-peddling-false-facts-and-only-he-can-be-trusted/2018/08/30/d7ac7c38-ac62-11e8-b1da-ff7faa680710_story.html?utm_term=.9caefe37507d.

Peters, Jeremy. 2018. *In a Divided Era, One Thing Seems to Unite: Political Anger*, August 17. Accessed September 25, 2018. https://www.nytimes.com/2018/08/17/us/politics/political-fights.html.

Power, Lis. 2018. *Fox News Has Gifted Trump Over $13 Million in Free Media Value by Airing His Rallies*, June 28. Accessed September 30, 2018. https://www.mediamatters.org/blog/2018/06/29/Fox-News-has-gifted-Trump-over-13-million-in-free-media-value-by-airing-his-rallies-/220565.

Reliable Sources Tipsheet. 2018. *Reliable Sources Tipsheet*, September 18. Accessed September 26, 2018. https://groups.google.com/forum/#!topic/haustus/CZbIqn7UmBA.

Renner, Nausicca. 2018. *First Comes the 'Shocking' News. Then Comes the Navel-Gazing*, September 25. Accessed September 26, 2018. https://www.nytimes.com/2018/09/25/magazine/first-comes-the-shocking-news-then-comes-the-navel-gazing.html?utm_source=CNN+Media%3A+Reliable+Sources&utm_campaign=51ae6e15d5-EMAIL_CAMPAIGN_2018_09_11_04_47_COPY_01&utm_medium=email&utm_term=0_e95cdc16a9-51ae.

Schwarz, Hunter. 2018. *Nearly a Quarter of Trump's Instagram Posts Are Reposts of Fox News Content*, August 26. Accessed September 26, 2018. https://www.cnn.com/2018/08/22/politics/trump-instagram-fox-news/index.html.

Schwartz, Ian. 2018. *Trump: "Don't Believe the Crap You See from These People on Fake News"*, July 24. Accessed September 25, 2018. https://www.realclear-politics.com/video/2018/07/24/trump_dont_believe_the_crap_you_see_from_these_people_on_fake_news.html.

Schwartz, Jason. 2018. *Media Boost Security as Trump Ramps Up 'Enemy' Rhetoric*, September 9. Accessed September 26, 2018. https://www.politico.com/story/2018/08/09/media-boosts-security-as-trump-ramps-up-enemy-rhetoric-768666.

Shashkevich, Alex. 2017. *Empathy, Respect for One Another Critical to Ease Political Polarization, Stanford Sociologist Says*, January 20. Accessed October 2, 2018. https://news.stanford.edu/2017/01/20/empathy-respect-critical-ease-political-polarization-sociologist-says/.

Skinner, Allison. 2018. *The Slippery Slope of Dehumanizing Language*, June 4. Accessed October 1, 2018. http://theconversation.com/the-slippery-slope-of-dehumanizing-language-97512.

Stanley-Becker, Isaac. 2018. In Trump's Right-Wing Media Universe, It Was a Day Like Any Other. *The Washington Post*, August 22. https://www.washingtonpost.com/news/morning-mix/wp/2018/08/22/how-right-wing-media-dealt-with-adevastating-day-for-trump/?utm_term=.da3063cffa60.

Stein, Sam. 2018. *New Poll: 43% of Republicans Want to Give Trump the Power to Shut Down Media*, August 7. Accessed September 25, 2018. https://www.thedailybeast.com/new-poll-43-of-republicans-want-to-give-trump-the-power-to-shut-down-media.

Stelter, Brian. 2017. *How Fox News and President Trump Create an Anti-Mueller 'Feedback Loop'*, December 16. Accessed September 26, 2018. https://money.cnn.com/2017/12/16/media/fox-news-campaign-against-fbi-robert-mueller/index.html.

———. 2018a. *Trump and His Media Boosters Live in a Hall of Mirrors*, August 14. Accessed September 26, 2018. https://money.cnn.com/2018/08/14/media/trump-media-hall-of-mirrors/index.html.

———. 2018b. *President Trump Helps Out Fox's Sean Hannity Before Rally*, September 21. Accessed September 26, 2018. https://money.cnn.com/2018/09/21/media/reliable-sources-09-20-18/index.html.

Stephens, Bret. 2017. *We're All Part of Trump's Show*, November 30. Accessed September 26, 2018. https://www.nytimes.com/2017/11/30/opinion/trump-putin-pomerantsev-show.html?rref=collection%2Fsectioncollection%2Fopinion-columnists&_r=0.

StoryCorps. 2018. *https://storycorps.org/*, September 30. Accessed September 30, 2018. https://storycorps.org/.

Sullivan, Margaret. 2018. *The Local-News Crisis Is Destroying What a Divided America Desperately Needs: Common Ground*, August 5. Accessed September 30, 2018. https://www.washingtonpost.com/lifestyle/style/the-local-news-crisis-is-destroying-what-a-divided-america-desperately-needs-common-ground/2018/08/03/d654d5a8-9711-11e8-810c-5fa705927d54_story.html?utm_term=.38c101302647.

Todd, Brad. 2017. *Why Republicans Need to Self-Deport from Washington DC*, December 28. Accessed October 1, 2018. http://thefederalist.com/2017/12/28/republicans-need-self-deport-washington-dc/.

Todd, Brad, interview by Alison Dagnes. 2018. *Partner, OnMessage*, July 19.

Trump. 2018. Tweet. *Twitter*, August 30.

VandeHei, Jim. 2017. *Trump's Mind-Numbing Media Manipulation Machine*, December 1. Accessed September 26, 2018. https://www.axios.com/trumps-mind-numbing-media-manipulation-machine-1513307286-fd-2cdc98-5399-41c4-84bd-f5aa74a267a3.html.

Wagner, Michael, interview by Alison Dagnes. 2017. *Associate Professor, University of Wisconsin at Madison*, April 7.

Wattles, Jackie. 2018. *Katie Couric: The News Needs More Diversity at the Top*, September 30. Accessed October 1, 2018. https://money.cnn.com/2018/09/30/media/katie-couric-reliable-sources/.

Wemple, Eric. 2018a. *Chuck Todd Blames Fox News for Americans' Cratering Trust in News Media*, August 26. Accessed September 25, 2018. https://www.washingtonpost.com/blogs/erik-wemple/wp/2018/08/26/chuck-todd-blames-fox-news-for-americans-cratering-trust-in-news-media/?utm_term=.aea444d6a1d1.

———. 2018b. *The 'Horror' of President Trump's Dependence on 'Fox & Friends'*, April 9. Accessed September 26, 2018. https://www.washingtonpost.com/blogs/erik-wemple/wp/2018/04/09/the-horror-of-president-trumps-dependence-on-fox-friends/?utm_term=.582efa56cf4e.

West, Darrell, interview by Alison Dagnes. 2018. *Director of Governance Studies, The Brookings Institution*, January 8.

Wise, Justin. 2018. *Trump References 'Legitimate Media and Fake-News Media' at Meeting with NATO Leader*, July 11. Accessed September 26, 2018. https://thehill.com/policy/international/396463-trump-begins-na-to-press-conference-by-referencing-legitimate-media-and?utm_source=CN-N+Media%3A+Reliable+Sources&utm_campaign=7dca7f3b9f-EMAIL_CAMPAIGN_2017_06_06_COPY_01&utm_medium=email&utm_term=0_e95cdc16a.

Zurawik, David, interview by Alison Dagnes. 2017. *Baltimore Sun, Media Critic*, October 6.

# Index

© The Editor(s) (if applicable) and The Author(s),
under exclusive licence to Springer Nature Switzerland AG 2019
A. Dagnes, *Super Mad at Everything All the Time*,
https://doi.org/10.1007/978-3-030-06131-9

Made in the USA
Monee, IL
05 June 2024